Fundamentals of Statistics for the Social Sciences

Mark B. Johnson

University of Maryland, College Park

KENDALL/HUNT PUBLISHING COMPANY
4050 Westmark Drive   Dubuque, Iowa 52002

Cover art is by D. Maurice Taylor, and is supplied by author.

Contents

Introduction to Statistics

Statistics is an important part of most quantitative research. Later in the book I will discuss research designs commonly used in the social sciences, describe strengths and weaknesses of different methodological approaches, and underscore why statistics is an essential step in the research process. At this point, however, I will say only that statistics describes a set of procedures that researchers use to process, clarify, and make sense of quantitative data generated through the research process. Often, researchers are not able to determine exactly what results their scientific studies have produced until statistical procedures have been applied to the data.

The purpose of this book is to introduce you to statistical techniques commonly used in social science research: it will illustrate when and why we use a particular technique, and what we hope this procedure will tell us about our results. Certainly, much of the work in statistics involves mathematical computation, and in introductory courses it is typical that students learn how to perform statistical computations by hand (in more advanced courses, students may use computer software to compute statistics). This book will describe and explain the hand calculations necessary to perform different statistical tests. It is important to note, however, that statistics courses are not math courses per se. None of the mathematical computations discussed in the book are particularly difficult (although they may be tedious), and no test described requires mathematical knowledge beyond simple algebra. However, carrying out the mathematical computations is only a part of the task in statistics; knowing when and why to use one statistical test v. another is a separate, but important, issue. Furthermore, having a firm *conceptual* understanding of statistics—knowing why these calculations inform us about our data, and seeing the underlying similarities among different statistical procedures—can only strengthen one's ability to appropriately use statistical procedures in real applications. In sum, it is not difficult to learn how to carry out the statistical computations, but neither is it sufficient to demonstrate mastery of the subject.

Any student who intends to attend graduate school in a social science invariably will be required to take several semesters of statistics as part of the their post-baccalaureate education. Statistics courses are required for many undergraduate degrees in part for the same reasons. Even for students who do not plan to conduct research in their graduate or undergraduate careers, gaining a basic understanding of statistics can be beneficial because we all are *consumers* of research. We all are exposed to brief reports on television or in the newspaper that describe the results of research studies; having basic understanding of statistics can aid in clarifying those study results. Most of us, I'm sure, have also heard the phrase that "statistics can lie," or that they can be used to support any position. Well, the truth is, statistics *can't lie*, but they **can** be presented in a way that is very misleading, especially to the uninformed. By gaining a basic level of statistical understanding, you can better separate the truth from misleading statistics when you are presented with research results.

The Purpose of Statistics

Statistics refers to a broad branch of applied mathematics that is concerned with the collection and interpretation of quantitative data. For practical purposes, statistics is an essential component of scientific research. In many (but not all cases), empirical research begins with the development of a *theory* that is used to predict or explain phenomena. Given that theories often are very broad and may be intangible, researchers typically derive specific and testable hypotheses or questions from the theory. However, scientists may develop research questions that are not deeply rooted in theory.

After identifying a testable hypothesis, a researcher may develop a study or method of collecting data to address this hypothesis. Although this book is not intended to discuss research methodology in great depth, an overview of research design is presented in Chapter 3. After conducting the study, the researcher is left with quantitative data, and must apply statistics to those data to clarify their meaning and value. Statistics involves a set of procedures that allow researchers to interpret the data and determine the implication of the data for the hypothesis (i.e., does the data support the hypothesis or does it fail to support the hypothesis?). Without statistics, it may not be possible to draw any conclusions from the research.

The process of research involves collecting data on one or more **variables.** *A variable is a characteristic or quality that takes on different values—or varies—between units of observation.* Frequently, in psychology, the units of observation we use are people, but in fields other than psychology, the units of observation may be cultures, or countries, or star systems, or atoms. In psychology, therefore, statistics typically concerns characteristics that vary in degree or value among people, and psychological research involves measuring or quantifying people along these variables. Almost anything you can think of can be a variable: height, weight, intelligence, self-esteem, extroversion, gender, occupation, favorite color, whether you drive a stick-shift or an automatic, hair color, number of tattoos, et cetera, et cetera. A *constant*, on the other hand, does not vary among units of observation.

Statistics play two broad purposes in the service of empirical research, and this depends on the nature of the research questions. The first broad purpose of statistics is **descriptive:** to describe or summarize some quality or characteristic of the people who make up the sample. Research designed to find out what percentage of students smoke cigarettes, or the average number of alcoholic drinks the typical student consumes per week are examples of descriptive statistics. Statistics can be used to take a "snapshot" of a group of people and describe what they are like on any number of different variables.

Statistics also are used to describe the **relationship between variables.** Remember, a variable is some characteristic or quality that people differ on. Sometimes, people differ on several variables in the same way, and statistics can be used to detect and assess this. For example, people differ in gender: some people are male, others are female. People differ in self-esteem—some people have higher levels of self-esteem, other people have lower levels. Some people are relatively taller, some are relatively shorter, have higher v. lower GPAs, etc. The question is, are people with a specific amount or level of one variable likely to have a particularly high or low level of another variable? If we collected data on these variables and analyzed them with statistics, what types of *relationships* might we find? Might we find that people who are male also tend to be taller? Do we see that people in our sample who are female tend to have higher amounts of self-esteem? Do people in our sample who have lower self-esteem tend to have lower GPAs?

Sample and Population

Generally, when we do research, we collect information about the variables we are interested in from a **sample** of people. The sample, by definition, refers to the group of individuals from which you actually gather information. In public opinion polls—for example, to estimate President Bush's popularity—researchers will often call up a couple thousand or so people and ask for their opinions. In this case, the group of people who actually were called and asked to give their opinion constitutes the sample. If a psychologist wants to see if self-esteem is related to academic success, she might get a group of students, obtain their GPAs, and measure their self-esteem. This body of students would make up the sample for her research.

However, researchers are very rarely interested in simply what is going on in their sample. Instead, they are interested in a larger **population** of individuals. The population refers to the body of people to which the results of the research are intended to apply. If I were interested in knowing the percentage of college sophomores that smoke, I might use my statistics class as my sample but I would want to be able to generalize the results to the population of all United States college sophomores. We are not merely interested in the sample of students involved in the study, but we would like to apply our results to describe sophomores in general. Or, if I found that in this class, students with higher self-esteem also tended to have higher GPA scores, I ideally would like to say something about the relationship between self-esteem and GPA for students in general. When public opinion pollsters try to examine President Bush's popularity, they're not just interested in the thousand or so people in their sample that they actually call; they want to say how popular President Bush is for the entire population of United States voters.

It is important to understand that whether we are engaged in research for descriptive purposes or to examine relationships between or among variables, in almost all cases we will be working with data from a sample. Whether I am surveying college freshmen on their typical drinking behavior, or conducting a study comparing men to women on voting preferences, chances are that I will have data from only a fraction of the people (i.e., the sample) to whom I would like to generalize the results (i.e., the population of interest). It simply is not practical, or even possible, to collect data from each college sophomore, or male and female voter. However, at the conclusion of our research we would like to be able to draw conclusions about the larger population of interest.

Another thing that statistics does is gives us information about how confident we can be that the results we find in our sample also hold true for the entire population of people we are interested in. If, in my research, I find that women tend to vote differently than men on a particular topic, it may be the case that men and women, in general, differ on this issue. However, it also is possible that the differences between men and women I discovered are specific to this particular sample; maybe the people in my sample poorly represent the voting preferences of men and women in general. Similarly, if my research finds that college students typically consume six alcohol drinks when they go out, I would like to know how confident I can be that six drinks is typical when considering the entire population of college students.

Inferential statistics refers to a broad set of procedures designed to make conclusions about the population of interest by using data from the sample. If we describe some quality or characteristic of a sample, we can use inferential statistics to estimate the value of the quality or characteristic in the sample. Similarly, if we find a relationship, trend, or pattern between two variables in the sample, we can use inferential statistics to estimate whether the same relationship, trend, or pattern exists in the population as a whole.

When we discuss some quality or characteristic of data within a sample, we refer to that as a **statistic.** For example, if I calculate the average height of everyone in this class, that average is a statistic. If I talk about the difference between the tallest and shortest persons in the class—sort of the range of different heights—I'm also talking about a statistic. But if I discuss the average height of everybody in the world, for example, I'm talking about a **parameter.** A parameter is a characteristic of the population we're interested in.

Remember that one purpose for doing statistics is to generalize information gathered from a sample of data to the entire population. We're really interested in knowing what goes on in a population; in other words, we're really interested in finding out the values of different *parameters*. Very, very rarely will we know for sure what the value of a parameter is. For example, we might be interested in knowing what the average height and weight are of everyone in the world; because they refer to the entire population, in this case average height and weight are parameters. However, the only way we can know for sure what the average height and weight of all people are is if we measure and weigh everyone in the world. This is impossible, so we *can't* really know what these parameters are. We use *statistics* from a sample taken from the population, to try to *estimate* what the population parameter is. We calculate statistics from the sample data and then use the sample statistics to try to infer what population parameters really are.

We cannot assume, however, that our sample statistics necessarily accurately reflect the corresponding population parameters. Consider that we may be interested in a the voting preference (parameter of interest) of all registered voters in the United States (population), and our study involves surveying a sample of 500 registered voters. The population that we are interested in contains over 150 million people, and the 500 persons in our sample is clearly a very small fraction of that population. How do we know that the people in our sample have preferences typical and representative of the population? It is plausible, at least, that our sample may be overrepresented by persons with a particular voting preference (e.g., Democrats) and underrepresented by persons with another voting preference (e.g., Republicans). In this case, we might expect our voting preference measured in our sample (statistic) to be discrepant with actual value in the population (parameter).

Sampling error refers to the difference between qualities and characteristics observed in the sample and the actual values that exist in a population. Note that as our sample size increases and grows closer and closer to the size of the population, sampling error is expected to decrease. This point is addressed more thoroughly in Chapter 10. Researchers attempt to minimize the problems caused by sampling error by ensuring, as much as possible, that the sample is collected randomly from the population.

PRACTICE PROBLEMS

1.1 Define a research **population** and contrast that to a research **sample.** Describe how these two terms relate to the terms **statistic, parameter,** and **inferential statistics.**

1.2 Identify and describe the two broad purposes of statistics.

1.3 Listed below are several research examples. For each one, indicate whether the research calls for *descriptive* statistics or statistics concerned with the *relationship between or among variables.*

1. A professor wishes to know how well his students performed on a midterm exam.
2. A professor wishes to know how long it took the typical student to complete the midterm exam.
3. A professor wishes to know whether students who sit closer to the front of the classroom performed better on the midterm exam than those who sit closer to the rear of the classroom.
4. A professor wishes to know how well students performed on the final exam relative to the midterm exam.
5. A researcher wishes to know what proportion of registered voters support the policy of the United States President.
6. A researcher wishes to know whether men and women differ on their support for the policy of the United States President.

1.4 Define **sampling error.**

Measurement

Statistics, and in fact quantitative research itself, is all about *measurement*. When we conduct research we typically are interested in *conceptual* variables—abstract concepts and phenomena such as "achievement motivation," "intelligence," "self-consciousness," etc. Conceptual variables, or "constructs," are believed to exist but not necessarily in tangible, material, or physical form. In order to examine these variables empirically, it is necessary to make them tangible by quantifying them: applying a process representing these concepts in terms of numbers. *Measurement* is the process of taking conceptual variables that we are interested in and operationalizing them by assigning quantitative values that reflect the level of the variable that each individual possesses.

There are numerous methods of measurement. In social sciences we often rely on surveys where research participants describe their own behavior and attitudes, but other methods include observation or direct measures of behavior, or even recordings of physiologic responses. While discussion of these different methods of measurement is beyond the scope of this book, suffice it to say that all these methods can produce quantitative values that reflect concepts in question.

Often, however, we cannot directly measure the concepts in question; this is true for social sciences in particular. For example, we cannot currently extract brain fluid from a person and from that determine definitively his or her intellectual capacity, or motivation, or introversion, etc. Instead we must develop scales, surveys, and tasks—measures, to be precise—that we believe will give us accurate insight into how much of a variable a person has. Rarely in social sciences do our measures inform us of absolute values of a variable, but more commonly allow us to make relative judgments: does Person A have more "introversion" than Person B, and so forth.

Measurement Reliability and Validity

But if we cannot measure a conceptual variable with absolute objectivity, how can we be confident that our operationalization of the variable, i.e., our measurement of it, truly reflects the variable that we wish to measure? How do we know that our introversion scale, for example, really measures our conceptualization of *introversion*, rather than some other similar, but meaningful distinct construct? The properties of reliability and validity deal specifically with this question.

Reliability describes internal properties of a measure, and refers to the extent that a measurement can be reproduced. Assuming that we are attempting to measure a stable construct, something that will not change greatly in value over time, we would hope that our measure would produce the same score if it were administered at multiple times. If a measure shows one value at time 1, and a considerably different value at time 2, even if the level of the conceptual variable has not changed, we would not consider that measure to be reliable. If we weigh 180 pounds and that weight does not change, we would hope that our bathroom scale would read close to 180 each time we stepped on it. A highly reliable scale would vary very little each time we stepped on it (assuming that our actual weight has not changed), whereas a poorly reliable scale might vary quite a lot. An IQ test that produced a score of 130 at one time, and then a score of 95 one year later from the same person would not be considered a reliable test. Thus, one way of assessing the reliability of a measure is to determine the correspondence among scores collected at different times. This is called test-retest reliability. Note that not all constructs are expected to be stable over time, and thus might not show high test-retest reliability. A measure of how much alcohol a person plans to drink that night would not necessarily be expected to generate a similar score if asked on a different night.

Some measures involve multiple items (questions) assessing the same basic conceptual variable. There may be a large number of possible questions to assess a single concept. For example, there are many questions that would inform us whether a person was relatively introverted or relatively extraverted. Asking about a person's social behavior and social comfort using several questions is not necessarily redundant; there may be different facets to the concept of introversion, and including an array of questions to reflect the different facets of the construct may produce an overall better measure. However, it is important for measurement reliability that these different items used on the scale all seem to go together, to cling together. This reflects *inter-item reliability*. If a participant taking a personality test gave very high scores for some questions, moderate scores for other items, and low scores for other items, this would suggest poor inter-item reliability. Since all items are meant to measure the same construct (introversion, in this example) we would expect similar response patterns to each item. Note, however, that some variables are measured with single questions, and thus inter-item reliability cannot be assessed.

Whereas reliability reflects a property of the scale, **validity** reflects the correspondence between the measure and the conceptual variable in question. For example, does our measure of introversion really distinguish between introverts and extroverts, or does it really measure some other variable? There are multiple ways of thinking about validity. Experimental design, for example, is concerned with internal validity, external validity, construct validity, and conclusion validity (see Cook & Campbell, 1979, for a thorough discussion on this topic). For understanding whether a scale, instrument, or item validly measures the conceptual variable that it is supposed to measure, however, it is common to consider convergent and discriminant validity.

Convergent and discriminant validity both are considered subcategories of construct validity. The idea behind convergent validity is that measures of constructs that theoretically should be related together in fact are observed to be related. For example, self-esteem and shyness are not identical constructs, but they are similar to each other. We would expect that people who score high on our introversion measure also would score high on a valid measure of shyness. Finding such a relationship would provide convergent evidence of the validity of the introversion measure. Discriminant validity, on the other hand, concerns the fact that constructs that theoretically should not be related to our target construct in fact are not observed to be related. For example, we would not expect introversion and "math skill" to be related; there is no reason to expect that people who are introverted would necessarily be better at math. Finding no relationship between these two variables would be evidence of discriminant validity. Typically, in order to determine whether a measure is valid, there needs to be both convergent and discriminant validity.

The relationship between **reliability** and **validity** is asymmetric. It is possible for a measure to be reliable but not valid; however, if a measure is valid, it also must be assumed to be reliable. A measure that produces a different score or value each time you administer it likely would not be considered a strong measure of the construct of interest. To clarify the relationship between the two, it may be useful to think of reliability as analogous with *precision,* and validity as analogous with *accuracy.* A person throwing darts at a dartboard may consistently hit the target several inches to the right of the bull's-eye. This dart thrower may be considered reliable because the outcome is always the same, but would not be considered valid because he never hits the bull's-eye. Similarly, a scale that always adds 10 pounds to a person's weight would be considered reliable, but not valid as the weight it reports does not reflect the actual weight of the person.

Scales of Measurement

Remember that measurement, in general, concerns taking abstract concepts and making them tangible by systematically quantifying different amounts of that variable. There are several broad categories of metrics or scales that can be used in the process of quantifying a conceptual variable. Each of the four scales of measurement described next contains different properties.

The most raw, least refined scale of measurement is the **nominal scale.** When we measure something using the nominal scale, we take participants' responses to a survey question or item and place each response in a category or group. The categories used in the measurement differ from each other *qualitatively,* but not quantitatively. We know that responses placed into one category are somehow different from responses placed in another category, but there is little way of defining these differences; we cannot, for example, use the nominal scale to indicate whether one person has more or less of a variable than another person, or whether one score is higher or lower than another. We cannot rank or order the data, or apply a quantitative label to them.

For example, questions that ask participants to describe their favorite color or indicate what type of car they drive are examples using a nominal scale for measurement. Regarding favorite color, we know that the response "yellow" is different than the response "blue" and accordingly would be placed into a different category (i.e., the yellow and blue categories, respectively). We can say that two people are different on the variable "favorite color," but we cannot say much more than that. It would not make sense to indicate that one person was higher on that variable, or had more of "favorite color" than another person, and such is the limit of the nominal scale.

When using the **ordinal** scale, responses are placed into categories that differentiate them from one another, but unlike the nominal scale, there is some inherent order or structure to these categories; responses can be ranked. For example, if we collected data on runners in a race, we could record whether a runner fell into the "first place," "second place," "third place," or "did not place" category. Using the ordinal scale, however, we can do more than determine that "first place" is different than "second place," but we can assign rank to those categories as well. It is clear that "first place" is higher than "second place," or that "first place" reflects more speed than "second place."

Military rank is another common example of the ordinal scale. Military personnel could be measured on whether they were privates, sergeants, lieutenants, captains, majors, colonels, or generals. There is a clear hierarchy to military rank, and it is possible to deduce whether one military rank is higher or lower than another. However, what cannot be deduced from the ordinal scale is the *size* of difference between categories. For example, we cannot quantify the difference between captain and major (other than it is a difference of one rank). Thus, neither can we compare differences. We might ask: is the difference between general and colonel smaller or greater than the difference between captain and major? Because it is not possible to measure the size of the difference between categories, it is not possible to address this question. This is a limitation of the ordinal scale.

On the other hand, variables measured using the **interval** scale not only can be ranked, but the differences between and among categories can be measured. Measuring variables using the interval allows us to make **additive** comparisons. Temperature, for example, is measured using an interval scale. If we measure temperature on two days and get scores of 70° and 50°, it not only is clear that the former day is warmer than the latter, but that in fact it is 20° warmer. If two other days were measured at 55° and 45°, we could state that the difference between the first pair of days (20°) is larger than the second pair of days (10°). The differences between categories can be quantified and have meaning across the range of scores.

One crucial limitation of the interval scale, however, is that the value of zero does not have special, absolute meaning; a score of zero is simply another value on the scale. When using the interval scale, we cannot conclude that a participant with a zero on some variable has none of that variable, only that he has less of the variable than someone who scored a 1, and more of that variable than someone who scored a –1. For example, if a temperature is measured at 0 degrees Fahrenheit, it does not indicate that there is no temperature; it simply means that it is cold out. We cannot make multiplicative statements when using the interval scale. Forty degrees is not *twice* as warm as 20°, since zero is not the starting point for temperature; zero is just another value on the scale.

The most refined scale of measurement is the **ratio** scale. Things measured on the ratio scale have all the properties of the interval scale, but the value of zero indicates that there is none of the variable in question. A vehicle that is traveling at 0 miles-per-hour has no speed, and an object that is 0 inches tall has no height. Unlike the interval scale, when a variable is measured using the ratio scale, we can make multiplicative comparisons: 30 miles-per-hour is twice as fast as 15 miles-per-hour, etc.

Continuous Variables

Some variables hold the distinction of being labeled **continuous** variables. Often, some ratio variables are considered continuous, but not all continuous variables are ratio, nor are all ratio variables necessarily continuous. A variable is considered continuous if it (theoretically) has an infinite number of categories, and an infinite number of categories between any two scores. Height, speed, distance, etc., each are continuous variables because, in theory, they can be measured with greater and greater precision. If we are measuring height of a group of people, one person might measure 67″ tall, and another person might measure 68″ tall. Although we may round off measurements to the nearest inch, in truth there is any number of measurements between those two: it is possible for a person to be 67.1″ tall, 67.01″ tall, 67.001″ tall, etc. When using continuous variables, the placement of participant responses into categories is artificial.

However, a measure of how many problems out of 10 a student answered correctly would be ratio but not continuous. The measure is ratio because a score of 0 means that no problems were answered correctly; however, the variable is not continuous because there are no possible values in between whole number categories. A student can get 8 problems correct or 9 problems correct, but not 8.5 problems correct.

Categorical v. Score Variables

A *practical* distinction regarding scales of measurement concerns whether a variable is categorical or a score variable; often this distinction parallels whether a variable is nominal or not. A variable is categorical if scores on the variable indicate which group or category a participant belongs to; sometimes the value does not indicate whether *how much* of a variable a participant has. For example, a data set might indicate a participant's gender by assigning "1" to men and "2" to women. However, women do not have *more* gender than men simply because they have a higher score; the score simply indicates they belong to one group v. another.

Categorical variables sometimes can be ordinal as well. A social psychological experiment on persuasion might expose some participants to a weak persuasive message, others to a moderate persuasive message, and still others to a strong persuasive message. The variable used to indicate to which group participants were assigned would be considered categorical even though the variable clearly is ordinal.

Variables are considered *score* variables when the variable value is used to indicate the relative level or extent of a variable in a participant. Score variables allow us to determine whether a given participant has more or less of a variable relative to another participant. Score variables typically are measured using ordinal, interval, or ratio scales. A measure of introversion would be a score variable; having a higher value indicates that the participant is relatively more introverted than a participant whose value is lower on the scale.

Whether a variable is considered categorical or score has implications for the type of research designs and statistical tests used to analyze the data. These issues are introduced in the next chapter and addressed more thoroughly when we begin to discuss statistical tests.

PRACTICE PROBLEMS

2.1 Define **measurement.**

2.2 Describe the difference between conceptual variables and measured variables.

2.3 Defined **reliability.**

2.4 List and describe two methods for assessing reliability.

2.5 Define **validity.**

2.6 How is the validity of measure assessed?

2.7 Describe the relationship between reliability and validity.

2.8 Describe and define each of the four scales of measurement: **nominal, ordinal, interval, ratio.**

2.9 Listed below are several examples of measured variables. For each one, identify the **scale of measurement** used.

1. whether a person's exam score is rated as: distinguished, passing, marginal, or failing
2. the square feet of living area in a house
3. team standings in Major League Baseball
4. scores on the SAT test
5. a person's personality type (e.g., Myers-Briggs Personality Type)
6. scores on an introversion-extroversion personality scale
7. the years in which important historical events occurred
8. telephone area codes

2.10 Describe and define each of following types of variables: **continuous, score,** and **categorical.**

1. the hiking distance of trails in the Shenandoah Valley
2. whether a person is defined, based on a test score, as an *introvert* or an *extrovert*
3. the number of correctly answered questions in a trivia game
4. people's ratings (on a 10-point scale) of the attractiveness of different celebrities
5. participants' response times on a reaction test
6. participants' assignment to receive Treatment A or Treatment B in a medical study

Research Design

As discussed in the introduction chapter, statistics is a process applied to data that has been collected in the process of conducting empirical research. Although it is not within the scope of this book to give a comprehensive examination of the variety of research methodologies used, it is important to introduce readers to two broad and distinct methodological approaches. But first, it is important to clarify and define scientific research.

What Is Science?

There are a variety of rules of thumbs—many of which are inaccurate—that guide people's beliefs about which topics and areas of interest should be considered scientific. Some people may believe that a field should be considering science to the extent that it involves math, or whether it involves strict, invariable laws, and even whether the topic matter is difficult to understand. While these may describe some sciences, science in fact is defined by the process through which knowledge about the field is gathered and how the field grows. This process is known as the scientific method, and disciplines that use the scientific method as the central approach for discovery are considered sciences. The scientific method is used to test hypotheses or research questions that (ideally) have been derived from a broad theory. Using the scientific method to test or examine a hypothesis informs scientists about the validity of related theory, and the process of developing, testing, and falsifying theories helps a scientific discipline grow and expand.

Although more thorough discussions of the scientific method are presented in research methodology text books, it is important to describe the basic components of this method. Key to the scientific method are the principles of empiricism, objectivism, and skepticism. Science advances via collection of *empirically observed* phenomena; i.e., the subject of interest must be measurable using sensory information. This is in contrast to knowledge that is based on intuition, presumption, or authority, where subjective beliefs or feelings serve as data without any direct evidence of veracity against the external reality. Ideally, collection of observations (i.e., measurements) occurs systematically. Following the scientific method, data collection should occur *objectively* to minimize bias and to separate the scientist's own presumptions from the data. Even scientists who try very hard to divorce their own expectations from the scientific procedures have potential to unintentionally bias the research results. Often, in experimental designs (discussed in this chapter), the person conducting the study will not be aware of the specific treatments that are administered to specific participants; participants, too, often are unaware of the purpose of the study and the specifics of their treatment in order to keep the results objective. Scientists also are encouraged to approach their research with *skepticism*; they should be willing to question their theories and hypotheses, and not be so quick to assume that data collected support their contentions. Scientists should attempt to interpret their research as if a scientist unconnected to the study were reviewing it.

What is crucial is that a field is considered a *science* not by the content of its theories, but rather by the process through which the field grows. Scientific research often—but not always—begins with (1) a broad theory—a set of principles for understanding the world that predict and explain a variety of phenomena. From theories, scientists derive (2) hypotheses—specific research questions. Often hypotheses are designed such that empirical support for the hypotheses contributes to support for the broader theory, but not all hypotheses are theory based. Sometimes researchers may wish to answer research questions that may have considerable practical value but that are not grounded deeply in theory. A researcher interested in knowing the voting preferences of registered voters might design a survey to measure this from a sample of voters, without their being any strong theory to predict the results.

After developing their hypotheses, researchers then (3) design studies in order to test these hypotheses. Two very broad research approaches—correlational and experimental—are introduced on the following pages. When developed and administered correctly, research studies generate data relevant to the research hypothesis. In order to make sense out of the data, researchers (4) conduct analyses of the data using statistical techniques (some of which are described in Chapters 11 through 18). Finally, researchers take the results of their analyses and (5) interpret them to help identify the implications of research (i.e., whether the data helped support or disconfirm the research hypothesis).

Correlational Methods

The purpose of correlational research designs is simply to establish that there is a relationship (covariation) between two variables. These methods may determine that people who score a particular way on variable X tend to score a particular way on variable (Y); consequently, knowing something about a person's score on one variable can be used to help predict scores on a second variable. It may be the case, for example, that the people with high school GPAs also tend to have high college GPAs. This example describes a positive relationship between those variables (as scores on variable X increase, scores on variable Y also tend to increase). However, some relationships may be *negative:* persons who watch a lot of TV per week (i.e., on the high end of the distribution for hours spent watching TV per week) may in fact have relatively low GPAs (as scores on X increase, scores on Y tend to decrease).

Correlational methods also can involve comparing differences between groups. For example, we may wish to compare men and women on their performance on a math exam. Men and women would take a math test, and the average test score for men would be compared to the average test score for women. Meaningful differences between men and women on the math test would indicate that a relationship exists between the two variables *gender* and math *performance.*

One key element of correlational research is that all of the variables involved are *measured* variables (as opposed to manipulated variables, as discussed under *Experimental Methods*). Participants come into the study with their a priori levels of the variables of interest, e.g., their own personality, intelligence, etc., and the researcher simply measures the extant levels of the variable. Statistical procedures (discussed later in this book) are applied to those measured variables to determine whether they are meaningfully related. Assuming that we have valid measures, statistical evidence of a relationship between our measured variables can indicate a relationship between conceptual variables.

Imagine that a researcher hypothesizes that there is a relationship between level of self-esteem and success on academic tests. In order to test this hypothesis, the researcher measures participants' self-esteem using a standard self-esteem scale, and then asks participants to take an exam designed to serve as an outcome performance measure. The researcher hypothesizes that people who score relatively high on the self-esteem scale also will tend to score relatively high on the test, and that persons who score relatively low on the self-esteem measure will score relatively low on the test. Assuming that the measures are valid and statistical techniques determine a relationship between the two measures, the researcher may conclude that her theory is supported.

Although this study will allow the researcher to determine whether or not there is an observable relationship between self-esteem and test performance, it does not explain why this relation may exist. Correlational research is limited in that it cannot determine *causality;* i.e., it cannot be used to determine whether change in one variable (self-esteem) causes change in the other variable (test performance). With any observed correlation between two variables, there usually are several possible causal explanations, and correlational approaches do not allow us to determine which explanation is correct. First, although the researchers may hypothesize that one variable caused the other variable, in many cases it is plausible that the reverse is true: that the latter variable influenced the former variable. For example, a researcher may observe a relationship between the extent of mental health problems and homelessness and hypothesize that individuals who suffer from poor mental health are particularly susceptible to losing their homes (i.e., that mental health problems *cause* homelessness). However, an alternative interpretation might suggest that individuals who are homeless and lack the social support networks of "mainstream" society develop mental health problems due to social isolation. A simple correlation, by itself, cannot indicate which of these two interpretations is likely to be correct.

It also is possible that an observed correlation between two variables is due to the presence of some "3rd variable" that has not been measured in the study (or even considered!). This 3rd variable may influence both of the measures and cause the two to become correlated. For example, if a researcher collected data on people's foot size and annual income and examined the relationship between the two, he probably would find a meaningful correlation. Astonishing as it may seem, people with larger feet do tend to earn higher salaries than people with smaller feet. However, the fact that this relationship is observed in the data by no means indicates that having larger feet *causes* a person to earn a higher income. In this example, participants' gender is a "3rd variable" that might explain the observed relationship between foot size and income.

Economic data suggests that women in the United States, on average, earn approximately $0.70 for each dollar men earn for the same occupation. It also is the case that women, on average, have smaller feet than men. The fact that women have smaller feet and lower incomes, and men have larger feet and higher incomes, creates a correlation between these two measured variables; the relationship that we find between them occurs because gender causes both. Note that if we conducted this study using only men or only women, it is likely that the correlation between foot size and income would go away (e.g., women with larger feet probably do not make more money than women with small feet). Note further that if children were included in our sample, age would explain the correlation in much the same way as gender (i.e., children have smaller feet and typically earn no money).

In the example introduced earlier, the hypothesized relationship between self-esteem and test performance could plausibly be explained by a 3rd variable such as participants' "global competence." For example, participants who are highly competent (e.g., intelligent, successful) likely have high self-esteem due to a history of success; at the same time, these highly competent people also are more likely to perform well on the test. On the other hand, participants who are low in competence may suffer from lower self-esteem because they have experienced more failure in life; and they also may be more likely to perform poorly on the test. Even if we find a relationship between self-esteem and test performance, we cannot conclude that high self-esteem causes people to perform well on tests because we cannot rule out the possibility that "global competence"—or some other variable not measured—really caused the relationship to exist.

Experimental Methods

In order to determine a causal relationship between variables, a special research design called an *experiment* must be used. Although a full treatise on experimental methodology cannot be produced in this chapter, the key steps in conducting experimental research are described.

In conducting experimental research, the researcher explicitly identifies and defines the **independent** and **dependent** variables. **Independent variables** are "causal" variables and are hypothesized to influence some outcome. The **dependent variable** is the outcome that should be affected by the independent variable. Unlike correlational research, where levels of both the independent "causal" variables and dependent "outcomes" variables existed within participants prior to the study, in experimental studies, the independent variable is explicitly manipulated by the researcher. The researcher controls (ideally) the amount of the independent variable in participants.

Experimental designs require first that participants are randomly assigned to groups. The number of groups involved in the research will depend on the nature of the independent "causal" variable that is being tested. The researcher will need a different group for each level of the independent variable that he or she is interested in. For example, if a researcher wishes to compare the relative efficacy of two teaching methods (Method A and Method B) on a standardized test, two groups may be used—one to reflect Method A and the other to reflect Method B. A researcher who wanted to test two types of pain killers (Medicine A and Medicine B) on two different types of pain (Headaches and Backaches) would need four groups.

The first key step to experimental design is that each person in the sample is assigned at random to one of the groups, and that probability of being assigned to any particular group is equal for all groups. The result of this random assignment is that the composition of participants within each group should be effectively equivalent among the groups. There no doubt will be variability within a given sample: people will differ in height, weight, sex, intelligence, attractiveness, introversion, motivation, sensitivity, etc.; however, if participants are assigned to groups at random, there is no reason to expect that the characteristics of people in one group will differ from those in other groups.

For example, if we assigned our sample to two groups, there is no reason to expect that people in group one would be smarter or more motivated than those in group two; nor is there reason to expect that people in group two would be smarter or more motivated than those in group one. Admittedly, within a single sample it is possible that random assignment would create disproportionate groups; however, in the long run, we expect that the composition of high intelligence and less intelligence, highly motivated and less motivated, etc., persons should be equal between the groups. Because we expect our groups to be equivalent (due to random assignment), if we gave participants a dependent measure (e.g., some test or outcome measure), we also would expect them to perform equally well; we would expect the groups to do just about the same (the average test scores would be approximately equal across the groups).

Note that participants are not considered to be randomly assigned if they select their own group, or if they are assigned to a group according to some *a priori* variable. For example, if a researcher decided to administer teaching Method A to students in his 8:00 class and Method B to students in his 11:00 class, this would violate the experimental requirement for random assignment; each individual student did not have the same probability of being assigned to one group or another, and it cannot be assumed that these two are equivalent. One can imagine, for example, that students who sign up for an 8:00 class may be more motivated than those who sign up for an 11:00 class; alternatively, students in 8:00 classes may have lower class standing (have fewer credits) and thus less choice over course selection. It is impossible to know whether these two groups differ before the start of the experiment. They may even differ on some important variable that we would never consider to measure!

The second key step in experimental methodology is for the researcher to **manipulate the independent variable.** Whereas the different groups in our study begin effectively equivalent (due to random assignment), the researcher now does something that creates a difference between or among the groups on the independent variable. For example, if the independent variable was teaching method and the researcher wanted to determine whether teaching Method A and Method B were differently effective, the researcher would implement teaching Method A to one group and Method B to another group. The previously equivalent groups now should differ (on average) on one and only one variable (i.e., teaching method). Now, if the researcher gave an exam to the participants in the two groups, and found that test scores from group A differed (on average) from test scores from group B, the only plausible explanation for these differences would be the fact that they received different teaching methods. Because the groups differ on only one variable, then that variable is the only thing that could be responsible for differences in test performance.

The crucial aspect of manipulating the independent variable is that the researcher must create the differences between or among the groups, rather than having participants come into the study with these differences. Comparing men to women does not constitute an experiment because the researcher does not randomly decide the gender of participants. Similarly, recall the correlational examples where the researcher hypothesized a relationship between self-esteem and test performance. If that researcher created one group of participants who scored high on a self-esteem scale and another group that scored low on a self-esteem scale, this also would not constitute an experimental design: although the groups may differ in self-esteem, it is possible that they differ on some other important variable as well. If these two groups produced different test scores (on average), it would not be possible to attribute this difference solely to difference in self-esteem. It would not be possible to rule out the possibility that another variable caused the differences.

So how might a researcher test the hypothesis that having high self-esteem causes higher test performance? A researcher might first take a sample of participants and assign them at random to two groups. We would expect that participants in the first group would have approximately the same level of self-esteem, intelligence, etc., as participants in the second group. At this stage, we would expect the two groups to perform equally well on the outcome test. But before administering the test, the researcher does something to raise the self-esteem of participants in one group relative to participants in the other group. Although it is beyond the scope of this chapter to describe in detail methods of experimental manipulation, one possible method is described.

Before giving the outcome test to participants, imagine that the researcher first gave participants on open-ended, abstract test (such as an inkblot test) where it is not clear what answers are correct v. incorrect. Without actually grading or examining these abstract tests, the researcher might use the test as an opportunity to provide participants with *bogus feedback.* All of the participants in one group might be told: "Your test results indicate hidden potential for great creativity. You might not realize it now, but one day this potential inside of you will blossom." Participants in the other group might be told: "Your test results suggest limited growth in creative capacity. You already have reached your peak in creative potential, and should not expect any additional growth." It is important to stress that this feedback is given to one group or another regardless of how they actually scored on the abstract test.

The only reason for administering the abstract test was to provide an excuse for giving them this feedback. The consequence of the feedback is that it might affect participants' self-esteem. Those participants who received positive feedback may have had their self-esteem boosted, and those who received the neutral/negative feedback may have had their self-esteem reduced.

On average, participants in one group should now have higher self-esteem than participants in the other group. This does not mean necessarily that all participants in group one have higher self-esteem than all participants in group two. A participant in group one who began with very low self-esteem might still have lower self-esteem than a participant in group two who began with very high self-esteem—even after the experimental manipulation. What is important is that *on average*, participants who received the positive feedback have higher self-esteem than participants who received neutral/negative feedback.

After manipulating the independent variable, the researcher then measures the outcome using the dependent measure. If the average test score in group one is meaningfully greater than the average test score in group two, the researcher can conclude that the high self-esteem causes higher test scores. Because the groups began as equivalent, and the only thing different between them was that one received positive feedback while the other received neutral/negative feedback, the manipulation is the only plausible explanation for the differences in test performance. Assuming that the manipulation successfully influenced the level of participants' self-esteem, the researcher can conclude that change in self-esteem caused the change in test performance.

Research Design and Type of Statistical Test

The examples used in this chapter foreshadow the fact that some statistical tests you will learn about later on involve comparing means among groups (e.g., comparing test scores between individuals who receive positive esteem feedback and those that receive neutral/negative feedback). Other statistical tests involve examining the relationship between measured variables (e.g., is there a tendency for people with relatively high high-school GPAs also to have relatively high college GPAs? is there a tendency for students who watch a lot of TV per week to have lower GPAs?). It is not too uncommon to assume that the former corresponds necessarily with experimental research, while the latter corresponds with correlational research. Although it is true that experimental research, by definition, involves comparing average scores among groups, correlational research can involve group comparisons as well. A comparison of men v. women, or high self-esteem participants to low self-esteem participants, would not be considered experimental because participants were not randomly assigned to be male or female, etc.

PRACTICE PROBLEMS

3.1   List and describe five steps involved in conducting scientific research.

3.2   Describe the key elements of the scientific method and a general approach to research.

3.3   Describe **correlational** research and differentiate between positive v. negative relationships.

3.4 Even if we demonstrate a correlation between two variables, why might this correlation not suggest causality? What are possible alternative explanations for this relationship other than a causal one?

3.5 Define **independent** and **dependent** variables.

3.6 What are two key components to **experimental research** approaches? What are the implications of each?

3.7 Described below are several examples of social science research. For each one, identify the hypothesized independent and dependent variables; indicate whether the research is *correlational* or *experimental.*

1. A traffic safety researcher wants to know whether active and visible police enforcement of drunk driving laws (e.g., using sobriety checkpoints) reduces alcohol-related crashes. Using data from 20 different state counties, the researcher examines how many sobriety checkpoints were conducted within each state and uses that to categorize each state as "high enforcement," "medium enforcement," and "low enforcement." He then compares the number of alcohol-related crashes that occurred within the counties among the three groups.

   a. What are the hypothesized independent and dependent variables?

   b. Is this research correlational or experimental?

2. A clinical psychologist hypothesized that many mental health problems that people experience stem from poor social skills and a lack of a social network. She has developed a social skills training course that she believes will help people. She randomly assigns one group of clients to receive this social skills training course, and randomly assigns another group of clients to receive standard "talk" therapy. Six months later she assesses their mental health using a standard instrument.

   a. What are the hypothesized independent and dependent variables?

   b. Is this research correlational or experimental?

3. An educational researcher wishes to assess whether requiring mandatory foreign language/culture classes in high school reduces cultural and racial tension in those schools. She has agreement from several school districts to conduct research in the high schools. Using a coin toss, she determines which schools will have a mandatory foreign language/culture requirement and which will not. After one year of having this policy in place, she measures the racial/cultural tension in the schools and uses valid observational techniques.

   a. What are the hypothesized independent and dependent variables?

   b. Is this research correlational or experimental?

4. A graduate student research assistant (RA) wants to test whether people are more influenced by a persuasive message when it is delivered by an attractive speaker v. a less attractive speaker. The RA posts a sign-up sheet in the psychology buildings inviting students to sign up and listen to a "guest lecturer" on either Monday or Wednesday. The research assistant randomly determines that participants signed up for Monday will listen to a talk by a less attractive speaker, and participants

signed up for Wednesday will listen to a talk by a more attractive speaker. Each speaker gives the identical lecture on "why the university needs to raise tuition next year." At the end of each talk, participants rate how much they agreed with the lecturer.

a. What are the hypothesized independent and dependent variables?

b. Is the research correlational or experimental?

CHAPTER
4

Probability

Probability is an essential component of statistics; it is a broad discipline and arguably the most complex and counterintuitive area within the field. A college math department concerned with *probability theory* may offer several courses on the topic; however, for this introductory course in statistics, only a basic understanding of probability is necessary. The statistical procedures taught in this course are rooted in probability, and so developing a solid comprehension of most fundamental probability concepts will greatly enhance understanding of the material presented herein.

In a nutshell, *probability* concerns the likelihood of a specific event occurring given the characteristics of all possible events. In the simplest form, we may wish to know the chance of drawing an Ace from a deck of cards, or determine the possibility that we can randomly select a person with a high IQ. In more complex forms, we may wish to determine the likelihood associated with any one of a number of events occurring (such as drawing an Ace or a Diamond from a deck of cards), or the probabilities associated with a particular series of events occurring (such as drawing three Aces in a row). Even more complex is combinatorial statistics (such as determining the total possible orderings of a standard deck of cards), which is beyond the scope of this book.

In its simplest form, the probability (chance) of an event occurring is equal to:

$$P = \frac{\# \text{ of specific events}}{\text{Total } \# \text{ of events}}$$

This produces a value between 0 and 1 (probabilities never are negative). A probability of 1 indicates that a given event is certain to happen (100% likely), while a probability of 0 indicates that it is impossible for a given event to happen (0% likely).

Consider that a standard deck of cards contains 52 cards, thus there are 52 total number of possible events that might occur when you randomly draw a card from the deck. A standard deck is composed of four different suits (Club, Diamond, Heart, and Spade) and thirteen faces (numbers two through ten, Jack, Queen, King, and Ace).

Therefore, the probability of drawing a King out of a deck of cards is equal to 4/52 because there are four Kings (four specific events) in a deck of cards (52 total number of possible events). Similarly, the probability of rolling a "5" on a die is equal to 1/6 because dice have six sides (six total number of possible events) but only a single value of "5."

Note that this formula for computing probability is true *assuming* that we are drawing from a *random sample*. The criteria for a sample being *random* are:

1. That each observation has an equal chance of being selected.
2. This equal chance remains *constant* across multiple draws.

Loaded dice, unfair coins, and sticky cards may violate the assumption of generating a random sample. When a true random sample cannot be assumed, this approach to computing probability is not necessarily valid. Some forms of survey sampling explicitly involve cluster and stratified sampling, and it becomes more complicated to compute probabilities in these cases. However, even assuming a simple random sample, there are other types of probabilities that require modification to the basic formula.

Compound Probabilities

Compound probabilities concern the likelihood of some combination of events occurring. There are two basic ways to "combine" events. Events can be combined such that (1) if any one of several specific events occurs, the criterion is met, and (2) if a particular serial order of events occurs, the criterion is met.

The OR Rule

We can refer to the former case as using the **OR** rule; we may be interested in knowing the probability of either Event A **or** Event B occurring. Imagine a poker player hoping to get a *straight* (five cards in serial order) currently holds cards of 4, 5, 6, and 7 in her hand, with one more card to draw. Drawing either a 3 **or** an 8 would give a straight. The rule of thumb when dealing with the OR rule is that individual probabilities are added together.

Probability A or B = Probability A + Probability B

For example, the chance of getting a King or a Queen on a single draw from a deck of cards is equal to $(4/52) + (4/52) = 8/52 = 2/13$. Determining the probability of each event individually and then adding the two events together gives the probability for the combined event.

This rule, however, assumes that the events are **mutually exclusive.** Two events can be considered mutually exclusive if it is impossible for both events to occur at the same time: the event must be one or the other, or neither, but not both. In this case, Kings and Queens are mutually exclusive events, because it is impossible to draw a card that is both a King and a Queen.

However, some events may not be mutually exclusive. This is the case when the possible events that we are interested in vary on multiple dimensions. Playing cards, for example, vary both in face value and in suit. If we are interested in computing the probability of drawing either an Ace or a Heart, we cannot simply add the two independent probabilities together because the two events are not mutually exclusive.

If we ignored the issue of non-exclusivity and simply added the probabilities, we would get (incorrectly):

Probability King or Heart = P(King) + P(Heart) = 4/52 + 13/52 = 17/52 = .327

Note that there are four Kings (thus 4/52) and thirteen Hearts (thus 13/52) in a standard deck.

The issue of mutual exclusivity becomes important because there is one card in the deck that is both a King and a Heart—the King of Hearts—and when the individual probabilities are added together, this one card is counted twice: it is counted as one of the four Kings, as well as one of the thirteen Hearts. When dealing with events that are not mutually exclusive, one must *subtract* the probability of joint events occurring. In this case, we must subtract the single King of Hearts from the computation.

Thus, the correct probability is:

Probability King or Heart = P(King) + P(Heart) – P(King and Heart)
= 4/52 + 13/52 – 1/52 = 16/52 = .308

The fact that the single King of Hearts has been counted twice is accommodated by subtracting it once from the equation. Note that when events are mutually exclusive, the probability of a joint occurrence is 0 (the probability of getting both a King and a Queen on a single draw is 0), and thus it drops from the equation.

The AND Rule

Whereas the OR rule concerns the likelihood of getting any one of several events on a single draw, the AND rule concerns the likelihood of getting a specific series of events on multiple draws. When we are interested in drawing multiple events from the pool of possible events, we *multiply* the probabilities of the individual events.

Probability A and B = Probability A × Probability B

For example, the probability of drawing a King and a Queen on consecutive draws from a deck of cards is equal to:

$$Probability\ King\ and\ Queen\ (on\ two\ draws) = Probability\ (King) \times Probability\ (Queen)$$
$$= (4/52) * (4/52) = 16/2704 = .006$$

Remember that there are four Kings and four Queens in a deck of 52 cards.

This probability computed using this formula assumes the exact order of events: King first, Queen second. Note, however, that if the problem asked to determine the probability of drawing a Queen first and then a King, the answer would be the same:

$$Probability\ Queen\ and\ King\ (on\ two\ draws) = (4/52) * (4/52) = 16/2704 = .006$$

If we needed to compute the probability of three events occurring in a row, we simply would multiply the third probability to the equation. For example, the probability of randomly drawing three Aces in a row would be:

$$Probability\ Ace,\ then\ Ace,\ then\ Ace = (4/52) * (4/52) * (4/52) = 16/2704 = .0005$$

But what if you were asked to compute the probability of getting a King and a Queen on two draws, *regardless of order?* This type of question borders on the field of permutations and combinatorials, but in simple cases we can calculate the answer without needing to understand these more complex probabilistic techniques.

In order to determine the probability of getting a King and Queen regardless of order, we first need to consider the possible number of orders that may occur. In this case, there are only two:

Order 1: King, Queen

Order 2: Queen, King

We already have calculated that the probability of either event occurring is .006. The problem of randomly drawing a King and Queen on two draws, regardless of order, is really the same thing as asking for the probability of getting a King and then a Queen **OR** a Queen and then a King. This type of problem requires us to combine the AND and OR rules. Since we know the probability of each, we simply can add the two together.

$$Probability\ of\ King\ and\ Queen\ (any\ order) = [P(King) \times P(Queen)] + [P(Queen) \times P(King)] = .012$$

Another similar example might involve coin tosses. If we flipped three fair coins, what is the probability of getting two heads and one tail (in any order)? The first step in computing this would be to determine the total number of different ways that tossing three coins could produce two heads and one tail. Careful consideration reveals that there are three different orders:

Head, Head, Tail

Head, Tail, Head

Tail, Head, Head

Assuming that the probability of getting a head or tail on any flip is equal to 0.5 (50–50), we can determine the probability of getting each combination.

P (Head, Head, Tail) = .5 × .5 × .5 = .125

P (Head, Tail, Head) = .5 × .5 × .5 = .125

P (Tail, Head, Head) = .5 × .5 × .5 = .125

The chance of getting the first order, OR the second order, OR the third order is equal to:

.125 + .125 + .125 = .375

This is the probability of flipping three coins and getting two heads and one tail in any order. It would not be so feasible to compute a probability using this approach if there were very many possible orders of events. That is the purpose of combinatorials.

Sampling With or Without Replacement

However, there is an additional concern that must be considered when using the **AND** rule, and this is whether or not the sampling is **with** or **without replacement.** In the previous examples using the AND rule, we were sampling *with* replacement: this means that each time an event was sampled (a card was drawn from the deck) that card was put back into the deck (i.e., replaced) before the next card was drawn. The implication of this is that the total number of events and composition of specific events does not change with each draw. If we are asked to compute the probability for drawing an Ace, King, and Queen on three consecutive draws while sampling *with* replacement, the total number of events (cards in the deck) remains at 52 for each draw, as does the number of Aces, Kings, and Queens.

While sampling *without* replacement, the total number of events decreases with each draw. After drawing the first card (Ace) and not replacing it, there remain only 51 cards in the deck; and after drawing the second card (King), only 50 cards remain before drawing the third card.

Therefore, while sampling *without* replacement, the probability of drawing an Ace, King, and Queen on three consecutive draws is:

Probability Ace, Queen, then King = (4/52) × (4/51) × (4/50) = .00048

If the problem called for drawing three Aces in a row (without replacement), both the total number of events (denominator) and the number of specific events (Aces; numerator) would be affected:

Probability Ace, Ace then Ace = (4/52) × (3/51) × (2/50) = .00018

There is no general rule for determining whether you are sampling with replacement v. without replacement: this will be stated explicitly in the problem. However, when the total number of events is extremely large (e.g., if we are sampling from an entire population) it almost is assumed that we are sampling *with* replacement.

Combining AND with OR Rules for Determining Probabilities

We already have discussed one type of problem where we need to combine the two rules in order to compute the probability (i.e., the chance of getting a King and Queen). However, problems that require combing these two rules also may be presented differently. Imagine that a bag contains 45 marbles that vary on two dimensions: color (Green, Yellow, and Red) and size (Large and Small).

	Large	Small	*Total*
Green	5	12	17
Yellow	10	10	20
Red	15	3	18
Total	30	15	45

This setup can be useful for presenting probability problems that use OR, AND, and both OR and AND rules.

For example, the probability of randomly sampling a Green marble or a Small marble on a single draw would be equal to:

$$(17/45) + (15/45) - (12/45) = 20/45 = 0.44$$

The probability of randomly sampling a Red marble on the first draw and a Green or Small marble on the second draw (assuming sampling with replacement) would be:

$$(18/45) * [(17/45) + (15/45) - (12/45] = (18/45) * (20/45) = \textbf{0.18}$$

It would be difficult to compute this problem using sampling without replacement because we do not know whether the Red marble that was sampled first is large or small, and that would have consequences for the probability of sampling a Small marble on the second draw.

PRACTICE PROBLEMS

4.1 Define **simple random sample.**

4.2 Listed below are paired examples of possible events. For each one, identify whether or not the events are **mutually exclusive.**

  1. The probability of sampling a vehicle that is front-wheel drive (as opposed to rear-wheel) or that has an automatic (v. manual) transmission

  2. Whether a crime occurred in a state with the death penalty or without the death penalty

  3. Whether a participant is male (v. female) or below age 21 (v. age 21 and older)

  4. Whether a person's first vehicle was a Ford, Chevy, Toyota, or Honda

  5. When rolling two dice, getting a total of "4" or rolling a "double" (getting the same number on both dice)

  6. When rolling two dice, getting a total of "7" or rolling a "double"

4.3 Define sampling **with** and **without replacement** and describe the implications for computing probabilities.

4.4 A political researcher has collected data on United States Senators. Out of the pool of 100 Senators, 45 are Democrats and 55 are Republicans. This researcher also has measured the voting patterns ("Yea," "Nay," and "Abstain") of these Senators regarding **Initiative Alpha.** Those data are below.

	Yea	Nay	Abstain	Total
Democrats	24	14	07	45
Republicans	37	03	15	55
Total	61	17	22	100

If we were to randomly select Senators from this population:

  1. What is the probability of sampling a Democrat or an opponent of Initiative Alpha?

  2. What is the probability of sampling a Senator who voted Yea or Abstained for Initiative Alpha?

  3. What is the probability of randomly sampling a Yea-voter and a Nay-voter on two consecutive samples (assuming sampling with replacement)?

  4. What is the probability of sampling three Abstainers in a row on three consecutive draws (assume sampling without replacement)?

  5. What is the probability of randomly sampling a Democrat on the first draw, a Republican or an Abstainer on the second draw, and a Yea-voter on the third draw (assume sampling with replacement)?

6. What is the probability of randomly sampling a Republican on the first draw, a Democrat or a Yea-voter on the second draw, and a Nay-voter or Abstainer on the third draw (assume sampling with replacement)?

4.5 A gambler wants to know the probability of rolling a total of "8" on two dice. What might this probability be? (Hint: Use the same approach for answering this problem as was used with the heads/tails coin toss example on page 26.)

Frequency Distributions

Frequencies and proportions (probabilities) for different values in a set of data can be tabulated and organized for clear presentation. One of the most useful and common practices of describing data is building a frequency distribution table. Frequency distribution tables involve ordering data by rank and condensing it into a table that characterizes the distribution of data, including frequencies, proportions, cumulative frequencies, and cumulative proportions.

There are several requirements for constructing frequency distribution tables. First, because the data is organized by rank, frequency distribution tables cannot be created from *nominal* data—only ordinal, interval, or ratio. Furthermore, under normal circumstances, data must not be truly *continuous* (i.e., have infinite values and categories). In order to create a frequency distribution from truly continuous data, the data first must be made discrete (by rounding, for example), or *class frequency distributions* (discussed later in this chapter) with real limits must be used.

Creating a Frequency Distribution Table

The first step in creating a frequency distribution table is to rank the data scores in order. Next, each possible value in the data set is listed in descending order (from high to low) in the first column of the table. Possible values are mentioned because we wish to include a value (category) that falls with the range of scores even if it happens not to have any observations. For example, if we were constructing a frequency distribution table using data that we collected on a 10-point scale (values from 1–10), but there were no cases with a particular value (for example, nobody in the sample scored a "7"), we still would include that value ("7") in our descending list of scores. It is important to organize score categories in descending order because this order gives meaning to how we interpret the cumulative frequency and cumulative proportion columns (described next).

In the second column of the frequency distribution table, list the number of subjects that fall within each category. This is the *frequency column (f)* that indicates how many participants from the sample have each score. Note that it is possible for a category or value to have a frequency of 0 if there are no cases of participants with a given value.

In the third column, list the *proportion (p)* of cases that fall within each category, where:

$$\text{Proportion (p)} = f/N$$

As a general rule, N reflects the total number of cases in the data set or distribution. Note the similarity in the formula for proportions and that for probability. Proportions, in fact, do reflect probabilities; the probability of randomly sampling a case with a given value from a distribution of scores is equal to the proportion of cases that have that score.

The fourth column in a frequency distribution table contains the *cumulative frequency (cf)* of the scores. The cumulative frequency describes the total number of cases with a given score as well as the total number of cases with scores below that. Assuming, for example, that our data was collected on a 10-point scale, the cumulative frequency for the score category "7" would include the total number of cases that scored "7" as well as the total number of cases that scored "6," "5," and so forth, down to "1." Basically, it includes the total number of scores contained within the "7" category and lower.

Typically, it is easiest to compute the cumulative frequency from the bottom up. At the lowest category, the cumulative frequency and frequency are always the same. The cumulative frequency for a given score ("7," for example) can be calculated by taking the cumulative frequency of the category directly below it ("6") and adding to that the frequency of the current category ("7"). In the example presented on page 33, the frequency associated with the category "7" is 2, as there are two cases in the distribution that scored "7." The cumulative frequency of "6" is 14, as there are 14 cases that scored "6" or lower. Adding the cumulative frequency of "6" plus the frequency of "7" produces 16 (i.e., 14 + 2 = 16), which is the cumulative frequency of the "7" category. The cumulative frequency for the highest category (in this example, "10") always equals the total sample size—the total number of cases in the distribution.

Note that it is because we organize the score categories in *descending* order that the cumulative frequency describes the total number of cases in a given category or above. Had the first column been organized in ascending order (from low to high), our cumulative frequency really would have reflected the total number of cases in a given category or above.

The fifth and final column in a frequency distribution table is the *cumulative proportion*. The cumulative proportion is the proportion of scores in a given category or below; it is similar to the proportion but is calculated from the cumulative frequency rather than the frequency. Thus:

$$\text{Cumulative proportion } (cp) = cf/N$$

Example

Twenty subjects were asked to indicate their impressions of a speaker on a 10-point scale. According to this scale, lower numbers reflect less favorable impressions, while higher numbers reflect more favorable impressions. Below are the ratings made by the 20 participants:

6, 4, 6, 8, 4, 3, 5, 10, 2, 8, 4, 5, 8, 7, 1, 6, 7, 6, 5, 6

We organize the scores in descending order to facilitate constructing the frequency distribution table.

10, 8, 8, 8, 7, 7, 6, 6, 6, 6, 6, 5, 5, 5, 4, 4, 4, 3, 2, 1

▶ Frequency Distribution Table

X (value)	f (frequency)	p (proportion)	cf (cumulative frequency)	cp (cumulative proportion)
10	1	1/20 = .05	20	20/20 = 1.0
9	0	0/20 = .00	19	19/20 = .95
8	3	3/20 = .15	19	19/20 = .95
7	2	2/20 = .10	16	16/20 = .80
6	5	5/20 = .25	14	14/20 = .70
5	3	3/20 = .15	9	9/20 = .45
4	3	3/20 = .15	6	6/20 = .30
3	1	1/20 = .05	3	3/20 = .15
2	1	1/20 = .05	2	2/20 = .10
1	1	1/20 = .05	1	1/20 = .05

Grouped Frequency Distribution Tables

Some types of data, however, do not work well with standard frequency distributions. In cases where the data are truly continuous, and even when data are not continuous but there are a large number of possible categories, summarizing the data in a frequency distribution table may become unwieldy. Tables are designed to make it easier to understand set, and a table with too many rows will not easily be comprehended.

The solution is to use a *grouped* or *class frequency distribution* table. These grouped frequency distribution tables contain the same columns as do standard tables; however, in the first column, score categories are represented as *intervals* or *score ranges*. Any case in the data set with a score that falls within the interval is included in the frequency for that interval. By organizing our data using intervals, rather than single score categories, we are able to describe a wider range of possible scores using relatively few rows. Whereas standard frequency distribution tables include one score or category per row, group frequency distribution tables include multiple scores to be placed in each row.

Although there are many ways a person could construct a set of intervals to include a wide range of scores, there are rules for creating class intervals that produce frequency distribution tables that are manageable and easily interpretable. To the extent that these rules are not followed, it is assumed that the group frequency distribution table created will be less clear.

The primary goal in creating a grouped frequency distribution table is to determine an appropriate *interval width* (i.e., the number of scores or range that fall within each category) that can span the entire range of scores in the data set. As described earlier, too many categories and the table becomes cumbersome and difficult to grasp; too few categories and there is considerable loss of precision in the data.

The first step in creating a grouped frequency distribution table is determining the total range of scores that need to be included in this table. The *range* of scores is equal to the high score in the data set minus the low score in the data. In some cases, a value equal to the smallest denomination of change in the data set is added to the difference score. This accommodates the fact that both the high score and the low score are included in the count. For example, in a distribution of scores ranging from 1 to 10, where scores differ in units of 1, the value 1 may be added; thus the *range* of scores using a 1 to 10 scale would be $10 - 1 + 1 = 10$, indicating that 10 possible values fall within that range (as opposed to 9 if the value of 1 had not been added). Similarly, SAT scores always are measured in units of 10 (e.g., 990, 1000, 1010, 1020, as opposed to 996, 1007), and thus 10 might be added to the difference between high and low SAT scores. In a data set with a high SAT score of 1420 and a low score of 830, the range of scores would be $1420 - 830 + 10 = 600$. The value of 10 is added because that is the smallest unit of measured change. If we measured blood alcohol concentrations, which often are measured to 2-decimal places (such as .00, .08, .16, etc.) we would add .01 to the difference between high and low scores to get the correct range.

The next step after computing the range of scores is to determine how many intervals, and of what interval width, is needed to cover the necessary range of scores. When determining the number of intervals and the interval width, we should consider two rules.

1. It is ideal for a grouped frequency distribution table to contain between 8 and 15 intervals.
2. Interval widths should be whole numbers that are common denominators, such as 5, 10, 20, 25, 50, 100, etc., depending on the range of scores we are using. It is easy for people to interpret data that is organized in groups of 5, 10, 25, etc., and less easy to interpret data that has been organized in groups of 7, or 13, or 17, or some other irregular number; thus we prefer to use the former when choosing interval widths.

The goal is to select an appropriate interval width that can include the entire range of scores using between 8 and 15 intervals. For example, imagine a distribution of scores where the high score was 127 and the low score was 33. The total *range* of scores in that distribution is: $127 - 33 + 1 = 95$. What interval width might we choose to represent these data in a group frequency distribution table? If we choose an interval width (i) of 5, for example, we could determine that it would take approximately 19 intervals to cover a range of 95 scores (because $95 / 5 = 19$). However, 19 intervals falls above the desired 8 to 15 range. Alternatively, if we choose an interval width of 20, we find that it would require 5 intervals to scan the range of 95 scores; 5 intervals seems too few. But if we select an interval width of 10 for this example, 10 intervals each containing 10 scores would be sufficient to cover the entire range of 95 scores in the data set. Note that interval widths of 8, 9, and 11 would cover the span of 95 scores using between 8 and 15 intervals, but those values would produce a table that is less clear than the interval width of 10.

Once an appropriate interval width is selected, the final step is to determine the starting point for the class intervals. The lowest interval in the series of class intervals:

3. Should include the lowest score in the distribution; and

4. The starting value of the lowest interval should be evenly divisible by the interval width.

The starting point for a series of class intervals should be the highest score that is below the low score in the distribution and also evenly divisible by the interval width.

In the prior example, we determined that an interval width of 10 would contain the entire range of 95 scores using the sufficient number of intervals, and the low score in the distribution is 33. The highest score below 33 that is evenly divisible by 10 is 30; thus, the series of class intervals should begin with 30, and increase accordingly by the interval width.

Note that expanding an interval by the interval width is not the same as simply adding the width to the starting value. For example, if the starting value in a series of class intervals is 30, and the width is 10, then the first interval will be $30 - 39$, and NOT $30 - 40$. There are 10 whole number scores between 30 and 39 ($39 - 30 + 1 = 10$), while there are 11 scores between 30 and 40. A person who constructed an interval ranging from 30 to 40 in fact would be using an interval width of 11.

Starting from lowest interval, then, an ideal series of class intervals for a distribution of data ranging from 127 to 33 would be:

30–39; 40–49; 50–59; 60–69; 70–79; 80–89; 90–99; 100–109; 110–119; 120–129

We start with 30 because that score is the largest value below the lowest score (33) that is evenly divisible by the interval width.

When constructing an actual table using these intervals, the intervals would be organized in the descending order (120–127 at the top, and 30–39 at the bottom). The total number of cases with scores that fall within each category would be recorded in the frequency column. Once appropriate frequencies are determined, proportions, cumulative frequencies, and cumulative proportions can be computed.

X	f	p	cf	cp
120–129				
110–119				
100–109				
90–99				
80–89				
70–79				
60–69				
50–59				
40–49				
30–39				

Real Limits

When the data is truly continuous (i.e., and therefore possesses an infinite number of categories), it may become difficult to determine how values all along the border should be categorized.

For example, in a data set of vehicle speeds measured on the highway, we may have two intervals such as:

80–89

70–79

Depending on our means of measurement, it is possible that we will collect data with scores such as 79.256 that fall between the upper boundary of the lower interval and the lower upper of interval. To accommodate this possibility, *real limit values* that lie directly in between 79 and 80 must be created.

Accordingly, the upper real limit for the 70–79 interval is 79.5000 . . . while the lower real limit for the 80–89 interval is also 79.500000 . . .

PRACTICE PROBLEMS

5.1   Consider the set of data below. For this data set, construct a frequency distribution table, including: (a) all the possible values in the distribution; (b) the frequencies of each value; (c) the proportion of each value; (d) the cumulative frequencies of each value; and (e) the cumulative proportion of each value.

01   08✓   05✓   02   06✓

09✓   03   09✓   04✓   10✓

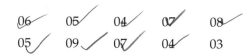

5.2 Discuss the relationship between the proportion scores with a particular value and the probability of randomly sampling that value.

5.3 Define **cumulative frequency** and **cumulative proportion.**

5.4 Why is it important to organize observations in *descending* (rather than *ascending*) order?

5.5 When might it not be appropriate to use a standard frequency distribution table?

5.6 Identify four rules of creating ideal **grouped frequency distribution tables.**

5.7 Consider that a large sample of blood alcohol concentration (BAC) scores ranged from .000 to .212. Generate a set of *class intervals* that would be ideal for constructing a *group frequency distribution* table for these data.

6

Measures of Central Tendency

A s useful as frequency distribution tables are at simplifying and characterizing a set of data, sometimes it is desirable to summarize the data set using a single value. Measures of central tendency describe a class of statistics used to characterize what value is typical, expected, or average in a distribution of data. Although there are a variety of measures of central tendency, this book focuses on the three most commonly used measures: the mean, the median, and the mode.

Mean

The arithmetic mean probably is the most widely used measure of central tendency, and is ideal for data that is relatively symmetric (i.e., "normally distributed," see Figure 6.1). In some circumstances the mean is described as the "expected value" because it is the value that we would expect to get over the long run if we randomly sampled a score from the distribution. Computationally, the mean of a sample is equal to the sum of scores in the data set divided by the number of observations, and is symbolized by an X with a bar over it ($\bar{X}$ stands for the "mean of variable X"; similarly, $\bar{Y}$ would reflect the mean of variable Y).

$$\bar{X} = \Sigma X / N$$

Note that the mean of a population is symbolized by the Greek character μ (mu). That, too, would be computed by summing all of the scores in a population and dividing by the total number of sores, but rarely is it the case that we have an entire population of data at our disposal. Typically, μ is not computed, but rather it is assumed from a theoretical distribution. The importance of μ becomes clearer as we discuss hypothesis testing.

The utility of the mean as a measure of central tendency diminishes as data sets become increasingly skewed (i.e., non-symmetric, see Figure 6.2 and 6.3). The mean is not particularly *robust* and can be influenced a great deal by adding extreme scores, or outliers, to the distribution of data. As will be discussed under the *median*, the mean typically is not used to characterize data that is highly skewed.

Weighted Means

Imagine that a test was given to a sample of college undergraduates spanning all four class levels. But rather than containing individual student scores, the data set included only the means and sample size of each class level. For example:

	$\bar{X}$	N
Freshman	72	13
Sophomore	83	25
Junior	87	28
Senior	75	10

6.1

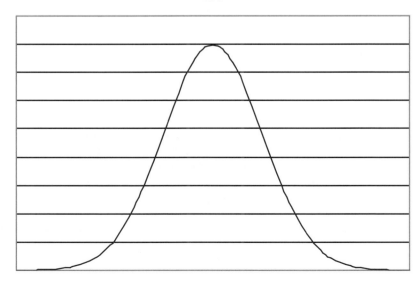

6.2

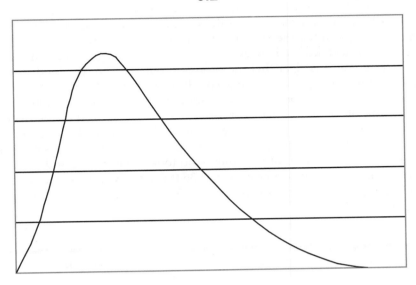

6.3

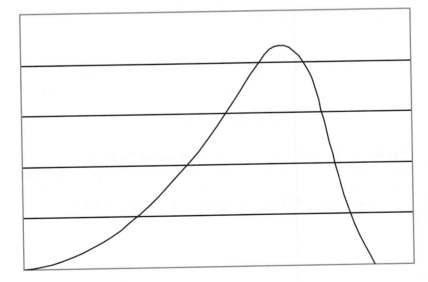

A researcher presented with such data who is interested in computing the overall mean test score may be tempted to simply average the means of the four groups. In this case: $(72 + 83 + 87 + 75)/4 = 79.25$. This approach treats the weight of each group equally; it assumes that the freshman mean, sophomore mean, junior mean, and senior mean all contribute the same to the overall mean of test scores. However, when we consider that the sample sizes of the four groups are different, it is clear that the groups should not be weighted equally. Groups containing more scores have greater influence on the overall mean of the data set.

The correct approach to calculating the overall mean from these data would be to compute the overall sum of the individual scores in the data set, as well as the overall N of the individual scores. Although we do not have the individual data, we can easily get the raw score sum of each group by multiplying each group mean by the group sample size. Using the previous example, if the mean of freshmen who took the test is 72 and 13 freshmen took the test, the sum of the freshman scores must be 936 (the only way a mean of 72 could be produced from 13 scores is if the scores summed to 936). We also can sum the sample size of each group to get the total N.

	$\bar{X}$	N	Mean × N
Freshman	72	13	936
Sophomore	83	25	2075
Junior	87	28	2436
Senior	75	10	750
Total		76	6197

The sum of the four Mean × N products reflects the sum of all the individual scores, even though individual scores were never available in the data set. Given these totals, we can correctly compute the overall mean of the test scores:

$$\bar{X} = 6197/76 = \mathbf{81.54}$$

Note that this mean of 81.54 is higher than the mean of 79.24 generated simply by averaging the four group means. This is due to the fact that the groups with higher test scores (sophomores and juniors) account for relatively more cases and thus contribute more to the overall mean than the groups with lower test scores (freshmen and seniors) who include relatively fewer cases.

Median

The median reflects the score that rests in the middle (i.e., 50th percentile) of the distribution; half of the scores in the distribution are above the median and half are below the median. If data already are organized in a frequency distribution table, the median can be identified as the score for which the value in the cumulative proportion column is the *lowest* proportion, that is at or above .50. In the frequency distribution table example in Chapter 5, the score of "6" marks the median (see page 33): 70% of scores are "6" or below, but 45% of scores are "5" or below, indicating the case at the 50th percentile is a "6." Note that it is not possible to determine the precise median from a *grouped* frequency distribution because it includes the range of scores.

When data are not already in a frequency distribution table (which is most of the time), the median can be computed by first placing all of the scores in order (ascending or descending). Unlike frequency distribution tables, however, each case, not just each score, must be represented. If there are five cases of the score "6," the "6" needs to be written out five times. If the sample size (N) is odd, then there is a single true middle score in the distribution . . . one value where half the scores are above and half the scores are below that score. Computing $(N + 1)/2$ indicates the number of spaces (cases) the researcher must count (in either direction) and that score is the median.

In the example below, N = 23, and $(23 + 1)/2 = 12$

$$10, 12, 12, 13, 13, 13, 14, 14, 15, 15, 15, 17, 18, 18, 19, 19, 20, 20, 21, 21, 23, 24, 25$$

Counting up 12 cases from the start of the ordered distribution results in the score "17." Counting down 12 cases from the highest score also ends on the "17." Thus, the median, the score in the center of the distribution, is 17.

In cases where the sample size is even, there will be two scores in the center of the distribution. The median in this case will be the arithmetic mean of those two middle scores. In the next example, we added an additional score (a second "25") to the distribution to make N = 24. Here, we may simply identify $(N + 1)/2 = 12.5$.

$$10, 12, 12, 13, 13, 13, 14, 14, 15, 15, 15, 17, 18, 18, 19, 19, 20, 20, 21, 21, 23, 24, 25, 25$$

Counting up 12.5 from the bottom of the distribution, and 12.5 from the top of the distribution indicates the score between 17 and 18. The median of this distribution is the mean of these two central scores, therefore $(17 + 18)/2 = 17.5$.

The median is a relatively robust measure of central tendency in that it is less influenced (compared to the mean) by the addition of extreme scores or outliers to the distribution. Note that adding an extremely high score will move the median only one "case" to the right, while adding an extremely low score will move the median one case to the left. Adding multiple, asymmetric extreme scores is required to have a profound affect on the median.

We can compute the mean and median of the ordered data set below (N = 17).

$$10, 12, 12, 13, 14, 14, 15, 15, 18, 19, 19, 20, 21, 21, 23, 24, 25$$

$$\Sigma X = 295 \quad \bar{X} = (\Sigma X/N) = (295/17) = \textbf{17.35}$$

$$(17 + 1)/2 = 9, 9 \text{ cases from low score} = \text{median} = \textbf{18}$$

However, if we add an outlier to the data set (a score of 37) to reach a sample size of 18:

$$10, 12, 12, 13, 14, 14, 15, 15, 18, 19, 19, 20, 21, 21, 23, 24, 25, 37$$

our new mean becomes (332/18) = 18.44, an increase of 1.09, and our new median becomes 18.5, an increase of only 0.5.

Note that if we add several outliers (three additional, in this case), so that N = 20, the difference between mean and median becomes more extreme.

10, 12, 12, 13, 14, 14, 15, 15, 18, 19, 19, 20, 21, 21, 23, 24, 25, *34, 37, 40*

The mean = 406 / 20 = 20.3, an increase of 2.95 over 17.35, whereas the median = 19, an increase of only 1 over 18. The effect of adding non-symmetric outliers to a data set has a larger affect on the mean as the number of outliers increases.

	Example 1 (N = 17)	Example 2 (add one outlier)	Example 3 (add three outliers)
Mean	17.35	18.44 [increase of 1.09]	20.3 [increase of 2.95]
Median	18.00	18.50 [increase of 0.50]	19.0 [increase of 1.00]

The median is commonly used to describe the central tendency of skewed data. Particular examples of skewed distributions include income and salary prices. It is easy to see why these variables are skewed: prices and income typically are grounded at $0 on the low end (there are not houses that sell for negative dollars, nor people who earn negative income), but there is a very high upper boundary. If you consider what the "typical" person earns during the year, or what the "typical" house costs, and then realize the incomes of famous celebrities and company CEOs, and the prices of the homes that those people can afford, it is clear that the positive tail of distribution is much longer than the negative tail. In many situations, therefore, income and price data are inherently skewed.

Note that in a normal, symmetric distribution, the mean and median typically are very close, if not identical. However, non-symmetric outliers have a larger influence on the mean than the median. The presence of multi-millionaires in a distribution of incomes, and the presence of a few mansions in a distribution of home prices, will pull the mean of the distribution to the right, so much so, in fact, that the mean no longer characterizes a value that is "typical" for the distribution. The median, by definition, always indicates the score in the middle of the distribution; thus, it is the preferred measure of central tendency when describing skewed data.

Mode

The mode is the least refined measure of central tendency and refers simply to the most frequent response. If data are organized in a frequency distribution table, the mode is the cate-

6.4

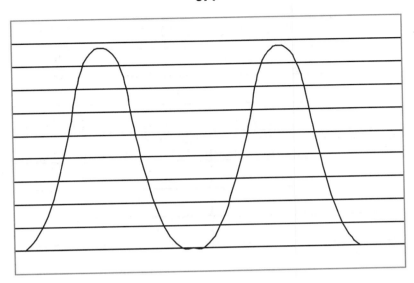

gory with the highest value in the frequency column. It is possible for a distribution to be bi-modal (see Figure 6.4) or tri-modal, etc., if several responses are tied for the highest fre-quency. In a frequency histogram, the mode is the value associated with the highest part (highest frequency) of the graph.

The mode is useful in that it is the only measure of central tendency that can be applied to nominal data. For example, a survey that collected data on participants' favorite colors would produce a set of data containing "red," "blue," yellow," etc., as responses. There is no way to quantitatively sum those responses to compute the mean, nor is it possible to order such that the median can be calculated. Only the mode, the measure of which responses (or responses) is most frequent, can be computed. The mode is highly robust, and typically does change when new scores are added to the data set.

Graphic Comparison of Mean, Median, and Mode

Figures 6.5 and 6.6 illustrate graphically how the mean, median, and mode separate as the skew of distribution increases. Note that the mode is most robust, while the mean is least robust, and moves the most as the distribution grows increasingly skewed.

6.5

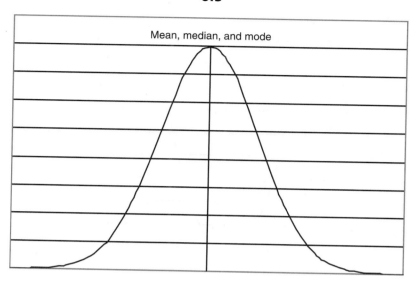

Mean, median, and mode

6.6

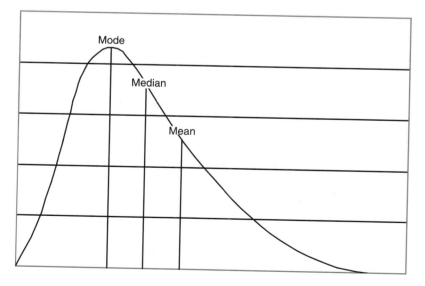

Mode

Median

Mean

PRACTICE PROBLEMS

6.1 Define the **mean, median,** and **mode.** Discuss special properties of each and describe when you would use one method over the other.

6.2 Consider the following set of data. Compute the *mean, median,* and *mode.*

21 ✓   08 ✓   05 ✓   18 ✓   17 ✓   11 ✓ 05 ✓
09 ✓   11 ✓   14 ✓   08 ✓   03 ✓   14 16 ✓
11 ✓   16 ✓   17 ✓   20 ✓   11 ✓   06 15 ✓

6.3 Consider the following set of data. Compute the *mean, median,* and *mode.*

02 ✓   07 ✓   01 ✓   09 ✓   10 ✓   05 ✓
05 ✓   03 ✓   04 ✓   06 ✓   05 ✓   03 ✓
07 ✓   04 ✓   02 ✓   08 ✓   06 ✓   05 ✓

6.4 Consider the same data set as above; however, assume that three large outliers were added to the data set. Compute the mean, median, and mode from this revised data set, and contrast those statistics to what you calculated in the previous example. What does this say about the *robustness* of the three measures?

02   07   01   09   10   05
05   03   04   06   05   03
07   04   02   08   06   05
21   27   18

6.5 Imagine that a survey on student alcohol use was administered to five different campuses. At each campus, from a sample of students, researchers calculated the *mean* number of alcoholic drinks consumed on a typical weekend night. From these group data, compute the overall mean number of alcoholic drinks consumed by the entire sample (across all five campuses).

	N	$\bar{X}$ # of Drinks
Campus A	036	5.2
Campus B	151	2.4
Campus C	052	8.6
Campus D	099	6.0
Campus E	123	4.2

6.7

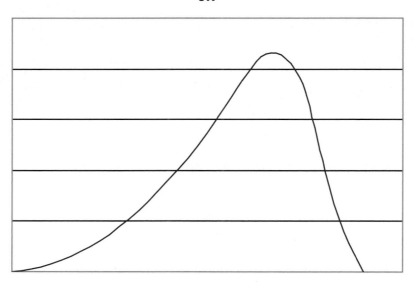

6.6 On the population histogram in Figure 6.7, identify (approximately) the location of mean, median, and mode.

Measures of Variability

Measures of central tendency are used to describe what value is "typical" in the distribution of data using a single statistic, and when data are relatively symmetric, the arithmetic mean is our preferred measure. But central tendency is not the only important characteristic of a set of data. We very often are interested in understanding the *variability* of the data as well.

Imagine that a researcher measured the height of a sample of college students, and the mean of this sample was 5'7". There are many ways that a sample of data could produce a mean of 5'7". It may be that almost all subjects in the data set were 5'7" tall, and this clearly would generate a mean of 5'7". It could be the case that most students were 5'7" but a couple were 5'8", 5'9", and 5'10", and a few more were 5'4", 5'5", and 5'6"; with the deviations above and below 5'7" effectively canceling each other out, this, too, might produce a mean of 5'7". It could be the case that there is considerable range in heights, and that scores vary greatly around 5'7".

In addition to understanding the central tendency of distribution, it is helpful to know something about the variability of scores in a distribution. Are scores spread out widely or is the distribution narrow? Are scores clustered tightly around the center of the distribution

7.1

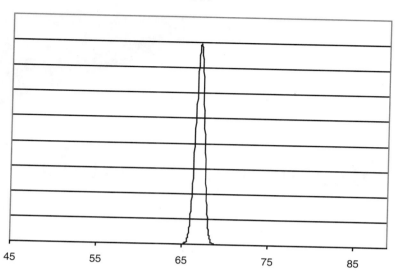

7.2

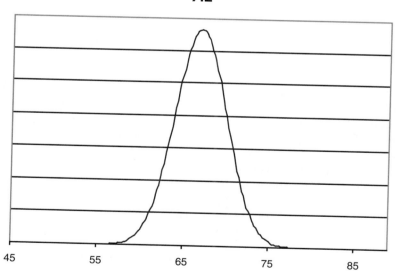

(see Figure 7.1) or do they deviate somewhat from the center (see Figure 7.2) or do they deviate considerably from the center (see Figure 7.3)? While knowing the variability of a distribution is an important descriptive characteristic, as will be shown in later chapters, understanding variability in data is essential to hypothesis testing; we become interested not only in
knowing the extent to which scores vary, but *why* scores vary.

7.3

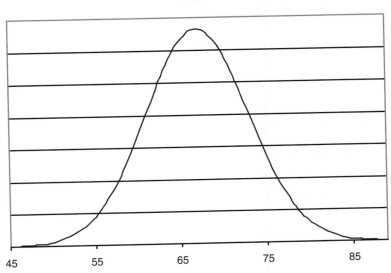

45   55   65   75   85

Range as a Measure of Variability

Perhaps the simplest and most straightforward measure of variability is the range of scores—the highest score in the distribution minus the lowest score in the distribution. (As described in Chapter 5, researchers sometimes add a value to the high—low difference in order to make it inclusive.) Evidence of a relatively large range suggests greater variability among scores; a smaller range indicates less variability.

   Although the range is very easy to compute, it is extremely limited as a measure of variability because it is based on only two points (the highest and lowest scores) of an entire distribution of data. While it characterizes the extreme values, it says nothing about most of the scores in the data set. The presence of a few *outliers*—extreme scores that fall well outside of what might normally be expected—will yield a range that is not at all descriptive of the distribution. Figure 7.4 illustrates how the range is influenced by extreme scores.

   To reduce the influence of extreme scores on the range, the *inter-quartile range* has been used as a measure of variability. The inter-quartile range is similar to the range in that it is computed by subtracting a low score from a high score, but here we identify the high score as the score at the 75th percentile, and the low score as the score at the 25th percentile. Accordingly, the inter-quartile range reflects the range of scores found in the middle 50% of the distribution. The upper and lower 25% of the distribution are trimmed away before the range is calculated, thus eliminating any outliers or extreme scores from the statistic.

   Although the inter-quartile range is computed directly from only two scores, it is important to note that the entire distribution plays a role in determining which scores mark the 75th and 25th percentiles. A frequency distribution table can be used to identify the appropriate "high" and "low" scores. The cumulative proportion column of a frequency distribution

7.4

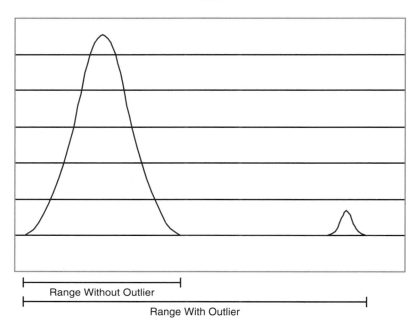

table depicts percentile rank. The category associated with the lowest cumulative frequency at or above .75 contains the "high score" at the 75th percentile, and the category associated with the lowest cumulative proportion at or above .25 contains the "low score" at the 25th percentile.

Variability Around the Mean

The range and inter-quartile range reflect "end-point" measures of variability in that the ends of the distribution are used to compute the variability. However, another way of conceptualizing variability is to think about dispersion around the center of the distribution. Assuming that we are using the mean as a measure of central tendency, a distribution may be thought to be more variable to the extent that scores are spread out from the mean, and a distribution may be thought to be less variable to the extent that scores are clustered tightly around the mean. The former describes a wider distribution, while the latter describes a distribution that is narrower (see again Figures 7.1 to 7.3).

The centerpiece of measuring variability in this fashion is the *mean deviation*—the extent to which each score in a distribution deviates from the mean of that distribution.

Consider the following set of data (N = 10). The sum of the data set is 50, and thus the mean is 50/10 = 5.0. We could compute a column of mean deviations by subtracting the mean (5) from each score in the data set.

X	$(X - \bar{X})$
3	−2
8	+3
2	−3
7	+2
9	+4
6	+1
5	0
4	−1
5	0
1	−4
$\Sigma X = 50$	

Note that in cases where the score was above the mean, the mean deviation is positive, and in cases when the score was lower than the mean, the mean deviation is negative. If we were to sum together the column of mean deviations, we find that $\Sigma(X - \bar{X}) = 0$. *In fact, one special property of the mean is that a complete distribution of mean deviations will always sum to 0.* No matter what is being measured, if the mean of a data set is subtracted from each score in that data, the sum of those difference scores (mean deviations) will always be 0. It is not necessarily the case that a distribution of median deviations or modal deviations, if they were computed, would sum to 0.

One way of measuring variability, therefore, might be to calculate the "typical" mean deviation; this would indicate how far from the mean scores "typically" tend to vary. An intuitive measure of variability would be to compute the *mean of the mean deviations*. However, any person who attempts this approach quickly will realize the problem: because mean deviations always sum to 0, the mean of the column of mean deviations will always be 0. The positive and negative mean deviations always cancel each other out.

Several approaches have been advanced to address this. One is to use the absolute value of the mean deviations to make them all positive. The *mean of absolute mean deviations* is one measure of variability. Using the same data as above, we find the that sum of the absolute values of the mean deviations, $\Sigma|(X - \bar{X})|$, is 20, and the mean is 20/10 = 2. The value of "2" reflects the extent to which the scores in the distribution tend to vary from the center of the distribution.

X	$(X - \bar{X})$	$|(X - \bar{X})|$
3	−2	2
8	+3	3
2	−3	3
7	+2	2
9	+4	4

(continued)

(continued)

X	(X – X̄)	|(X – X̄)|
6	+1	1
5	0	0
4	−1	1
5	0	0
1	−4	4
ΣX = 50	0	20

Sums of Squares, Variance, and Standard Deviation

However, there is another approach to examining variability around the center of a distribution that has proved superior to the *mean of the absolute mean deviations*. This approach is to square each mean deviation before summing them together. Through squaring, all mean deviation scores become positive. Using data from the previous example, we find that the *sum of squared mean deviations* (sum of squares, or SS, for short) is equal to 60.

X	(X – X̄)	(X – X̄)²
3	−2	4
8	+3	9
2	−3	9
7	+2	4
9	+4	16
6	+1	1
5	0	0
4	−1	1
5	0	0
1	−4	16
ΣX = 50	0	60

It should be clear that the *sum* of the squared mean deviations does not tell us how much variability is typical because it is based on the total number of cases. All else being equal, a data set with many cases will invariably produce a larger sum of squares than will a data set with fewer cases. The *mean of the squared mean deviations* (*mean square*, or more commonly, *variance*) in this case is $60/10 = 6$.

However, even the mean of the squared mean deviations is not quite ideal for describing the extent to which scores vary because in the process of squaring the deviation scores, we lose the original scale of measurement. For example, if our data set contained temperatures measured on a sample of days, our mean square would not indicate the number of degrees that temperatures typically vary from the mean, but rather the number of degrees-*squared* that temperatures vary from the mean.

In order to transform the mean of squared mean deviations back into the original scale of measurement we must take the square root of the value. The square root of the mean square is called the *standard deviation*.

The *sums of squares, variance,* and *standard deviation* are not separate measures of variability, but are three stages in the same measure of variability. As we will see later in this book, some statistical tests use the variance, others use the standard deviation, and others use the sum of squares as part of the calculation.

Symbols

Separate symbols are used to distinguish the variability of scores in a population from the variability of scores in a sample.

The *variance* of a population is indicated by the Greek letter sigma-squared: σ^2.

The standard deviation of the population is indicated simply by the sigma: σ.

Given the fact that the standard deviation is simply the square root of the variance, the difference between the variance and standard deviation symbols is quite literal.

Sample statistics do not use Greek letters. The variance of a sample is indicated by S^2, while the standard deviation of a sample is indicated with an S.

There is no special symbol to represent the sums of squares of a population; SS typically is used to describe SS computed from a sample.

Sample Variance

The distinction between sample and population variance is important because they are not calculated the same way. The formula indicated previously for the variance, literally the mean of squared mean deviations, or $\Sigma(X - \bar{X})^2 / N$ in fact is the formula for the variance of a *population*. It should be noted that it is rare for data from an entire population to be available; thus it is unlikely that you will have the opportunity to compute the population variance and standard deviation.

The formula for calculating the variance and standard deviation for a sample is very similar to that of a population, except that instead of dividing by N (to get the *mean* of the squared mean deviations), we divide by N − 1.

$$S^2 = \Sigma(X - \bar{X})^2 / (N - 1)$$

The reason for dividing by N − 1 instead of N is complicated, but it has to do with the fact that in a data set where sample size = N, there really are only N − 1 useful pieces of data. Once the sample mean is known, only N − 1 of the scores (and not N) are free to vary. Once the second to last value is determined, that final score is fixed because there is only one value that will produce the final mean. Imagine, for example, that N = 5 and the $\bar{X}$ is 7. If four of the five scores were determined to be 4, 7, 8, and 9, the final score must be "7," because only a final score of "7" will produce an $\overline{X}$ of 6: $(4 + 7 + 8 + 9 + 6)/5 = 7$. Because the value of the final score does not provide additional information (it is predetermined), essentially subtract that case from the denominator when dividing sample size into sums of squares to get the *variance*.

The sample standard deviation is computed the same way as the population standard deviation: once the sample variance is calculated, taking the square root produces the standard deviation.

$$S = \sqrt{\Sigma(X - \overline{X})^2/(N - 1)}$$

*Note that sums of squares, variance, and standard deviation will always be **positive**.* If you get a negative value for any of these, you made a mistake somewhere along the way.

Computational Approach

The formulae for sums of squares, sample variance, and sample standard deviation described previously can be described as *raw score* approaches. The formulae are simple, and it is easy to see where the value (SS, S^2, etc.) comes from. To the extent that scores vary a far distance from the mean of the distribution, i.e., to the extent that the mean deviations are large, the larger the variance will be. Distributions where scores cluster tightly around the mean produce small mean deviations and generate relatively smaller variances.

The sums of squares formula presented earlier is not, in fact, the easiest or most efficient to use. In order to compute the sum of squares using the formula, a person must subtract the mean from each score and then square each mean deviation. Note if the sample size is small and if the mean is a whole number, this process is relatively quick. But if the sample mean is not a whole number, then fractional values must be subtracted from the scores, and fractional differences must be squared. This increases exponentially the effort involved in computing the sum of squares, as well as the risk of making mathematical error.

The *computational formula* for computing the sum of squares *looks* more complicated, but in fact is easier to perform, and is mathematically equivalent to the raw score formula. The computational formula for SS is as follows:

$$SS = \Sigma X^2 - (\Sigma X)^2/N$$

This formula requires us to calculate the sum of the squared Xs (ΣX^2) and the square of the summed Xs $[(\Sigma X)^2]$. The former involves taking each score in the data set, squaring it, and then adding up the squared values. The latter involves adding together each score in the data set, and then squaring the total. Almost invariably, the squared total will be larger than the sum of the squared Xs. The squared total is divided by the sample size (N) before it is subtracted from the sum of the squared Xs. Once the sum of squares is calculated, variance is computed by dividing by $N - 1$, and the standard deviation is computed by taking the square root of the variance.

$$S = \sqrt{\frac{\Sigma X^2 - \frac{(\Sigma X)^2}{N}}{N - 1}}$$

Below are two data sets, for variables X1 and X2. Each data set has as a sample size of 16, a sum of 116, and a mean of 7. Despite these similarities, however, the variability of the data differs for the two variables.

		X1	X2
		6	1
		9	16
		3	3
		6	2
		11	9
		2	12
		5	5
		8	3
		14	2
		12	10
		5	13
		6	1
		9	9
		10	8
		4	7
		2	11
	Σ	112	112
	N	16	16
	$\overline{X}$	7	7

	X1	X2
ΣX^2	978	1,118
$(\Sigma X)^2$	12,544	12,544
SS	$978 - (12,544/16) = \mathbf{194}$	$1,118 - (12,544/16) = \mathbf{334}$
S^2	$194 / (16 - 1) = \mathbf{12.93}$	$334 / (16 - 1) = \mathbf{22.27}$
S	$\sqrt{12.93} = \mathbf{3.60}$	$\sqrt{22.27} = \mathbf{4.72}$

Note that the range of the first set of scores (high = 14, low = 2) is smaller than the second set (high = 16, low = 1). This increased variability in range is reflected in the higher standard deviation of variable X2; scores within X2 are more varied around the mean of that distribution, while the scores in X1 are clustered more tightly around the mean of that distribution.

To demonstrate the equivalency of the raw score and computational approaches, the data for variable X1 is computed using the raw score approach. The fact that the mean of this data set is 7 makes the computations easier.

X1	(X – X̄)	(X – X̄)²
6	–1	1
9	2	4
3	–4	16
6	–1	1
11	4	16
2	–5	25
5	–2	4
8	1	1
14	7	49
12	5	25
5	–2	4
6	–1	1
9	2	4
10	3	9
4	–3	9
2	–5	25
SS = 194		S² = 194/(16–1) = **12.93** S = **3.60**

Note that the results from the raw score calculations are identical to those found using the raw score computations.

PRACTICE PROBLEMS

7.1 Define **variability**.

7.2 Describe the use of **range** as a measure of variability. Discuss one limitation of the range, and describe a modification to the range that addresses this limitation.

7.3 Consider the following data set. Compute the mean of these data, and then compute a **mean deviation** for each observation in the data set. Finally, compute the *sum* and *mean* of these mean deviations.

01✓	13	07	08	12
03	05	11	10	09
04	04	08	07	02
04				

7.4 Using the same data as above, compute the sum and mean of **absolute mean deviations**.

7.5 Using the same data as above, computer the **sum** of the **squared mean deviations**.

7.6   From the data in the previous example, compute the **variance** and **standard deviation.**

7.7   From the data below, compute the standard deviation. Identify the sums of squares and variance in the process.

12	16	17	10	15	11
18	13	14	14	10	19

7.8   Consider the same data set as above, however, with the addition of three outlier scores. Re-compute the standard deviation and compare that to the standard deviation obtained in the previous example (without the additional outliers).

12	16	17	10	15	11
18	13	14	14	10	19
25	30	35			

Z-Scores

A nytime two scores are compared to each other with the intention of determining which score is larger or smaller than the other, the scale used to measure the scores is ultimately important. In order to make valid comparisons, the scores being compared must be measured on the same scale. For example, grade point average (GPA) and SAT scores both are measures that reflect academic aptitude, yet scores on these two measures cannot be compared directly. A combined (math + verbal) SAT score of 400 is an extremely low SAT score, but clearly it is a larger number (in absolute magnitude) than is a near perfect GPA of 3.9 (i.e., 400 > 3.9). Despite 400 being larger than 3.9, we know intuitively that a GPA of 3.9 suggests greater academic aptitude than does a SAT score of 400 because we understand the distributions of the two variables: the GPAs range from 0.0 to 4.0, and SATs (math and verbal combined) range from 200 to 1600. We are able to say that a GPA of 3.9 is meaningfully greater than a SAT of 400, but because they are measured on different scales, it is not possible to directly determine the size of the difference between the two scores.

Often, variables that measure the same things may be transformed to a common scale. A vehicle traveling 160 kilometers per hour may be compared to a vehicle traveling 80 miles per hour because it is possible to transform kilometers to miles (and vice versa) quite easily. But what if we wished to compare two variables that were measured such that they could not be transformed easily into a common scale? What if we wished to compare two variables that measured different concepts altogether?

Imagine, for example, data were available from two groups of athletes: a group of sprinters, for whom data on time to run a 40-yard dash were available, and a group of weight lifters, for whom data on weight lifted during a bench press were available. One subject from the sprinter distribution, Person S, has a recorded speed of 4.4 seconds to run the 40-yard dash. One subject from the weight-lifter distribution, Person W, has a recorded bench press of 370 pounds. What if we posed the question: Is the sprinter faster than the weight lifter is strong, or is the weight-lifter stronger than the sprinter is fast? How might it be possible to make such a comparison? Clearly, 4.4 seconds and 370 pounds cannot be compared directly because they are measured on completely different scales. Furthermore, because lower times (seconds) reflect greater speed, but higher pounds reflect greater strength, it is even less clear how such a comparison would be possible. Understanding Z-scores sheds light on how such a comparison might be possible. First, a more practical example will be presented to demonstrate how Z-scores work.

Imagine that Person A took a test and scored an 85, while Person B took a test and scored a 56. Assume in both cases that test scores reflect the percentage of material correct on the test, and thus scores range from 0 to 100. Because test scores are measured on the same scale, the two scores, on one hand, are immediately comparable, and we might easily conclude that Person A scored better on her test than Person B did on his (85% > 56%).

But what if the tests were from completely different courses, and the two distributions had completely different means. Test A, for example, might have come from an introductory psychology course, while Test B came from an organic chemistry course. Presumably, Test B is considerably more difficult than Test A, and thus lower scores on Test B might be expected. We could examine the means of the two tests. Imagine that the mean test score of Test A was a 77, while the mean test score on Test B was a 51.

In order to accommodate the fact that the means of the two tests were different, we might examine the test scores of Person A and Person B in terms of *mean deviations*.

$$\text{Person A} \quad X = 85 \quad \mu = 77 \quad \text{mean deviation} = 85 - 77 = \mathbf{8}$$

$$\text{Person B} \quad X = 56 \quad \mu = 51 \quad \text{mean deviation} = 56 - 51 = \mathbf{5}$$

In this example, using *mean deviations* as a measure, we still might argue that Person A performed better on her test than did Person B because Person A was *8* points above average while Person B was only *5* points above average. This comparison, however, assumes that the two *mean deviations* are directly comparable, and this concerns the variability of the two distributions. Remember that the standard deviation reflects the extent to which scores tend to vary in a distribution. If one variable has a relatively large standard deviation it indicates it is not uncommon for scores to vary quite a distance from the center of the distribution. Although the score from Person A might be 8 points above the mean, it is possible (depending on the standard deviation of scores for Test A) that many people were 8 or more points above average on Test A. On the other hand, it might be the case that there was very little variability in scores for Test B, and that relatively few people performed as well as 5 points above the mean on Test B.

Imagine that the standard deviation of Test A was 10 and the standard deviation of Test B was 4. Accordingly, Test A scores were much more variable than were scores from Test B. Figures 8.1 and 8.2 graphically depict the population distributions of Test A and Test B.

Remember that the height of the graphs represents relative frequencies, and that scores become increasingly less common as they deviate further from the mean of distribution. In distributions with larger standard deviations, a score must deviate even further from the

8.1

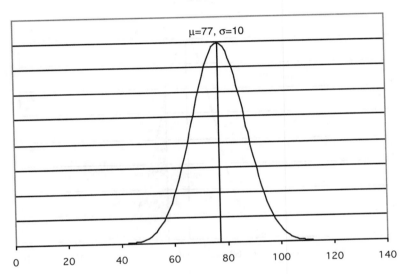

8.2

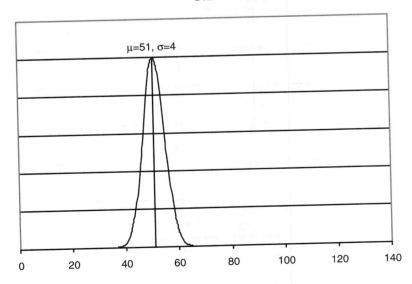

mean before it can be considered extreme, uncommon, or rare. In distributions with smaller standard deviations, a relatively small mean deviation might fall at the extreme end of the distribution.

Figures 8.3 and 8.4 graphically depict the distributions for Test A and Test B, but also indicate the locations of Person A and Person B's test scores (X = 85 and 56) in their respective distributions. The shaded area represents the proportion of test scores that fall at or above the

8.3

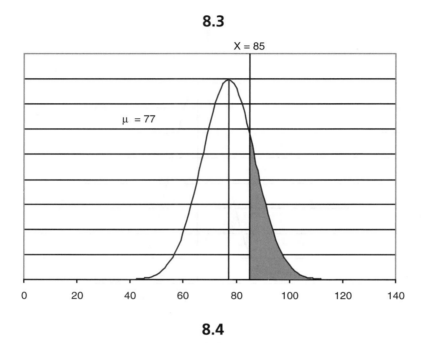

X = 85

μ = 77

8.4

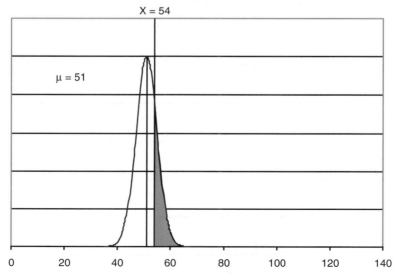

X = 54

μ = 51

two individuals' scores. Note that even though Person A's test score is further from the Test A mean than Person B's score, Person A's score is not as extreme as Person B's score: as indicated by the shaded area, the proportion of people who scored better than Person B is smaller than the proportion who scored better than Person A. The standard deviation of 10 associated with Test A suggests that it is not too uncommon for students taking introduction to psychology to get scores that deviate 10 points from the mean; thus Person A scoring 8 points above the mean should not be considered that unusual of an accomplishment. However, the standard deviation of 4 for Test B indicates that organic chemistry scores tend to vary only 4 points from the mean; the fact that Person B scored 5 above average indicates that his performance was a little more than "typical."

In research, we like to avoid qualitative judgments such as Person A's score is "not uncommon" and Person B's score is "more than typical." We prefer to quantify this difference. We can do so by taking a given score from a distribution and indicating how far it is from the mean in terms of standard deviations. Person A, for example, scored 0.8 standard deviations above the mean for her distribution (8 points mean deviation / 10 point standard deviation = 0.8), while Person B scored 1.25 standard deviations above the mean of his distribution (5 points mean deviation / 4 points standard deviation = 1.25). By transforming scores into "standard-deviations-from-the-mean" we can identify where scores lie relative to other scores in the distribution.

A *Z-score* is a score represented in terms of standard deviations from the mean. Anytime the mean and standard deviation of a distribution are known, a Z-score can be computed for each score in the data set. For Person A, her raw score of 85, given a test mean of 77 and standard deviation of 10, produces a Z-score of +0.8. For Person B, his raw score of 56, given a mean of 51 and standard deviation of 4, produces a Z-score of 1.25. By simply comparing Z-scores we can determine that Person B did better on his test (*relative to other people who took Test B*) than Person A did on her test (*relative to other people who took Test A*).

If the population mean and standard deviation are known, then Z-scores can be computed for a given X according to:

$$Z = \frac{X - \mu}{\sigma}$$

If population parameters are not known (i.e., they are not provided), then Z-scores can be computed from sample statistics.

$$Z = \frac{X - \bar{X}}{S}$$

Properties of Z-Scores

Each score in the data will have a Z-score, and identical scores will have identical Z-scores. Raw scores that are below the mean will produce negative Z-scores (remember that standard deviations cannot be negative). Raw scores that are above the mean will produce positive Z-scores. A raw score that is equal to the mean will produce a Z-score of 0.

If a Z-score is computed for every score in a data set, a Z-score distribution will result. One special property of Z-scores is that a distribution of Z-scores will always produce a mean of 0 and a standard deviation of 1. The significance of this cannot be overstated. Regardless of what we are measuring and regardless of the scale—SAT scores, introversion, height, temperatures across days, etc.—the distribution of Z-scores that result will have a mean of 0 and a standard deviation of 1. By sharing these common parameters, Z-scores always are on the same scale and thus always are comparable (i.e., a Z-score of 1.25 will always be greater than a Z-score of 0.8). By transforming raw scores into Z-scores, we can make comparisons that otherwise might not appear possible. Referring to the example at the beginning of the chapter, if we wanted to compare a weight lifter's bench-press weight to a sprinter's speed on a 40-yard dash, we could determine the Z-scores for each (assuming we had the means and standard deviations of the two distributions). These Z-scores would indicate where the raw scores rested relative to other scores in the distribution. The larger Z-score (in absolute value, in this case) would indicate whether the weight lifter or the sprinter had a better score.

Consider the distribution of scores below ($N = 6$).

	X	X²	X – X̄	Z-Score	Z-Score²
	10	100	+4.17	+1.42	2.02
	03	09	−2.83	−0.97	0.94
	02	04	−3.83	−1.31	1.72
	07	49	+1.17	+0.40	0.16
	07	49	+1.17	+0.40	0.16
	06	36	+0.17	+0.06	0.00
ΣX	35	247	~0	0	5
$(\Sigma X)^2$	1,225				

$\bar{X} = 35 / 6 = \mathbf{5.83}$

$SS = 247 - (1225/6) = \mathbf{42.83}$ $S^2 = 42.83/(6-1) = \mathbf{8.57}$ $S = \sqrt{8.57} = \mathbf{2.93}$

The mean of X is equal to $(35/6) = 5.83$, and the standard deviation of X is computed to be 2.93. A Z-score can be computed for each score in the data set by first computing the mean deviation $(X - \bar{X})$ and then dividing the mean deviation by the standard deviation. Note that Z-scores are smaller (in absolute value) for scores that are closer to the mean, and become larger (in absolute value) as they deviate further from the mean. Note that the sum of the mean deviations and Z-scores both are 0 (within rounding).

We can compute the sum of squares for the Z-scores simply by squaring and then summing each Z-score (because the mean of the Z-scores is 0). Doing so in this case produces a sum of squares of 5. Thus, the standard deviation of the Z-scores is 1.

$$SS_Z = 5 \qquad S^2 = 5/(6-1) = 1 \qquad S = \sqrt{1} = 1$$

Some tests and measures have been designed to produce certain population parameters, or have been used enough that the population parameters are known. For example, IQ tests have been shown to produce population means (μ) of 100 and population standard deviations (σ) of 15 (however, the actual parameters may be different depending on the specific IQ test being used). Similarly, the SAT test has been shown to produce a combined score μ of 1000, where σ = 200. Z-scores can be computed from raw scores samples from populations with known parameters. For example, assuming a distribution of IQ scores where μ = 100 and σ = 15, an IQ score of 125 corresponds with a Z-score of +1.66 ((125 – 100) / 15 = +1.66).

Using Z-Scores to Determine the Area Under the Curve

Because Z-scores always form a distribution with μ = 0 and σ = 1, it is possible to identify proportions associated with specific Z-scores. For example, not only does a Z-score of "1" tell us that our data point is one standard deviation above the mean, we can use it to locate the precise percentile rank associated with that score. Regardless of what we were measuring originally—IQ scores, height, introversion, etc.—the score associated with a given Z-score will always fall at the same percentile rank; an IQ score associated with a Z-score of "1" has the same proportion of scores above and below as an introversion score associated with a Z-score of "1" has above and below it.

Fortunately, most of the work involved in determining the proportions associated with Z-scores has been computed for us; we must merely learn to use a pre-established table in order to identify percentile ranks.

The appendix in this book contains the unit normal table—a table of Z-scores and associated proportions. This table contains three columns: (A) the Z column; (B) the greater proportion column; and (C) the lower proportion column. The Z column contains Z-scores ranging from 0 to 3 in increments of .01, and the two proportion columns contain values that always sum to 1.0 when added together. Depending on the specific Z-score, values in columns B and C represent the proportion of scores in the population that fall below the specific Z-score and the proportion of scores in the population that fall above the specific Z-score.

A greatly reduced version of the unit normal table is presented below.

► Reduced Unit Normal Table

A Z-SCORE	B GREATER	C LESSER
0.00	.5000	.5000
0.50	.6915	.3085
1.00	.8413	.1587
1.50	.9332	.0668
2.00	.9772	.0228
2.50	.9938	.0062
3.00	.9986	.0014

How we interpret columns B and C depends on whether the Z-score in question is positive or negative (see Figure 8.5). Note that column B always contains a larger proportion than column C. If a Z-score is positive (i.e., the raw score is above the mean and to the right of the center of the distribution) then clearly the larger portion (B) of the distribution will fall to the left (below) the Z-score and the small portion (C) of the distribution will fall to the right (above) the Z-score. Therefore, if we have a positive Z-score, column B will reflect the proportion of scores *below* the Z-score and column C will reflect the proportion of scores above the Z-score.

If the Z-score is negative (i.e., the raw score is below the mean and to the left of the center of the distribution) then the larger area (B) falls to the right (above) and the smaller area falls to the left (below). Thus, for negative Z-scores, column B indicates the proportion of scores above the Z-score, while column C reflects the proportion of scores below.

Imagine a distribution of scores with known population parameters, where $\mu = 50$ and $\sigma = 10$, and Person A has a score of 65. The Z-score for Person A is $(65 - 50) / 10 = 15/10 = $ **1.5.** Examining the unit normal table (see example on p. 67) we find that a Z-score of 1.5 is associated with .9332 in column B and .0668 in column C. Because 1.5 is a positive Z-score, this means that a score of 65 falls at the 93.3% of the distribution, and that 6.7% of scores were above Person A's score of 6.

Imagine that Person B's score was 45. The corresponding Z-score is thus $(45 - 50)/10 = -5/10 = $ **−0.5.** The unit normal table shows a .691 in column B and .309 in column C. Because the Z-score is negative (i.e., the score of 45 is below average), the larger proportion (found in column B) clearly reflects the proportion of scores in the population above 45. Person B's score of 45 rests at the 30.9 percentile and 69.1% of scores are larger.

8.5

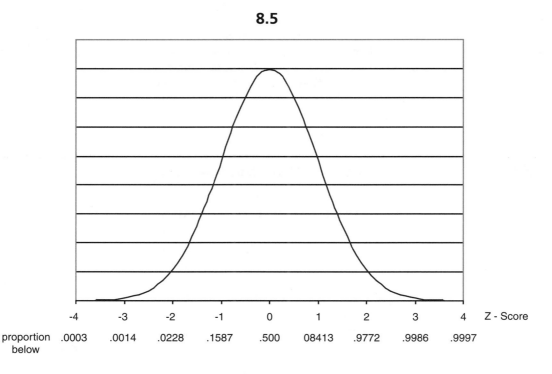

									Z - Score
	-4	-3	-2	-1	0	1	2	3	4
proportion below	.0003	.0014	.0228	.1587	.500	08413	.9772	.9986	.9997

Finding the Area Between Two Scores

We may have two Z-scores and wish to determine the proportion of scores in a population that fall between those two Z-scores. For example, assuming the same parameters used in the previous example, we might want to know what proportion of scores falls between 40 and 60. The first step is to determine the Z-score for both raw scores of 40 and 60.

$$Z40 = (40 - 50)/10 = -10/10 = -1$$

$$Z60 = (60 - 50)/10 = 10/10 = +1$$

In this example we get Z-scores of +1 and −1. If we examine the unit normal table we find that a Z-score of 1 marks the 84.1 percentile, and a Z-score of −1 marks the 15.9 percentile. But what is the area between these two scores?

The key to solving these problems is to realize that the area between Z-scores of 1 and −1 is the same as the area below a Z-score of 1 *minus* the area below a Z-score of −1. Figure 8.6 illustrates how the remainder from this subtraction is in fact the area between Z-scores of 1 and −1:

$$\text{Area below } Z = 1 \text{ minus area below } Z = -1: .8413 - .1587 = \textbf{.6826}$$

68.3% of scores in a distribution fall between the raw scores of 40 and 60.

8.6

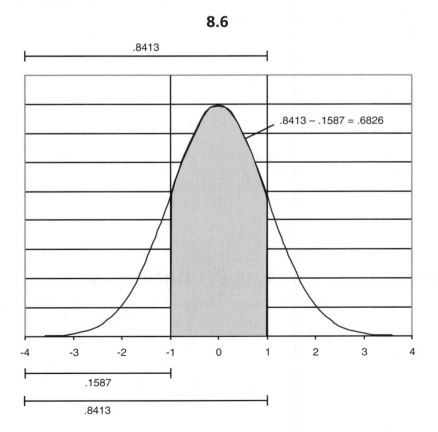

Note that the same answer would have been obtained had we calculated the proportion of scores above 40 *minus* the proportion of scores above 60. This approach, too, isolates the scores in between.

Working Backwards from Proportions to Raw Scores

Imagine a distribution of scores with $\mu = 100$ and $\sigma = 15$. Many IQ tests, for example, generate scores that tend to follow this distribution. What if a person was interested in knowing what score marked the upper 15% of the distribution, and what score marked the lower 25% of the distribution?

In cases where the proportion or percentages are provided and the goal is to determine the corresponding raw score, the first step is to determine which Z-scores correspond to those proportions. Specifically, in this example, we are in the 85th percentile (with .15 score above) and the 25th percentile (.75 scores above). We can search columns B and C in the unit normal table until we find proportions that approximate .85/.15 and .75/.25, respectively. Note that we might not find those precise values in the table, but we should come as close as possible.

Looking through columns B and C we find that a Z-score of 1.04 corresponds closely to the 85th percentile (.851/.149 in columns B/C). Because the 85th percentile clearly is above average, we can be confident that the Z-score in question (1.04) in fact is a positive Z-score. We also find that a Z-score of 0.67 is associated with 0.749/.251 in columns B/C; however, because we know that the raw score associated with the 25th percentile is *below* the average, the Z-score must be negative. When the Z-score = –0.67, the value in column C (in this case .251) will reflect the proportion of scores below the Z-score.

Once Z-scores that correspond to the upper 15% and lower 25% points in the distribution are located, the Z-scores can be transformed back to raw scores according to:

$$X = \sigma Z + \mu$$

Thus, the raw score marking the upper 15% of the distribution, where Z-score = 1.04, equals: $(15)(1.04) + 100 = 115.6$, rounding up to 116. The raw score marking the 25th percentile, where Z-score = –0.67, equals: $(15)(-0.67) + 100 = (-10.05) + 100 = 89.95$, rounded to 90. Thus, a raw score of 116 marks the 85% (upper 15%) and a raw score of 90 marks the lower 25%.

Treating Proportions as Probabilities

The proportions and "areas under the curve" identified through using Z-scores and the unit normal table can be treated as probabilities. If we were to randomly sample one case from a population, we could use Z-scores to determine the probability of sampling a value from within a given range.

In a previous example, we determine that the area under the curve between –1 and +1 standard deviations from the mean is .6826. The probability of randomly sampling a case from that range is equal to .6826; a random draw will produce a Z-score between −1 and +1 68.3% of the time. Note that all of the probabilistic techniques discussed in Chapter 4 can be used here. For example, the probability of randomly sampling 3 scores in a row between −1 and +1 Z-scores is equal to: .6826 × .6826 × .6826 = .3181. Similarly, the probability of randomly sampling a score above Z-score +1 *or* below Z-score −1 is equal to: .1587 + .1587 = .3174.

P R A C T I C E   P R O B L E M S

8.1 From the following set of data, compute the mean and standard deviation, and then the Z-scores for each observation. The ΣX^2 and $(\Sigma X)^2$ already have been computed for you.

08	09	01 04
02	08	10 05
05	04	07 13

$N = 12$

$\Sigma X^2 = 614$

$(\Sigma X)^2 = 76^2 = 5776$

8.2 Consider the Z-scores that you just computed from the data above. Treating each Z-score as a data point, compute the *mean* and *standard deviation* of the Z-scores. (Hint: Make sure you use the Z-score from all 12 observations.)

8.3 Use the same set of data as in the original example, but now add a single extreme outlier of 50. With this new outlier included, re-compute the mean, standard deviation, and Z-scores for each observation. Compare these new Z-scores to the Z-scores computed from the sample that did not include the outlier. How do they differ?

8.4 Describe how adding an outlier might influence the *numerator* in the Z-score formula. Describe how adding an outlier might influence the *denominator* in the Z-score formula. Consider how outliers influence the numerator and denominator and discuss how this relationship influences the practical ranges of the Z-score distribution.

8.5 Consider a population where $\mu = 50$ and $\sigma = 10$.

1. What is the probability of randomly sampling from this population a score as high (or higher) than 65?
2. What is the probability of randomly sampling a score as low (or lower) than 33?
3. What is the probability of randomly sampling a score between 41 and 63 from this population?
4. What is the probability of randomly sampling two scores in a row (assuming sampling with replacement) between 42 and 48?
5. What score marks the 35th percentile?
6. What score is needed to mark the 95th percentile?

Logic Behind Hypothesis Testing

Research often is used to examine the relationship among or between variables. Researchers test whether different groups of people vary on some important variable (e.g., whether men and women differ in math ability); whether a given treatment or intervention influences some outcome (e.g., whether taking an SAT prep course really increases SAT scores); or whether knowing something about Variable X helps them to predict Variable Y (e.g., does knowing a person's age help predict their risk for causing a traffic accident). Researchers test their hypotheses regarding relationships between or among variables by conducting studies and examining the patterns of results that emerge from the data.

In this chapter, we will use a single, simple example to demonstrate the logic behind hypothesis testing. Keep in mind that the research described in this example is for illustrative purposes only; we would not actually conduct the study the way it is described.

Imagine that a researcher developed a pill that he believed would make people smarter. He conducted a very simple study to test his pill: first, he randomly selected one person from the phone book and recruited this one person to take part in the study. Second, he had the participant take the "intelligence boosting pill." Third, he gave the participant an IQ test.

Imagine that this study was conducted, and the participant produced an IQ score of 130. Assume the IQ test that was used had known population parameters $\mu = 100$ and $\sigma = 15$. The participant's IQ score produces a Z-score of $(130 - 100) / 15 = +2.0$. Examining the unit normal table we find that the IQ score is in the upper 2.3% of IQ scores (97.7 percentile).

The essential question is this: Why was this participant's IQ score so high? There are two possible "realities" that might explain this.

Reality A

We will refer to this reality as the *null reality* and it states that this "intelligence boosting pill" had *no effect* whatsoever, and it did nothing to increase the participant's IQ score; the person's IQ score was the same before taking the pill as after taking the pill. The reason why this study produced an IQ score as high as 130 was simply that we just happened to randomly sample a very bright person (with an IQ of 130) to begin with. The results of this study are due entirely to random chance—the fluke probability that we sampled a person to be our participant from the extremely high end of the IQ score distribution.

One implication of this null reality is that if an entire population of people took this "intelligence boosting pill," this population would look identical to the population of people who did not take this pill (i.e., because the pill does nothing). Both populations would have $\mu = 100$ and $\sigma = 15$. Note that if the null hypothesis was true, we would *expect*, on average, that our participant would have an IQ score of 100.

The *null hypothesis* states that the null reality is true. Symbolized by H_0, the null hypothesis for this example can be written formally as:

$$H_0: \mu_P = \mu = 100$$

where μ_P represents the population mean of people who take the "intelligence boosting pill" and μ represents the mean of the "normal" population (who have not taken the "intelligence boosting pill"). According to the null hypothesis, people who take the pill are not different from those who did not take the pill in terms of intelligence.

Reality B

The second reality is the *alternative* to the null. According to this reality, the "intelligence boosting pill" had at least *some* influence on the participant's measured IQ score. It is not clear whether the pill boosted the participant's IQ score by 1 point, 5 points, or by 30 points, etc., only that it had some effect. Nor is it clear whether our randomly sampled participant had an initial IQ of 129, 125, 100, etc. All that we conclude is that the results of our study are not due *entirely* to a random fluke.

One implication for this alternative hypothesis is that if we gave this "intelligence boosting pill" to an entire population of people, the mean of the population of people who take the pill (μ_P) is *not the same* as the population mean of people who do not take the pill (μ).

$$H1: \mu_P \neq \mu$$

Or, specifically, because we predict the "intelligence boosting pill" to increase IQ scores, we might hypothesize

$$H1: \mu_P > \mu$$

Researchers generally are interested in showing that the *alternative* hypothesis (Reality B) is correct; rarely are researchers interested in showing that the null hypothesis (Reality A) is true. Unfortunately, for a number of reasons, we can't test the alternative directly. However, we are able to test the null hypothesis directly, and if we are able to reject the null hypothesis it implies that the alternative must be true.

So how do we go about testing the null hypothesis? Every statistical test has a null hypothesis, and every null hypothesis is essentially the same. Formally, the null hypothesis states "that there are no differences between observed and expected data." Colloquially, the null hypothesis states that there are no differences between or among groups, that there is no effect of our treatment, or that there is no relationship between variables. Essentially, the null hypothesis states that nothing special is going on in our data and that any apparent patterns or relationships simply are a result of randomness. According to the null hypothesis, if we conducted the exact same study a second time, we would not expect to get the same pattern of results.

For the example involving the "intelligence boosting pill," the null hypothesis states that the pill had absolutely no effect on the participant's IQ score, and whatever IQ was produced through the study was obtained through the process of randomly sampling our participant. Assuming that the null hypothesis is true and the pill does not work, we would expect, *on average,* that our participant would have an IQ score of 100. This is because the population mean of IQ scores is 100. However, we also know that there is variability ($\sigma = 15$) among IQ scores, and so the IQ score of any randomly sampled participant may vary around the *expected* score of 100.

In this example the participant's IQ score was 130. Previously we demonstrated that the participant's IQ score produced a Z-score of $(130 - 100) / 15 = +2.0$, which falls at the 97.7 percentile and thus is in the upper 2.3% of the IQ score distribution. What this means is that *if the null hypothesis is true,* we will only obtain an IQ score as extreme as 130 (i.e., Z-score = 2) by random chance 2.3% of the time. It seems very unlikely—although still possible—that this study could have produced data as extreme as it did if the pill had no effect whatsoever. Given this, the researcher must decide between two possibilities: (A) the pill does not work and the study results are simply a 2.3% fluke, or (B) the pill must have played some role in producing such a high IQ. Note that if the research concludes that option B (the alternative hypothesis) is correct, there is still a small chance that he or she is incorrect in making this conclusion because it is possible that the results could have been obtained due to random chance.

Assume that instead of getting a score of 130, the participant's IQ score obtained through this study is 110. In this case, the corresponding Z-score would be $(110 - 100) / 15 = +0.67$, and this is associated with a percentile rank of 74.9. Accordingly, the probability that we could randomly sample an IQ as extreme as 110 from a population where $\mu = 100$ and $\sigma = 15$ is .251 (upper 25.1% of distribution). Although an IQ score of 110 is above average, it neither is extreme nor rare, and we would expect that if approximately 1/4 of the time a score was randomly sampled from the population, it would be at least as high as 110. In this case, if the researcher decided to reject the null hypothesis and conclude that the pill had an effect, he or she would be in error 25.1% of the time, because we would expect to get an IQ score as high as 110 due to random sampling 25.1% of the time, even if the "intelligence boosting pill" had no effect on intelligence whatsoever.

How extreme must data be for a researcher to be confident that the results are not simply random fluctuation? How unlikely must it be that the data could have been obtained due to random sampling before rejecting the null hypothesis? An important variable in statistical testing is the alpha-level (α). Alpha is a value that is set by the researcher at the beginning of the study (before data collection) that defines the *threshold of risk* that a researcher is willing to take before rejecting the null hypothesis and concluding that the treatment had some effect. Whenever a researcher rejects the null hypothesis and concludes that the study results are not merely an artifact of randomness, there is always risk that he or she has made a mistake because it is always possible (although unlikely) that such data *could* have been obtained simply due to chance. In the first example, when the participant's IQ score was 130 and in the upper 2.3% of the distribution, this risk was relatively low. In the second case, when the participant's IQ score was 110 and the data fell in the upper 25.1% of the distribution, this risk was much greater.

In social science, it is standard for researchers to set a risk threshold where $\alpha = .05$. If the probability that the data could have been obtained simply by random chance is less than 5%, the researcher is allowed to reject the null hypothesis because the chance of drawing this conclusion in error is small enough. In some cases, however, researchers may lower α to a smaller value (such as .01), or raise it to a higher value (such as .10). The implications for this are discussed further in this chapter. Note that in the first example, the probability of obtaining an IQ score as extreme as 130 simply by chance if the "intelligence boosting pill" does not work is less then 5% (i.e., it is 2.3%). In that case, assuming $\alpha = .05$, the researcher is allowed to reject the null hypothesis and conclude that the pill must have had some effect: it is unlikely that such extreme data would have been obtained if the pill did nothing. On the other hand, when the IQ score was 110, the likelihood that such data could have been obtained by chance even if the pill did not have an effect is greater than .05% (i.e., it is 25.1%). In this case, the researcher could not confidently reject the null hypothesis and must conclude that there is not strong evidence to say the "intelligence boosting pill" had any effect whatsoever.

Errors in Conclusion

We already have indicated that every time a researcher rejects the null hypothesis there is a chance that he or she has done so in error: we can never rule out completely the possibility that our results are due to a random fluke; however, we can identify when it is extremely unlikely. Whenever a researcher has rejected the null hypothesis when the results really are due entirely to random chance, he or she has made a **Type I error.** A Type I error can be considered a "false alarm," an instance where the researcher claims to have found a meaningful effect, relationship, or difference, but in fact this discovery is spurious. Using our example, if our researcher just so happened to randomly sample a participant with an IQ of 130 to begin with, the data would be extreme enough to reject the null hypothesis even if the pill did not influence the IQ score. The researcher would conclude that the pill had some effect, even if it did not, thus making a Type I error.

Note that if the data is not extreme enough, if it plausibly could be obtained randomly even if the null hypothesis was true, the researcher must retain, or fail to reject, the null hypothesis. Failing to reject, however, does not mean that the treatment had no effect; it only means that data were not strong enough to conclude with sufficient confidence (at the set alpha-level) that the pill had an effect. Sometimes the treatment will have an effect, or the groups will be meaningfully different, but our study failed to detect these differences. This circumstance is a **Type II error,** and can be considered a "miss." For example, imagine that the "intelligence boosting pill" really did work, and on average it increased people's IQ by 5 points. (Note that even if the pill truly and reliably boosted IQ by only 1 point, it still would be considered to work.) Imagine that we randomly sampled a person for the study with an initial IQ of 105, and after taking this "intelligence boosting pill," her IQ score was 110. As illustrated previously in this chapter, an IQ of 110 produces a Z-score of +0.67, which is associated with the upper 25.1% of the distribution. Because it is plausible enough to obtain an IQ score as extreme as 110 even if the null hypothesis is true (25.1% > 5.0%), the researcher in this case cannot reject the null hypothesis, and cannot conclude that the pill had any effect, even if it truly increased the participant's IQ score by 5 points.

The probability of making a Type II error is known as beta (β); however, unlike α, β is not set beforehand by the researcher. Although researchers can do things to minimize the risk of Type II errors, the actual value of β is not known. The term **statistical power** refers to the ability of a study to detect effects or differences that actually exist (i.e., the ability to avoid making Type II errors). Statistical power, in fact, is equal to $1 - \beta$. For example, if the "intelligence boosting pill" did have an effect on IQ scores, a more *powerful* study would be able to detect smaller effects of the treatment, while a less powerful study would require larger effects (e.g., larger increases in IQ from taking the "intelligence boosting pill") in order for the researcher to reject the null hypothesis. Statistical power can be increased by increasing sample size (see Chapter 10) and reducing error variance (see Chapter 11).

The table below illustrates the correspondence between the researcher's decision (to retain or reject the null hypothesis) and an unknown reality. It should be clear that anytime the researcher decides to reject the null hypothesis there is a chance (equal to the alpha-level) that the researcher has made a Type I error. Further, anytime the researcher fails to reject the null hypothesis, it is possible that a Type II error has been made (β). Note, however, that under conditions where the researcher does reject H0, there is no chance of making a Type II error, and under conditions where the researcher fails to reject H0, there is no chance of making a Type I error.

	Reality	
	H0 Is False	**H0 Is True**
Researcher Rejects H0	CORRECT	TYPE I ERROR α
Researcher Retains H0	TYPE II ERROR β	CORRECT

One-Tailed v. Two-Tailed Alpha

Recall that it is the researcher's prerogative to set the alpha-level before any analyses are conducted. The alpha-level defines the size of the area under the curve where data must fall in order to reject the null hypothesis. This area is called the *region of rejection*. Thus when $\alpha = .05$, the region of rejection marks the extreme 5% of the distribution (see Figure 9.1): only when the data falls in the extreme ends of the distribution, and thus is very unlikely to have been sampled at random, can the researchers reject the null hypothesis.

It is standard in social science to conduct statistical tests using *two-tailed tests*. When a two-tailed test is conducted, the alpha-level essentially is split in two such that a region of rejection the size of $\alpha/2$ is indicated in both the upper and lower ends of the distribution. In the common case where $\alpha = .05$, a two-tailed test places the lower 2.5% of the distribution and the upper 2.5% of the distribution in the regions of rejection (see Figure 9.2). If data falls in the upper or lower 2.5% extremes of the distribution, then the researcher can reject the null hypothesis with confidence. If the researcher decided to set $\alpha = .10$, then the two-tailed regions of rejection would include the upper and lower 5.0% of the distribution, and obtaining data in the upper and lower 5% extremes would allow the researcher to reject H0.

In some circumstances, researchers may opt to use *one-tailed tests*, in which case all of the alpha-level is dedicated to either the upper or lower extremes of the distribution. If a researcher anticipates an increase in scores following some treatment, she might elect to indicate the region of the rejection as the upper 5% of the distribution (assuming $\alpha = .05$). If she anticipates a decrease in scores following some treatment, she might indicate the region of rejection as the lower 5% of the distribution. Using a one-tailed test increases the statistical power of the research for detecting one direction of chance. However, the researcher cannot reject the null hypothesis if the data occur in the opposite direction. Using a one-tailed test to analyze the increase in IQ of the "intelligence boosting pill" would prohibit the researcher from determining at all whether the pill in fact had deleterious effects on IQ. Two-tailed tests generally are more conservative and widely accepted in the scientific community. One-tailed tests typically are only appropriate if there is a strong theoretical basis for anticipating only one direction of change, and not allowing for both.

Adjusting Alpha-Level

The relative risk of making a Type I or a Type II error can change by altering the alpha-level. Recall that α literally defines the size of the region of rejection, and typically is set at .05. Assuming a two-tailed test, the null hypothesis can only be rejected if the data falls in the upper or lower extreme 2.5% of the distribution. If the researcher had set $\alpha = .10$, the regions of rejection are now twice as large: the null hypothesis can be rejected if the data falls in the extreme 5% areas.

Assuming $\alpha = .05$, an IQ score of 130 (Z-score = +2.0) would be sufficient to reject the null hypothesis because it falls in the upper 2.3% of the distribution (within the upper 2.5% region of the rejection). The probability of obtaining that data due to random chance is small enough that the researcher can be confident that it did not merely occur by chance. An IQ score of 125 (Z-score = +1.67) is not sufficient because the likelihood of sampling that by

9.1

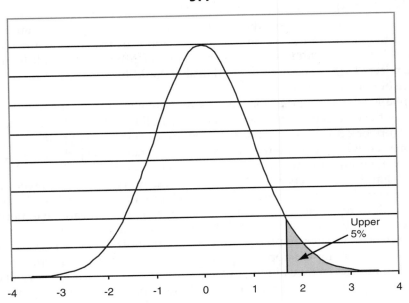

9.2

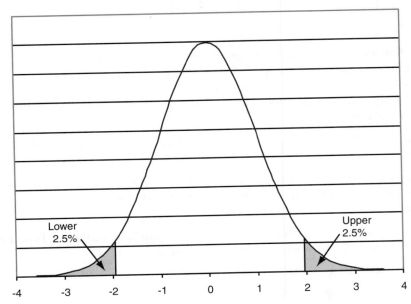

chance is too great; according to the unit normal table, the probability of sampling an IQ of 125 or greater is .095. However, if α was set at .10, an IQ score of 120 would be sufficient to reject H0. It becomes easier to reject the null hypothesis with a larger α because less extreme data is needed to fall within the region of rejection, and thus the chance of making a Type II error is reduced. However, due to the larger regions of rejection, the null hypothesis more often will be rejected when the data quite plausibly could have occurred randomly, increasing the chance of making a Type I error.

If the alpha-level was reduced, for example to two-tailed α = .01, the data must fall in the extreme 0.5% of the distribution in order to reject the null hypothesis. In this case, an IQ score as high as 130 (upper 2.3%) would not be sufficient to reject the null hypothesis. Quick calculations reveal that an IQ score as high as 139 would be needed to reject H0 using a two-tailed α = .01. However, because the alpha-level is so low, it is very unlikely that the data could have been obtained simply due to chance. Although decreasing α decreases power and increases the chance of a Type II error, it greatly reduces the chance of making a Type I error. Although it is more difficult to reject H0 as α becomes smaller, a researcher can have more confidence that she was correct in her rejection and avoided a Type I error when α is set to a smaller level.

In social sciences, greater emphasis is placed on minimizing Type I errors. For example, the consequences for failing to support a psychological theory (Type II error) are considered less important than incorrectly claiming evidence in support of such a theory (Type I error). However, in some medical research, greater emphasis is placed on avoiding Type II errors. A study designed to determine whether there were side effects from taking a particular medicine would want to make sure it detects every negative side effect, even at the risk of falsely detecting side effects. In this case, researchers may choose an increase in alpha-level. An alpha of .05 is thought to ideally balance between minimizing Type I and Type II errors.

PRACTICE PROBLEMS

9.1   In everyday terms, define **null hypothesis.**

9.2   Imagine that a clinical scientist has developed a new therapy to treat depression. To test this, he randomly selects a group of depressed people, administers his new therapy, and then measures their behavior. He observes that the people exhibit much fewer signs of depression than he would expect from this population. According to null hypothesis, what explains these results?

9.3   How are the null hypothesis and the alternative hypothesis related to the difference between *sample data* and *population means?*

9.4   Hypothesis testing involves using the population μ and σ to compute Z-scores. What precisely do these population parameters (μ and σ) reflect? What precisely does the Z-score reflect?

9.5   Define Type I and Type I errors. Under what circumstances might a Type I error occur, and under what circumstances might a Type II error occur?

9.6   Define α without using the term "Type I error."

9.7   Using everyday language, define **statistical power.**

9.8   Discuss the relationships among alpha, power, and Type I and Type II errors.

Sampling Distributions, Standard Errors, and Z-Tests

The prior example used to illustrate the logic behind inferential statistics is unrealistic in several ways, not the least of which is the fact that it employed only a single participant. Typically, studies in social science involve tens, hundreds, or even thousands of participants. However, when conducting research on groups of people (rather than on a single individual), our approach to estimating the probabilities associated with the data (in order to determine whether it falls within the region of rejection) must be adjusted. The logic behind hypothesis testing remains the same, but we now are working with the mean of the group, rather than with a single score.

When data on groups are collected, we must compute the mean score of all participants in the group, and determine the likelihood that we could have sampled that mean by chance if the null hypothesis was true. Following the previous example, in order to test the "intelligence boosting pill," we would sample a group of participants, give each participant in the group an "intelligence boosting pill," and then measure the IQ of each person in the group.

Imagine that the researcher sampled six people, gave each one the "intelligence boosting pill," and then gave them an IQ test. The data from this N=6 sample are:

130, 107, 95, 112, 90, 120

Thus

$$\Sigma X = 654$$

$$\overline{X} = 109$$

We would like to determine the Z-score and corresponding probabilities associated with a mean of 109. If this mean fell in the extreme upper or lower 2.5% of the distribution (assuming a two-tailed $\alpha = .05$), then we could reject the null hypothesis and conclude the pill must have increased the participants' IQ scores.

However, although we can compute the Z-score for a single *score* (X) according to:

$$Z = \frac{X - \mu}{\sigma}$$

it is *not* appropriate to use this formula to compute the Z-score associated with a mean.

In understanding why this is the case, it is important to remember several things. First is that when sampling at random, the population mean can be thought of as the *expected* value. If we were to draw a case from a normal distribution of scores, the mean of that distribution is our best guess of what the score would be. The variability of that distribution describes to what extent to which the scores we might sample might deviate from the population mean. Second, if you recall the AND rule from probability, the likelihood of several uncommon or rare events happening in a row becomes increasingly small as the number of samples increase. For example, the probability of drawing four aces in a row is much smaller than the chance of drawing three aces in a row, than is the chance of drawing two aces in a row, etc.

According to the null hypothesis, the group mean we produce in any study is merely the result of random sampling, and has nothing to do with any treatment or intervention. In order to determine the likelihood that we could have obtained our sample mean if the null hypothesis is true, we first must determine what data we should *expect* to get via sampling randomly from the population.

If we are drawing scores randomly from a population, we would expect the population mean to be the most frequently sampled score. Below average and above average scores would occur in approximately equal numbers, and in the long run (were we to sample group means from the population over and over), we would expect above average scores and below average scores to cancel each other out. Consequently, the most common sample mean we would expect to obtain from random sampling would be equal to the population mean. In randomly sampling IQ scores, the expected sample mean would be 100; there is no reason to expect that the mean of a random sample would exceed the population mean, and there is no reason to expect the sample mean to be below the population mean.

Despite expectations, however, in any given sample, above average and below average scores might not cancel each other. Sometimes, merely due to chance, we will disproportionately sample scores that are above average, and sometimes we will disproportionately sample scores that are below average. Our sample mean may be higher than expected or lower than expected, and in rare cases where our random sample is grossly disproportionate, our sample mean may deviate from the population mean by a considerable degree. Thus there potentially is variability among means generated via random sampling. According to the null hypothesis, the mean of 109 generated in the earlier example (where six participants were given the "intelligence boosting pill") is due to our sampling (at random) a disproportionate number of above average IQ scores, and had nothing to do with the pill itself.

Although there are an unlimited number of ways to obtain a mean of 109 from six scores, it is clear that it would require a number of unlikely flukes (e.g., sampling mostly above average scores or sampling one or two extremely above average scores) for this to occur. Whereas randomly sampling a *single* score as high as 109 might be considered marginally uncommon (27.4% of IQ scores are above 109), sampling *six* scores sufficient to produce a mean of 109 is less likely. Randomly sampling 10 participants that yield a mean of 109 is even less likely still because it requires even more unlikely events to occur.

It is a fundamental property of probability that as our sample size grows it becomes increasingly likely that our data will approximate expected values, and that deviations from expected values due to random chance become increasingly rare. If we are to think of deviations from expectancy as fluke occurrences, we would expect over time that these fluke occurrences would balance out (i.e., for every above average fluke we might expect, eventually, a below average fluke to occur). With a limited sample size, it would not be too uncommon for fluke occurrences not to even out, but it would be rare not to achieve balance with larger sample sizes.

Consider this analogy: If you flipped a coin 10 times, you would expect to get 5 heads and 5 tails (assuming that it is a fair coin), but it would not be greatly out of the ordinary to get ratios of 6 and 4, or even 7 and 3. If you flipped 100 coins, you would expect to get 50 heads and 50 tails, but if you get ratios of 60 and 40, or even 70 and 30, you might begin to suspect the veracity of the coin. If you flipped 1000 coins and achieved 600 or 700 of one outcome, you probably would be quite confident that the coin was not fair.

Similarly, we test the null hypothesis by determining whether our data represents a "fair sample" from the population. If our data consists of a single IQ score of 110, although it deviates from the expected value of 100, it seems quite plausible that such a score could be generated from a fair random sample. If our data consisted of 10 participants that produced a mean of 110, we would be less confident that the data could be a fair sample from the population because we would expect deviations from the mean to be more balanced. Finally, if our data consisted of 100 participants that produced a mean of 110, we would be quite confident that the data was not a fair random sample from the population. It is extremely unlikely that we could sample 100 persons and so disproportionately overrepresent, simply due to chance, above average scores.

The primary message of this discussion is that the probabilities associated with sampling a given mean from a population differ systematically as a function of sample size. As sample size increases, the extent to which sample means will deviate from the population mean decreases. It may be somewhat unlikely that we could obtain a mean IQ of 110 from a random sample of six participants (assuming $\mu = 100$), but it would be extremely unlikely for us to obtain a mean IQ of 110 from a random sample of 100 people because as N increases, random flukes would be expected to cancel each other out.

Sampling Distribution of Means

We have discussed the fact that a sample mean will be expected to deviate less from the population mean than will an individual score. However, in order to reject the null hypothesis that a given mean (instead of an individual score) was due merely to random chance and not due to any treatment, we need to quantify specific probabilities. Whereas the standard deviation describes the variability in individual scores, it overestimates the variability we would expect to find among sample means, and thus cannot be used to identify the Z-score associated with the sample mean.

Assume a distribution of IQ scores were $\mu = 100$ and $\sigma = 15$. Imagine that six cases were randomly sampled (with replacement) from this population, and the mean of the $N = 6$ sample was computed and recorded. Now imagine that six more cases were sampled and that the mean was recorded. Imagine further that this procedure of sampling six cases and recording the mean was conducted an infinite number of times. In the end we would be left with an infinite distribution of means based on a sample of six. This resulting distribution is a **sampling distribution of means.** This is a theoretical distribution that describes the expected variability in means based on a sample size of six. According to the null hypothesis, the sample mean collected in our study—the mean IQ of 109 produced from our sample of six participants who took the "intelligence boosting pill"—in fact is a random sample from this sampling distribution. If we were able to compute the standard deviation from this infinite list of means, we would have the appropriate denominator for computing a Z-score for a mean of 109 based on six cases. This Z-score would be able to tell us whether the likelihood of obtaining a mean of 109 (where $N = 6$) from a distribution where $\mu = 100$ and $\sigma = 15$ is less than 5% (alpha-level), and this would inform us whether we should retain or reject the null hypothesis.

The standard deviation of a sample distribution of means is called the **standard error,** which is symbolized as $\sigma_{\bar{x}}$. Note, however, that sampling distribution of means does not really exist; we never actually go through the process of sampling means over and over, and there is no list of sample means from which to compute a standard error. Nevertheless, there is a direct relationship between the standard deviation of the individual scores and the standard deviation of the sampling distribution of means. When a sample of size N is drawn from a population with a standard deviation of σ, the standard error (that describes the expected variability of sample means) is equal to the standard deviation divided by the square root of N. Thus,

$$\sigma_{\bar{x}} = \sigma / \sqrt{N}$$

It should be clear from this formula that variability among means decreases as sample size (N) increases. Similar to the prior example involving coin tosses, the variability of individual scores (see Figure 10.1) will be greater than the variability of sample means based on a sample size of 9 (see Figure 10.2), which will be greater than the variability of means based on a sample size of 25 (see Figure 10.3).

Thus, the Z-score associated with a mean of sample size N that was randomly drawn from a distribution with population mean μ and population standard deviation σ equals:

$$Z = (\bar{X} - \mu) / \sigma_{\bar{x}}$$

where $\sigma_{\bar{x}} = \sigma / \sqrt{N}$

10.1

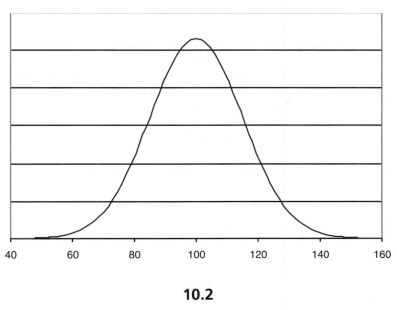

10.2

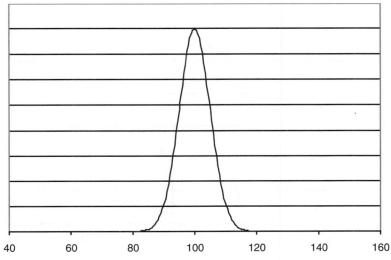

In the example where six participants (N = 6) produced a mean IQ of 109, we find that the standard error associated with that mean is equal to $15/\sqrt{6} = 6.12$. Thus, according to the null hypothesis, our mean of 109 is merely a random sample from a distribution of means with a population mean of 100 and population standard deviation of 6.12.

The Z-score associated with a mean of 109 (based on a sample size of 6) is equal to:

$$Z = (109 - 100)/6.12 = 1.47$$

10.3

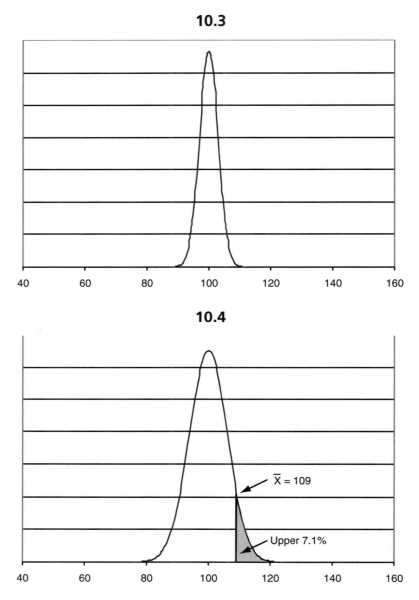

10.4

Examination of the unit normal tables reveals that a Z-score of 1.47 is located at the upper 7.1% of the distribution. Thus, the probability of randomly sampling *six scores* from the normal distribution of IQ scores and getting a mean as high as 109 is .071 (see Figure 10.4). The probability of obtaining a mean of 109 by chance is too plausible for us to reject the null hypothesis (i.e., the data does not fall in the extreme upper or lower 2.5% of the distribution).

Note, however, in Figure 10.5 that the probability of sampling a single score as high as 109 is much higher—27.5% (based on a Z-score of $(109 - 100)/15 = 0.60$). Sampling a mean as high as 109 based on six cases is much less common than sampling a single score as high as 109.

10.5

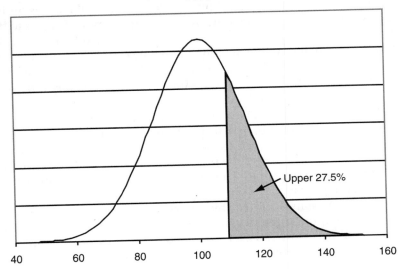

Upper 27.5%

If our study had involved 25 participants and still yielded a sample mean of 109, the expected variability of the means (i.e., standard error) would be:

$$\sigma_{\bar{x}} = 15/\sqrt{25} = 3$$

and the corresponding Z-score would be:

$$Z = (109 - 100)/3 = 3$$

If we examine the unit normal table, we find that a Z-score of 3 falls at the upper 0.14% of the distribution. It is rare enough (less than 5% chance) that a sample mean of 109 based on 25 cases could have been randomly drawn from a population where $\mu = 100$ and $\sigma = 15$ that we can confidently conclude that it did not come from such a distribution and reject the null hypothesis. In rejecting the null hypothesis, we imply that the population of people who took the "intelligence boosting pill" have different (higher) IQs than the population of people who did not take the pill.

This is evidence of the increased *statistical power* obtained by using larger sample sizes in the research. As N increases, it becomes easier and easier to reject even small effects (small deviations). Studies with very large sample sizes may have sufficient power to detect small mean deviations, whereas studies with very small effect sizes may require very large effects (mean deviations) in order to reject the null hypothesis.

Single Sample Z-Test

The first statistical test introduced in this book is the single sample Z-test. This is precisely to test was that conducted in the example above.

In order to conduct a single sample Z-test, the population mean (μ) and population standard deviation (σ) of the variable of interest must be known; thus the test is limited to examinations of IQ scores, SAT scores, etc. The purpose of a single sample Z-test is to determine the likelihood that a given sample mean ($\overline{X}$) could have been obtained by random chance from a population with a known μ and σ. Presumably, these parameters describe the "normal" population, and the researcher believes that his or her sample is something other than "normal." Specifically, the null hypothesis states that the sample data was merely a random sample of observations from the "normal" population (for which μ and σ are known), and is described symbolically as H0: $\mu\overline{X} = \mu$ (where $\mu\overline{X}$ represents the population mean of all persons who received the same "treatment" as those participants included in our sample). This essentially means that the treatment has no effect; if the treatment did affect scores on our outcome (dependent) measure, we would expect the population of people who received the treatment to be different from the mean of people who did not receive the treatment. Thus, the alternative hypothesis states H1: $\mu\overline{X} \neq \mu$.

We conduct a single sample Z-test by computing the mean of our sample (on the dependent measure), computing the deviation between the population mean, and dividing by the population standard error. Thus, as illustrated in the previous example, the test statistic for a single sample Z-test is computed following:

$$Z = (\overline{X} - \mu)/\sigma_{\overline{x}}$$

where $\sigma_{\overline{x}} = \sigma/\sqrt{N}$.

Assuming a two-tailed $\alpha = .05$, if the Z-score exceeds ± 1.96 (the Z-scores that mark the upper and lower 2.5% of the distribution) then we can reject the null hypothesis. It is unlikely enough that our data could have come from a population distribution of a given μ that we can conclude with confidence that our data must have come from a distribution with a different μ. This conclusion, in effect, says that our treatment must have had some effect: receiving the treatment changes, on average, the score on our variable of interest.

PRACTICE PROBLEMS

10.1 Using the probability formulas described in Chapter 4, compute the likelihood of obtaining three heads and one tail from tossing four coins. Note that while we expect a 50/50 split, we can compute the probability of getting a 75/25 split (favoring heads) on four coins. Note this probability. Next, compute the probability of getting a similar 75/25 split on eight coin tosses (i.e., six heads and two tails). Note that there are 28 different ways of getting six heads and two tails on eight coin tosses (this information is provided because the math involved in determining the total number of ways to obtain is beyond the scope of this book). Compare the probabilities of getting a 75/25 split from flipping four coins to the probability of a 75/25 split from flipping eight coins. This demonstrates the extent to which sample size influences the likelihood of events deviating from the *expected* values.

10.2 Define the **sampling distribution of means** and contrast this with a distribution of scores.

10.3 Define the **standard error** and contrast this with the **standard deviation.**

10.4 Consider a population where $\mu = 40$ and $\sigma = 12$.

1. What is the probability that a sample of $N = 4$ could be randomly sampled from this population such that $\bar{X} = 105$?
2. What is the probability of sampling a mean of 105 from this population when $N = 16$?
3. What is the probability of sampling a mean of 110 from this population if $N = 9$?
4. What is the probability of sampling a mean of 110 from this population if $N = 25$?

10.5 Why is the critical value for a single sample Z-test equal to ± 1.96?

10.6 An educational researcher is interested in knowing whether SAT prep courses really are effective in increasing students' SAT scores. This researcher obtains a random sample of 25 high school juniors and has each attend a commercial SAT prep course. After the course, each participant is given a standard SAT test. The sample mean SAT score is 1080, while the known population parameters of the SAT scores (verbal and math combined) distribution are $\mu = 1000$ and $\sigma = 200$.

1. What is the null hypothesis of the study?
2. What is the test statistic (Z-score) associated with the sample mean?
3. What can the researcher conclude from these data about the null hypothesis?
4. What would the researcher's conclusion be if the data ($\bar{X} = 1080$) was based on $N = 12$?

T-Tests and Confidence Intervals

U sing a single sample Z-test requires that both the population mean (μ) and population standard deviation (σ) are known. Knowledge of these parameters allows researchers to identify the location of a sample mean within a sampling distribution of means under the assumption of the null hypothesis. Knowing this location subsequently allows us to determine the probability that such a mean *could have* been sampled by chance and thus might occur even if our treatment or intervention had no effect. This probability allows us to determine whether or not we can reject the null hypothesis.

For all practical purposes, however, there are relatively few circumstances where the population mean or standard deviation is known. Typically, only if a dependent (outcome) measure has been tested on very large samples are population parameters known. Lacking information on the population values, it is unclear how to determine the location of the sample mean in the sampling distribution of means.

There may be circumstances where a researcher has a hypothesized population mean (μ) to use as a comparison in the numerator, but has no information on the population variability of that measure. In this case, the researcher may estimate the population standard deviation by computing the sample standard deviation from the data at hand. Imagine that on a scale used to measure depression, a score of "15" represents the threshold beyond which a clinician can label her client as clinically depressed. She takes a sample of 20 depressed persons and has them undergo depression therapy for three months, after which she asks them to take the depression measure. She hypothesizes that after the therapy, her clients no longer will be clinically depressed (thus, the sample mean on the depression measure will be significantly lower than "15"). The null hypothesis in this study would be that the sample depression scores are a random sample from a population with a μ of 15. Because the population standard deviation is not known, the researcher must compute standard deviation from the scores of her sample.

T-Distribution

Although we hope that standard deviation computed from our sample reflects the true population σ, we cannot be completely confident in its accuracy. This is true particularly when our sample is relatively small. Consider that σ is based upon an entire population of scores, whereas S is based on our sample (which may include only a small number of cases). If we randomly sample 10 people (for example) from a population, and compute the standard deviation from that sample, it would not be surprising if the computed value differed somewhat from the true (but unknown) population σ. It is plausible that we might sample cases more clustered, or more diverse, than the true variability in the population. It should be noted, however, that as our sample size increases and gets closer to the population size, we would expect our sample variability to approximate better the population σ.

Because the sample standard deviation (S) may not accurately reflect σ, we cannot conduct the same analysis as if σ was known. We cannot conduct a single sample Z-test using the sample standard deviation as a replacement for σ in computing the standard error. Because σ is unknown and we are forced to use the sample value S as an estimate, we must incur a penalty. Because the inaccuracy of the sample standard deviation decreases as the sample size increases, the size of this penalty also decreases as sample size increases.

The penalty incurred by having to estimate the population σ using the sample standard deviation is that we can no longer use the z-distribution (unit normal table) to determine the location of a sample mean, but instead must use the **t-distribution.** The t-distribution is very similar to the z-distribution in that it is symmetrical and has a population mean t-score of 0, but unlike the z-distribution, the variability of the t-distribution varies with sample size. The practical implication of using the t-distribution rather than the z-distribution is that the t-tests involve larger critical values in order to reject the null hypothesis. In the z-distribution, a score of ± 1.96 is always associated with the upper and lower 2.5% of the distribution. In the case of the t-distribution, the critical value (assuming a two-tailed α = .05) invariably will be larger. As the sample size increases, the critical value needed to reject the null hypothesis becomes smaller. Under the circumstance where the sample size equals infinity (thus, the sample is the population), the critical t-score for a two-tailed α = .05 is ± 1.96—the same as for the z-distribution.

In order to determine the critical value using the t-distribution, we first must determine the degrees of freedom for our study. If we wish to determine the probability of randomly sampling a given mean from a population with a known μ and unknown σ (estimated by S), the degrees of freedom **(df)** is equal to N – 1.

Below is a reduced t-table, indicating critical values associated with several different **dfs** and several different alpha-levels. Note that whereas the unit normal table (z-table) provides proportions associated with each Z-score, the t-table only provides t-scores associated with the critical values used for rejecting the null hypothesis at different alpha-levels.

Reduced T-Table

df = N − 1	Two-tailed $\alpha = .10$	Two-tailed $\alpha = .05$	Two-tailed $\alpha = .01$
3	2.353	4.303	5.841
7	1.895	2.365	3.499
20	1.725	2.086	2.845
50	1.676	2.009	2.678
100	1.660	1.984	2.626
∞	1.645	1.960	2.576

Thus, in a study where μ was known and a sample of 21 persons (df = 20) was used to compute the sample standard deviation (and subsequently, the standard error), t-scores of ± 2.086 would mark the upper and lower 2.5% of the distribution and indicate the *region of rejection* for rejecting the null hypothesis (assuming two-tailed α = .05). As discussed in Chapter 9, at lower alpha-levels, the critical t-scores are larger (i.e., the region of rejection is smaller), and at higher alpha-levels the critical t-scores are smaller (i.e., the region of rejection is larger).

Single Sample T-Test

A single sample t-test mirrors the single sample Z-test in Chapter 10 but is used when σ is not known. The standard error is computed from the sample standard deviation, and t-table is used to indicate the critical value. The test statistic is computed from:

$$t = (\bar{X} - \mu)/S_{\bar{x}}$$

where $S_{\bar{x}} = S/\sqrt{N}$ and S = sample standard deviation.

In order to conduct a single sample t-test, we must make a number of assumptions. This introductory text does not stress the assumptions underlying statistical tests, but it is important to identify them nevertheless.

First, we must assume that the population distribution of scores is normally distributed. It is not required that our sample necessarily be normally distributed, but the population from which the sample was drawn must be normal. If the population distribution was skewed, for example, the probabilities that we estimate may not be correct.

Second, we must assume that our data are *independent*. In essence, this means that the fact that one participant is sampled does not influence the relative likelihood that a particular other participant will be sampled. Thus, recruiting a group of friends to be participants might violate this assumption of independence; the fact that one friend has been sampled increases the likelihood that his or her other friends also will be sampled. This could be problematic for a number of reasons, but a detailed account of this is beyond the scope of this book. Reliance upon random sampling and/or random assignment (when appropriate; see Chapter 3) helps ensure that observations are independent.

For an example of single sample t-test, consider the following:

The manager of an assembly line wishes to reduce the number of errors made by factory workers, and develops a training program to achieve this end. Preliminary data collection indicated that workers made an average of 11 errors per day. After administering the training program to factory workers, data were collected from a sample of eight employees.

The null hypothesis (H0) of this study is: $\mu_{\bar{x}} = \mu$; i.e., the sample from which data was collected came from a distribution with a μ of 11. This would mean that people who go through the program are no different from those who do not go through the program in terms of errors made on the assembly line. However, if the training program is effective, then we would expect the population that produces the sample mean to have a lower population $\mu_{\bar{x}}$ than the "normal", and thus we would expect a sample mean that is significantly lower than 11 to indicate that the program had an effect.

The sample data follows:

X	X²	
10	100	N = 8
09	81	ΣX = 65
13	169	(ΣX)² = 4225
06	36	ΣX² = 589
08	64	X̄ = 65/8 = **8.125**
07	49	SS = 589 – (4225/8) = **60.88**
03	09	S² = SS/(N – 1) = 60.875/7 = **8.70**
09	81	S = √8.70 = **2.95**

$S_{\bar{x}} = S/\sqrt{N} = 2.95/\sqrt{8} = $ **1.04**

$t = (8.125 – 11)/1.04 = –2.875/1.04 = $ **–2.76**

The degrees of freedom **(df)** in this study is equal to N – 1 = 7. If we examine the reduced t-table (p. 93), we find that the critical t-score (assuming two-tailed α = .05) is 2.365. If the t-score that we *compute* exceeds the critical value—whether it is larger than +2.365 or lower than –2.365, then we can reject the null hypothesis while keeping the chance of making a Type I error lower than 5%. Because our t-score of –2.76 is lower than the critical value of –2.365, we reject the null hypothesis. It is unlikely that we could have randomly sampled eight workers from a population where μ = 11 and obtained a mean of 8.125. We can conclude, therefore, that this sample must have come from a population different from the "normal" population of workers.

Rejecting the null hypothesis implies that our sample mean is *meaningfully* different (i.e., statistically significant) than the population mean (i.e., that the differences are not merely due to random chance). When (and only when) we reject the null hypothesis, we can interpret the

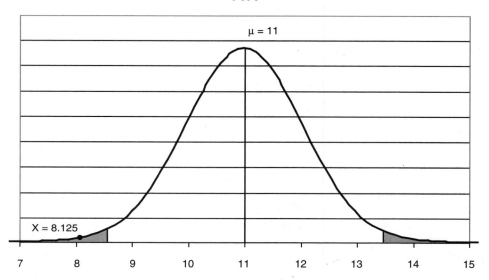

mean of our sample. In this case, our sample mean is lower than the population mean (8.125 < 11); thus the workers who took the training program performed better (made fewer errors) than what would be expected if the training program did not work. We can conclude from this that the training program successfully reduced assembly line errors. Note that had we failed to reject the null hypothesis, we would conclude that even though our sample mean was lower than the population μ, the evidence is not strong enough for us to conclude that the difference is a result of anything other than random chance; it is plausible enough that we could sample eight workers who produce a sample mean as extreme as 2.875 errors from the expected population mean simply due to chance—even if the training program had no effect whatsoever.

Independent Sample T-Test

In most cases, neither the population mean (μ) nor the population standard deviation (σ) are known. For the single sample t-test, we estimated σ from the sampled standard deviation; however, it is not clear how to estimate μ, as $\overline{X}$ already is used as an important part of the equation.

In cases where neither μ nor σ is known, a different type of research design must be used. Whereas the single sample t-test involves sampling data from a single group, when μ is not known we must collect data from two independent groups. Using the previous example of assembly line workers, if there was no information regarding the population mean errors per day, a researcher might randomly sample one group of workers, put them through the training program, and measure their errors, and then sample another group of workers and measure their errors without putting them through the training program. Thus we would have two sample means (of assembly line errors): one from the training program group, and one from the non-training group (i.e., control group). To test the efficacy of the training program, we would be interested in comparing the mean errors per day from these two groups.

If the training program has no effect whatsoever, we would expect the mean of the sample that went through the program to be pretty similar to the mean of the sample that did not go through the program. If the program did have some effect, we would expect the mean of the training group to be different from the mean of the non-training group; and if the program worked as intended, we would expect the mean of the training group to have a lower mean (fewer errors, on average) than the non-training group. However, it is possible to get differences in sample means simply due to chance; thus, we must conduct a statistical test rather than merely eyeball the mean differences to determine whether the program worked.

Consider a scenario where a group of participants wrote their favorite number between one and twenty onto a sheet of paper, and that a researcher collected these papers and randomly shuffled them into two piles—Pile A and Pile B. Imagine that the mean favorite number was computed for each pile. What would we expect to find? There is no reason to expect that the favorite number in Pile A would be larger than in Pile B; nor would we expect that the favorite number in Pile B would be larger than in Pile A. In fact, because we shuffled the papers into two groups at random, we would expect the two means to be equal. However, because we did this at random, we also would not be surprised if the means of the two groups were not perfectly identical. It is possible that through the process of randomly shuffling papers into piles, we just so happened to put a few papers with above average scores into one pile, and below average scores in the other pile. Thus we may find that the means of the two piles differ simply because of chance. Furthermore, if we did find different means between the two piles, we would not believe that the difference indicated important or meaningful differences about the piles themselves. If we re-shuffled the papers, we would not expect the same difference to necessarily reoccur.

If we conducted the study of the assembly line training program and found that the mean number of assembly line errors differed between the training and non-training groups, how could we be confident these differences were not due to random error, much in the same way that we might find mean differences if we randomly shuffled participants' favorite numbers into two groups? We would need to determine how likely it is that we could sample two groups (of given sample sizes) from the same population and obtain mean differences as large as we found in our sample.

The null hypothesis of the assembly line study is that the training group and non-training group are random samples from the same population (or populations with identical μs), i.e., that there is nothing meaningfully different from those two groups. Thus,

$$H0: \mu_T = \mu_{NT}$$

Alternatively,

$$H0: \mu_T - \mu_{NT} = 0$$

where μ_T = population mean of workers who go through the training, and μ_{NT} = population mean of workers who do not go through the training.

Recall from Chapter 9 that we expect (in the long run) the mean of a sample to approximate the population mean from which it was drawn, and that this expectation is stronger as our sample size increases. Similarly, if we sample two groups from the same population, we would expect both means to approximate the population mean.

Thus,

$$(\bar{X}1 - \mu1) = (\bar{X}2 - \mu2)$$

or

$$(\bar{X}1 - \mu1) - (\bar{X}2 - \mu2) = 0$$

Because the null hypothesis states that $\mu1 = \mu2$, the expectation under the null hypothesis can be reduced to:

$$\bar{X}1 - \bar{X}2 = 0$$

Due to random variability, however, it is possible that two samples from the population might produce different means. In order to determine whether the means of our two samples are significantly different from each other, we need to estimate the expected variability in mean differences.

In Chapter 9 we described the standard error as the standard deviation of a sampling distribution of means; this value is used as the denominator in calculating the test statistics (Z-score or t-score) for a single sampled Z-test or t-test. In order to test the null hypothesis that our groups are randomly sampled from the same population, we compute the **standard error of the differences between means.** This reflects the expected variability in mean differences if two means (of a given sample size) were sampled from the same population, and the differences were calculated, an infinite number of times.

There are several important facts to consider before we address the computations for obtaining the standard error of differences between the means. First is that the **independent t-test** does not require that our two groups be of equal size. Thus, while N indicates the total number of people in our sample, n1 and n2 represent the number of people in groups 1 and 2, respectively. However, it assumes that these groups are independent of each other (a participant in group 1 cannot also be in group 2, and cannot influence scores in group 2).

Second, it assumes that the population variances are normally distributed, and third, that the standard deviations within each group are equal. Approaches that deal with violations of this last assumption (e.g., Satterthwaite's Method) may be discussed in more advanced statistics courses.

The computation of standard error of the differences between means in fact is based upon the variability *within* each group. The first step in computing the standard error is to calculate the **pooled variance,** in essence, the variance within each group combined together. Note that this pooled variance is different than the variance we would find if both groups were combined into a single group. For the former, we compute the extent to which scores vary around the mean of each group and then combine those two variances, while in the latter we first combine the groups and then compute the total variability around the mean.

For the pooled variance:

$$S_P^2 = (SS1 + SS2)/(df1 + df2)$$

where SS1 and SS2 represent the sums of squares for groups 1 and 2, separately, and df1 and df2 represent the degrees of freedom $(n-1)$ for groups 1 and 2, respectively.

Once the pooled variance has been calculated, the standard error of the differences between mean can be calculated. Thus:

$$S_{x1-x2} = \sqrt{(S_P^2/n1) + (S_P^2/n2)}$$

In the case where the sample size of group 1 is the same as the sample size for group 2, $S_P^2/n1$ will equal $S_P^2/n2$. The pooled variance in the numerator will remain the same regardless.

Once S_{x1-x2} is calculated, the test statistics for the independent sample t-test can be computed as:

$$t = (\bar{X}1 - \bar{X}2)/S_{x1-x2}$$

Imagine that a researcher was interested in studying the effectiveness of a new anti-anxiety drug. Using an experimental design, one group of four participants was given this new drug (Drug A) while another group of six participants was given a placebo. After administering either Drug A or the placebo, participants' anxiety was measured using a measure of reduced anxiety (higher scores mean less anxiety). The data are as follows:

▶ Drug A	Placebo	N = 10	n1 = 4	n2 = 6
11	03		$\Sigma X = 37$	$\Sigma X = 21$
13	02		$(\Sigma X)^2 = 1369$	$(\Sigma X)^2 = 441$
04	07		$\Sigma X^2 = 387$	$\Sigma X^2 = 91$
09	04		$\bar{X}1 = 9.25$	$\bar{X}2 = 3.5$
	02			
	03			

Note that although our sample means are different (9.25 v. 3.5) it is possible that two groups with such a mean difference could be sampled by chance from the same population (or from populations with identical μs). To determine this likelihood, we must compute the expected variability for a sampling distribution of means. The steps in accomplishing this involve computing the sums of squares for each group, getting the pooled variance, and finally getting the standard error of differences between the means.

11.2

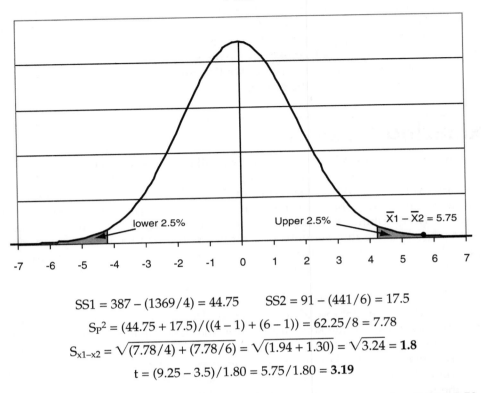

$$SS1 = 387 - (1369/4) = 44.75 \qquad SS2 = 91 - (441/6) = 17.5$$

$$S_P^2 = (44.75 + 17.5)/((4-1) + (6-1)) = 62.25/8 = 7.78$$

$$S_{x1-x2} = \sqrt{(7.78/4) + (7.78/6)} = \sqrt{(1.94 + 1.30)} = \sqrt{3.24} = \textbf{1.8}$$

$$t = (9.25 - 3.5)/1.80 = 5.75/1.80 = \textbf{3.19}$$

In order to determine whether the mean difference from our samples (9.25 – 3.50 = 5.75) is statistically significant, we must compare our test statistic against a critical value obtained from the t-table.

For an independent sample t-test, the degrees of freedom is equal to N – 2, or (n1 – 1) + (n2 – 1). In this case, N – 2 = 10 – 2 = **8 df.**

Assuming a two-tailed α = .05, cross-indexing 8 dfs on the t-table reveals a critical t-value of 2.31. In order to reject the null hypothesis, the t-score that we computed must exceed (in absolute value) the critical value. In this case, our computed t-statistic does exceed the critical value, 3.19 > 2.31. Figure 11.2 depicts the sampling distribution of differences between means. It indicates that the difference between sample means (X̄1 – X̄2 = 5.75) is large enough that we can be confident that the two means were not randomly sampled from populations with identical μs. The likelihood of getting mean differences this large by chance is less than α = .05.

The fact that the mean difference is statistically significant allows us to interpret the samples mean differences as indicating differences in population means. Generally, it is not sufficient to end a statistical test by stating simply whether or not the null hypothesis can be rejected. If the null hypothesis is rejected, we want to state whether the mean of group A was greater than the mean of group B, or whether the mean of group A was lower than the mean of group B. In this example, the mean anxiety reduction for the new anti-anxiety drug

(Drug A) was greater ($\bar{X} = 9.25$) than was the mean anxiety reduction for the placebo ($\bar{X} = 3.5$). Therefore, we conclude not only that the two samples are meaningfully different, but the people who take Drug A experience significantly greater anxiety reduction than do people who take a placebo. Thus Drug A appears to have an effect. Note that if we failed to reject the null hypothesis, we would not bother to examine the sample means, because we already have concluded that any samples mean differences we find are due to random chance, and not due to meaningful differences between the groups.

Maximizing T-Scores

Given that researchers generally wish to reject the null hypothesis, it is in their best interest to obtain as large (in absolute value) a t-score as possible when conducting a t-test. Examination of the t-score formula illustrates what types of data will produce the largest t-scores. First, note that larger differences between the sample means will produce a larger numerator, which invariably contributes to a larger t-score. Thus researchers can attempt to maximize their t-scores by choosing interventions or treatments that will have as large an effect, and produce as large a difference between groups as possible. However, in many cases the researcher has little or no control over the strength of the treatment. Medicines and treatments usually are designed already to be as effective as possible, and it is unlikely the researcher could make them more effective.

It also should be clear that researchers can maximize the t-score that they compute by minimizing as much as possible the standard error in the denominator. Using smaller standard errors invariably yields larger t-scores. Of course increasing the sample size will reduce the standard error, given that standard errors (for both t-tests and Z-tests) are computed by dividing the standard deviation by the square root of the sample size. However, it also is in the best interest of the researcher to try to minimize the standard deviations themselves. The standard error and the standard error of differences between the means are derived primarily from the variability within the groups. The numerator in the formula for the standard error in fact is the standard deviation, and the standard deviation of differences between means is based on the sums and squares (and eventually variance and standard deviations) within our two sample groups. If the standard deviations of our sample groups are relatively large, our standard errors will be relatively large, and thus t-scores will be smaller. If our group standard deviations are relatively small we will have smaller standard errors, and thus our t-scores will be larger.

Taken together, we can conceive of the t-score the *ratio of the difference **between** the group means relative to the variability of scores **within** the groups*, i.e., the spread of group means relative to the spread of scores within groups. The difference between group means is reflected in the numerator of the t-score formula, while the variability within the groups is reflected in the standard error in the denominator. Large deviations between group means relative to small within-group deviations (scores deviating from the mean of the particular group) will produce larger t-scores. Small differences between group means relative to large variability within groups will produce smaller t-scores.

This ratio of between-group differences relative to within-group differences can be illustrated graphically. The degree of overlap between the two groups is reflective of the magnitude of the t-score, where little overlap indicates larger t-scores. Figure 11.3 depicts relatively large differences between groups, and relatively small variability within groups, and would produce the largest t-score of Figures 11.3–11.6. Figure 11.4 reflects relatively large differ-

11.3

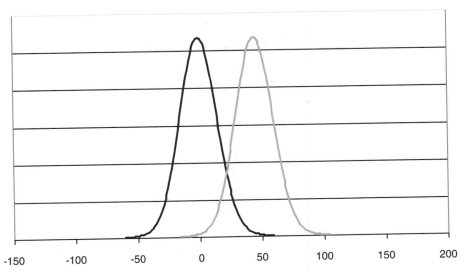

11.4

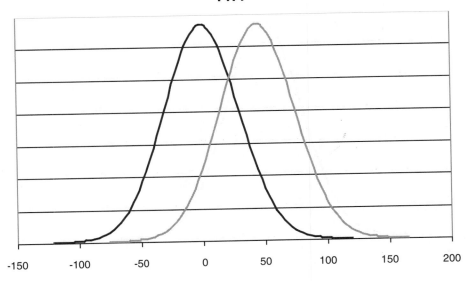

ences between groups, but also large variability within groups. This within-group variability blurs the distinction between the two groups, and reduces the t-score that we would obtain. In Figure 11.5 we have smaller differences between groups but also relatively small within-group variability. The t-score computed from this example may be comparable to one computed from Figure 11.4, although clearly it would be larger than the one associated with Figure 11.6. Here, the group means are relatively close, and the within-group variability is relatively large. The overlap between the two groups is so great that it may be difficult to

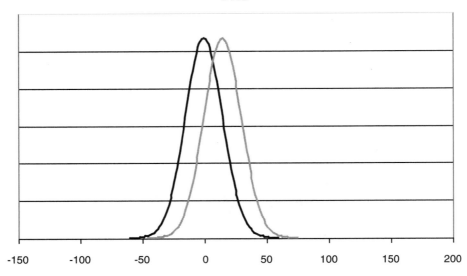

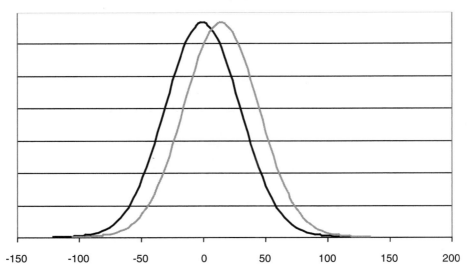

determine that there are two distinct groups. It may seem intuitively clear to readers that in Figure 11.3, the two groups are quite distinct, in Figures 11.4 and 11.5 they are less distinct, and in Figure 11.6 they are least distinct. This visual "distinction" is directly related to the t-score that we would expect to find.

Although these illustrations apply directly to the independent sample case, the underlying logic holds true for the single sample case and the related-samples case (discussed later in this chapter). Maximizing the comparison indicated in the numerator while minimizing the standard deviations (and subsequently, standard errors) implied in the denominator will result in large t-scores and a greater likelihood of rejecting the null hypothesis.

Error/Unexplained Variance

We have discussed in the previous section that it is advantageous for researchers to try to minimize the standard deviations (variability within the groups) of our samples, as this will increase the likelihood of rejecting the null hypothesis. Understanding how to reduce within-group variability requires an understanding of the factors that create within-group variability in the first place.

Imagine that an educational researcher wishes to determine whether taking an SAT prep course in fact really increases students' SAT scores. To test this question, the researcher collects a sample of participants and randomly assigns them to one of two groups. Participants who are assigned to group A complete an SAT prep course and then take a standard SAT exam. Participants who are assigned to group B are asked to complete a standard SAT exam without first taking an SAT prep course. At the end of the study, the research has SAT scores from the entire sample (N) of participants.

Without doubt, there will be variability among these SAT scores. Some participants will have high SAT scores, others will have low SAT scores, and still others will have SAT scores near the middle of the distribution. Note that if we did not have variability in SAT scores, or if there was very little variability in SAT scores, it would imply that everyone in the sample did just about the same on the SAT test. If everyone did just about the same on the SAT test, it will be very difficult to show that taking the SAT prep course helps (i.e., that people who took the course did just about the same as people who did not take the course). In fact, it is necessary for there to be variability (differences) among our outcome scores in order to conduct statistical tests of our hypothesis.

Another way to phrase the hypothesis that "taking a SAT prep course influences (increases) SAT scores" is to state that "whether or not a participant takes a SAT prep course helps to *explain the variability* in SAT scores"; that is, the fact some people took a prep course while others did not contributes to why some SAT scores are higher and others are lower.

Assume that we conducted this study to test the SAT prep course and that there was considerable variability in the SAT scores collected. What are some of the possible factors that might *cause* some scores to be high and other scores to be low? We already hypothesize that whether or not a participant was assigned to take the SAT prep course contributes to this variability. But there are many other factors that probably contribute to variability in scores as well. A participant's natural intelligence, for example, probably plays a large role in how he scored on the SAT. The fact that some people are relatively bright while other people are less bright is one factor that explains why some people have relatively high SAT scores and other people have relatively low SAT scores. Furthermore, some people may study more efficiently than others, and this may contribute to why some scores are higher or lower than other scores. Some people may have gotten more sleep the night before the test; some people may have been in a better mood; some people may have been particularly lucky, etc. The truth is, we probably cannot identify or list all of the factors that contribute to variability in SAT scores—that cause some people to score better than others on the SAT—but we must acknowledge that such factors exist. By randomly assigning participants to a condition, we help keep the influence of these variables comparable across groups (i.e., the amount of effect on scores due to these variables is approximately equal in each group); however, random assignment does not minimize the magnitude of this influence.

Note that in this research we did not <u>measure</u> any of the possible factors (*other* than taking the SAT prep course or not) that might have contributed to variability in SAT scores (e.g., intelligence, study habits, sleep). We do not know individual participants' IQs, or how much they slept, etc. However we very much would like to measure the extent to which these factors contributed to variability in the scores. The term **error variance** or **unexplained variance** (used interchangeably) is used to reflect the extent to which scores vary for reasons *other* than the independent variable in question (i.e., prep course). Thus we lump together all of the factors that influence SAT scores—natural intelligence, study habits, sleep, luck, and all of the other factors that we did not even think about—*except* whether or not the participant took the prep course, and refer to the influence of all these factors as error.

How can we measure the variability due to all of these unmeasured factors (i.e., error variance) and separate it from the variability that may be due to whether or not the participant took the SAT prep course? The answer comes from examining the variability (standard deviations) *within* each group. All of the participants in Group A were randomly assigned to take the SAT prep course. Whatever variability in scores exists within that group must be due to the fact that people differ in intelligence, study habits, sleep, etc., but cannot be due to whether or not they took the prep course (because everyone in that group did take the prep course). Similarly, if we look at the variability of scores within Group B, the fact that some scores are higher and some scores are lower cannot be due to the fact that some people took the prep course and others did not, because nobody in that group went through the prep course.

The variability (i.e., standard deviations) computed within each group are estimates of error, i.e., 100% unexplained variability, because we did not measure any of the variables (intelligence, sleep, etc.) that could explain why scores vary within the groups. It is important to note that if we examined SAT scores as if they were in a single group (and did not separate the data in groups according to whether or not they took the prep course), the variability of those scores would include both error (unexplained) variance as well as any variance due to taking the prep course or not. By separating the data into two groups and examining the standard deviations separately within the groups, we tease out any variability that might be due to our independent variable (prep course v. no prep course).

The standard errors that we use as denominators in our t-tests are labeled such because they are derived (based upon) our sample estimates of unexplained, or error, variability. The fact that we use the term "error" to describe *within group variability* should not lead readers to think that the presence of variability within groups implies some "mistake" in the study. Error variance probably is a poor term to use, because error (unexplained) variability should be thought of as natural variability—the extent to which scores vary naturally due to individual differences (in intelligence, study habits, etc.). In our study of SAT prep courses, the ratio implied by our t-test reflects the extent to which taking the SAT prep course v. not taking it spreads the group means apart above and beyond the extent to which we expect scores to vary "naturally". This point will be stressed more thoroughly in Chapter 12: One-Way Analysis of Variance.

Minimizing Error Variance

In the previous section we learned that the presence of individual differences in variables that influenced the outcome (e.g., intelligence, study habits, sleep) creates error/unexplained variance, which is measured by computing the variability within our groups. The standard deviations within our groups are used to derive the standard error that in turn is used as the denominator in the t-test. If we can reduce the standard deviations of our groups, we reduce our standard errors, use smaller denominators when conducting the t-test, and produce larger t-scores which makes it more likely that we will reject the null hypothesis.

It follows that if we can eliminate or control some of these other factors that contribute to the error variance, we will get smaller standard deviations. For example, in conducting this SAT prep course study, we could have first administered IQ tests to all participants, and selected only persons with IQ scores of 100 to participate in the study. In this case, all participants in the study would have the same IQ, and the fact that some people are naturally more intelligent than others would have a much smaller contribution to the variability of SAT scores within each group. If we could remove individual differences in natural intelligence as a source of error variance, we would increase the statistical power of our research by reducing the standard error (denominator) in our t-test.

Related Samples T-Test (Also Known as Dependent-Sample, or Repeated Measures, T-Test)

Some research designs allow us to minimize error variance due to individual differences by allowing each participant to serve as his or her own control. In the most simple version of such a design, a single group of participants is involved, but each participant is measured twice and thus each provides two scores. For example, using the SAT prep course study, we could have approached the research by having a single group of participants take the SAT, then having the entire group of participants take the SAT prep course, and finally, having everyone in the group take the SAT again. Thus each participant provides two SAT scores—one before the course (time 1), and one after the course (time 2). This design is quite different from having two independent groups of subjects where one group takes the prep course and the other does not take the prep course.

Another version of this simple design would involve a single group of participants, where each participant provides two ratings or evaluates two items. For example, a researcher may be interested in knowing whether people prefer Cola A or Cola B. She could recruit a single group of participants and have each person taste Cola A and rate how much they like it and then taste Cola B and rate how much they like that. This design is quite different from an approach where two independent groups would be sampled, and one group would be assigned to taste and rate Cola A, and the other group would be assigned to taste and rate Cola B.

In the case of an independent sample design, at the conclusion of the research we have two separate groups of data, and the organization or order of one group has no bearing on the organization or order of the other group. In the case of a related-samples design, we will still have two separate groups of data (e.g., pre-test v. post-test, or Cola A v. Cola B); however, the data are organized such that each row of data is paired. The person who produced the first score in the first data column also produced the first score in the second data column (thus the scores are "related"). The person who produced the second score in the first data column also produced the second score in the second data column, and so forth. See the table below for an example.

	Pre-Test	Post-Test
Participant 1		
Participant 2		
Participant 3		
. . .		
Participant N		

The consequence of this is that each pair of scores within a row was generated by the same person, and thus the influence of individual difference factors such as intelligence, study habits, sleep, etc., are the same for each score. Because the scores are paired, we can create a difference score for each participant by subtracting each second column score from the first (i.e., Pre – Post, or Cola A – Cola B). Creating a column of difference scores, in fact, is the first step in conducting a related samples t-test.

Imagine that we included a sample of five participants in an SAT prep course study. Each participant took the test before, and then after, going through the prep course. The difference column reflects the change in SAT score from time 1 (pre-test) to time 2 (post-test).

Pre-Test	Post-Test	Difference
0980	1030	–50
1120	1150	–30
1020	1000	+20
0810	0900	–90
1280	1290	–10

The null hypothesis states that there should be no difference (no change) between scores at time 1 and time 2 (or that there should be no difference in rating 1 and rating 2, depending on the exact nature of the research). Accordingly, both sets of scores are sampled from the same population, and thus we would expect the population mean of the differences scores (μ_D) to be 0. The primary assumptions underlying related samples t-tests are that (1) scores *within* conditions (i.e., pre-test v. post-test; rating of item A v. item B) are independent, and (2) the population variance of difference scores is normal (although in larger samples, this latter assumption can be relaxed).

Given this expected value for μ_D (assuming that H0 is true) we now are in the position to conduct a single sample t-test using the difference column of scores. Recall that single sample t-tests require a known μ, with which the sample mean ($\overline{X}$) is contrasted. Given the presence of paired data, we can compute a group mean deviation by comparing the sample mean of the difference scores ($\overline{D}$) to the known μ_D of 0. In order to add meaning to this group deviation, however, we must determine the appropriate standard error of the difference scores as a denominator.

Recall that for the single sample t-test, standard error that serves as the denominator is computed from the standard deviation of the sample divided by the square root of the sample size, N. In the case of the related samples t-test, the standard error is computed from the standard deviation of the difference scores divided by the square root of N.

Thus,

$$S_{\overline{D}} = S_D / \sqrt{N}$$

where

$$S_D = \sqrt{\frac{\Sigma D^2 - (\Sigma D)^2/N)}{N-1}}$$

and

$$t = \overline{D}/S_{\overline{D}}$$

Given the difference scores (D) computed from the five participants in the SAT prep course study

D	D²	N = 5
−50	2500	$\Sigma D = -160$
−30	0900	$(\Sigma D)^2 = 25600$
+20	0400	$\Sigma D^2 = 12000$
−90	8100	$\overline{D} = -32$
−10	0100	

$SS_D = 12{,}000 - (25{,}600/5) = 6880$

$S_D^2 = 6880/(5 - 1) = 1720$

$S_D = 41.47$

$S_{\overline{D}} = 41.47/\sqrt{5} = 18.55$

$t = -32/18.55 = -1.725$

11.7

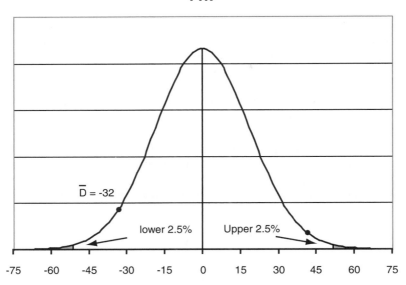

The related samples t-test essentially is a single sampled t-test conducted on a column of differences scores obtained from a single sample of matched or paired data. The degrees of freedom for a related samples t-test is based on N – 1, where N represents the number of participants in the study, and not the number of observations. Thus in the current example, df = 5 – 1 = 4. Assuming two-tailed α = .05, our critical value at 4 df is 2.78.

Because our computed t-score of –1.725 does not exceed (in absolute value) the critical value of 2.78, we cannot reject the null hypothesis. Although the scores from the post-SAT test sample were greater, on average, than scores from the pre-SAT test sample (1074 v. 1042), as shown in Figure 11.7, the evidence is not strong enough for us to conclude with sufficient confidence (based on α = .05) that these differences are due to anything other than random error. In other words, we cannot conclude in this case that the SAT prep course had any effect, and post-test scores were not significantly different than pre-test scores.

Comparing Independent Samples and Related Samples T-Tests

When the related samples t-test was introduced, it was described as a method of reducing the standard error by allowing each participant to serve as his or her own control. Although it is not always the case that a study using a related-samples design (pre v. post, or rating 1 v. rating 2) will be more powerful than an independent samples design, there are reasons to expect that it may be.

In the next example, consider that participants evaluated and then rated two objects, X1 and X2. The same set of data will be analyzed twice, once using an independent samples approach, and then again using a related samples approach. The first analysis will assume

	X1	X2	X1²	X2²	D	D²	
	10	06	100	036	+4	16	N = 12 (assuming independent sample)
	08	05	064	025	+3	9	n1 = 6
	05	02	025	004	+3	9	n2 = 6
	02	03	004	009	−1	1	$(\Sigma X1)^2 = 1296$
	05	04	025	016	+1	1	$(\Sigma X2)^2 = 484$
	06	02	036	004	+4	16	
Σ	36	22	254	094	+14	52	
$\bar{X}$	6.0	3.67			+2.33		

that the data came from two independent groups, while the second analysis assumes that the data reflect matched pairs of scores from a single sample.

For the *independent samples* test:

$$SS1 = 254 - (1296/6) = 254 - 216 = 38$$

$$SS2 = 094 - (484/6) = 094 - 80.67 = 13.33$$

$$S_P^2 = (38 + 13.33)/((6 - 1) + (6 - 1)) = 51.33/10 = 5.13$$

$$S_{x1-x2} = \sqrt{(5.13/6) + (5.13/6)} = \sqrt{(.855 + .855)} = 1.31$$

$$t = (6.00 - 3.67)/1.31 = 2.33/1.31 = \mathbf{1.78}$$

$$df = 12 - 2 = 10 \qquad T_{CRIT}(10) = 2.23$$

$$\text{Because } |1.78| < 2.23, \text{ fail to reject H0}$$

For the *related samples* test: N = 6

$$SS_D = 52 - (14^2/6) = 52 - (196/6) = 52 - 32.67 = 19.33$$

$$S_D^2 = 19.33/(6 - 1) = 3.87$$

$$S_D = \sqrt{3.87} = 1.97$$

$$S_{\bar{D}} = 1.97/\sqrt{6} = .80$$

$$t = 2.33/.80 = 2.91$$

$$df = 6 - 1 = 5 \quad T_{CRIT}(5) = 2.57$$

Because $|2.91| > 2.57$, reject the null hypothesis.

Note that in both the independent samples and related samples t-test, the numerator was 2.33. However, the related samples t-test was statistically significant, while the independent samples t-test was not. The difference between the two tests was the standard error. In the case of the independent samples t-test, the standard error was 1.78; it was over twice as small for the related samples t-test. It will not always be the case that the standard error produced using a related samples t-test will be smaller than the standard error produced if the data were analyzed as independent groups, but one clear advantage of the related samples t-test is that variability due to individual differences is removed from the error term. One disadvantage to the related samples t-test is that degrees of freedom will invariably be smaller than an analogous independent sample test.

There also are many circumstances where a related samples design is not appropriate, or even possible. The interpretation of repeated samples tests sometimes can be challenged by the presence of learning effects. Recall the research example where a single group of participants took the SAT, then went through a SAT prep course, and afterwards took the sample again. If we reject the null hypothesis and conclude that SAT scores are higher at time 2 than at time 1, we would like to attribute that increase to the SAT prep course, but it is possible that the increase was due entirely to *learning*. The process of taking the SAT at time 1 might have provided participants an opportunity to practice and to become familiar with the nature of the test. If the SAT prep course has no real effect, participants might still score better on the SAT at time 2 simply because of the practice they received at time 1. Although the researcher would be correct in rejecting the null hypothesis, his or her explanation for the increase in SAT scores may not be correct.

This example implicitly compares a SAT prep course treatment to a non-prep course treatment using repeated measures. What if the research wished to compare two different prep courses—prep course A or prep course B—to determine which was most effective. It is not clear how such a study would be conducted in a related samples way; it does not make sense that each participant in a group would go through prep course A, then take the SAT, and then go through prep course B and then take another (different) SAT. Because participants will not forget what they learned from the earlier prep course, it would be difficult to determine whether the two courses truly have differential effects.

Confidence Intervals

All t-tests explicitly involve a *comparison*—either between two sample means, or between a sample mean and a known population mean (μ). Sometimes, however, a researcher may wish to address sampling error with using statistics for descriptive purposes. The standard error we compute when calculating our t-test statistics can be used in indicating the extent to which sample data may accurately reflect population parameters.

Imagine that a researcher is interested in studying alcohol use by undergraduate students at a university. This researcher obtains a random selection of student email addresses from the campus registrar and administers a survey to this sample. Part of the survey asks students to indicate how many alcoholic drinks they consume on a typical night when they party.

Following this example, the researcher collects data from 50 students and computes a sample $\overline{X}$ of 5.4 number of drink per night. However, the researcher really is interested in knowing the population μ number of drinks, and realizes that her sample value of 5.4 is only an estimate of that parameter. In order to express the accuracy of the study statistic, she computes a *confidence interval* around the sample mean.

A confidence interval is an interval or range around a statistic (such as a sample mean), where there is a specific level of confidence that the actual population parameter falls within the interval. Following the tendency for researchers to use α = .05, confidence intervals often are set at the 95% level (i.e., 1 – .05 = .95). Accordingly, with 95% confidence, the interval range specified will contain the population parameter. Confidence intervals sometimes are constructed at the 99% confidence level (assuming α = .01), but in theory may be constructed at any confidence level.

For example, the researcher may use her sample data to indicate that with 95% confidence, the population μ number of drinks falls between 4.7 and 6.1 drinks per night. The same 95% confidence interval may be written alternatively as 5.4 drinks $\pm$ 0.7, to indicate the range of scores that might contain the population value.

The value of 0.7 (in the example) describes the variability around the mean and is based on the standard error of our sample. When our standard errors are relatively large, we have larger confidence intervals, and our estimation of the population parameter is less precise. When our standard errors are relatively small, we have smaller confidence intervals and our estimation of the population parameter can be said to be more precise. If the researcher claimed a 95% confidence interval of 3.4 to 7.4 drinks (i.e., 5.4 $\pm$ 2.0), it would suggest that the study was unable to pinpoint to any degree the actual average amount of drinks consumed per typical night in the population. Alternatively, if the 95% confidence interval was 5.1 to 5.7 (i.e., 5.4 $\pm$ 0.3), it would be clear that the study was able to pinpoint more closely what the population parameter might be.

In order to compute the confidence interval around any sample mean, the researcher must (1) compute the standard error around the mean, and (2) identify the critical t-value for the appropriate degrees of freedom and alpha-level.

Assume that the researcher did collect data from 50 students and that the sample mean was 5.4. Furthermore, she computes the standard deviation for her sample (because the population σ is unknown) and finds that S = 2.46. Because her N = 50, she can determine that the standard error around her sample mean is equal to $S/\sqrt{N}$ = 2.46/$\sqrt{50}$ = 0.348. This standard error reflects the expected variability of a distribution of sample means, and would serve as the denominator in a single sample t-test if the researcher had planned to contrast her sample mean to some population μ. In this case, however, the researcher does not wish to contrast her sample mean to anything; rather she wishes to determine how accurately it might reflect the population μ.

In order to determine the appropriate interval at a specific level of confidence, one must go to the t-table and determine the appropriate critical value. In order to construct a 95% confidence interval, the researcher must find the critical t-value assuming a two-tailed α = .05. In this example, where df = 49 (i.e., 50 – 1), the critical value equals 2.01. If the researcher wished to construct a 99% confidence interval (i.e., α = .01), the critical value would be 2.68.

Once the appropriate critical value is determined, the 95% confidence interval is computed according to:

$$\bar{X} \pm (T_{CRIT})(S_{\bar{X}})$$

In this example, the sample mean is 5.4, the standard error is 0.348, and critical t-value (where α = .05) is 2.01. Thus, the confidence interval is:

$$5.4 \pm (2.01)(.348)$$

which reduces to:

$$5.4 \pm 0.7$$

and that also can be expressed as:

$$4.7 \text{ to } 6.1$$

The researcher can be 95% confident that the population μ drinks per night falls between 4.7 and 6.1. Only 5% of the time will our sample mean and interval be sufficiently off-target that the population mean will not fall within that range.

If the standard deviation of the sample is larger—for example 4.3—then standard error would be 0.651 and the confidence interval would have been 5.4 ± 1.31. Furthermore, if the mean had been based upon a much smaller sample (assume N = 10 and S = 2.46), the standard error would be 0.78 and the confidence interval would be 5.4 ± 1.56. Samples with larger standard deviations and that are based on smaller sample sizes produce confidence intervals that are larger (wider) and thus relatively less precise. Confidence intervals constructed using smaller alpha-levels (and thus larger critical t-scores) produce wider intervals but greater confidence. Confidence intervals constructed using larger alpha-levels (and thus small critical t-scores) produce more narrow intervals but less confidence.

Confidence intervals typically are used in descriptive statistics to describe not only the sample mean, but also to express the variability around that mean. Confidence intervals allow consumers of research to assess the precision of a sample estimate. Confidence intervals that are extremely wide (for example, 5.4 ± 4.2) hold relatively little value because they contribute little to identifying the population μ.

In addition to computing confidence intervals around a single sample mean, it is possible to compute confidence intervals around mean differences, $\bar{X}1 - \bar{X}2$, and $\bar{D}$, from independent samples and related samples t-tests, respectively. In these cases, it is important to use the appropriate standard error (S_{x1-x2} or $S_{\bar{D}}$). Note that according to the null hypothesis, the population μ for both cases is 0 (under the null hypothesis, we expect the mean differences to be 0). If the value 0 falls within the confidence interval, it is analogous to retaining the null hypothesis. If the value 0 falls outside of the confidence interval, it is analogous to rejecting the null hypothesis.

In the example independent sample t-test (see p. 98) that tested a new anxiety medication, the difference between the sample means was $9.25 - 3.5 = 5.75$, and the standard error of the difference between the means was 1.80. Given a total N of 10 and degrees of freedom of $10 - 2 = 8$, we learn that our critical t-score (assuming two-tailed $\alpha = .05$) is 2.31. Our confidence interval, therefore, would equal:

$$5.75 \pm (2.31)(1.80)$$

which reduces to:

$$5.75 \pm 4.16$$

and can be expressed as

1.59 to 9.91

Thus, we can be 95% confident that the population μ of the differences between the mean *does not* include 0 (i.e., the interval only goes as low as 1.59). Thus, we can be 95% confident that two samples did not come from the same population (or from populations with identical μs). This is equivalent to rejecting the null hypothesis. If our confidence interval had included 0, then we could be confident that the two samples may plausibly have come from populations with the same μs, thus requiring us to retain the null hypothesis.

PRACTICE PROBLEMS
(unless stated otherwise, assume a two-tailed α = .05)

11.1 Compare and contrast the t-distribution to the z- (unit normal) distribution.

11.2 What is the disadvantage of having to estimate σ by using the sample standard deviation?

11.3 When would the results of a single sample Z-test and single sample t-test be identical?

11.4 Correctly identify the conditions under which the following tests might be conducted:

Single sample t-test

Independent samples t-test

Related samples t-test

11.5 A researcher wants to know if students in a Maryland undergraduate statistics course have a higher average IQ score than the population mean of 100. The 38 students in the class had an average IQ of 106 and the sample standard deviation was calculated as 20. What test would he use and what would he conclude?

11.6 A clinical researcher wants to find out if an anti-anxiety drug (Drug X), which is commonly used for people with Generalized Anxiety Disorder (GAD), is even more effective on people with Social Anxiety Disorder (SAD). She knows that the population mean of GAD patients is 6 on a measure of reduced anxiety. Her SAD participants score 11,13,4, and 9. State the null hypothesis, indicate what test she should conduct, conduct that test, and describe the results.

11.7 Another clinical researcher wants to see if Drug X is more effective than a placebo. Participants who receive the drug scored 11,13,4, and 9 on a measure of reduced anxiety.

The placebo participants scored 3,2,7,4,2, and 3. State the null hypothesis, indicate what test she should conduct, conduct that test, and describe the results.

11.8   Yet another clinical researcher wants to test Drug X using a different method. Participants first complete an anxiety measure, then take Drug X, and shortly thereafter complete the anxiety measure again. Scores on the anxiety measure are:

Subject	Time 1	Time 2
1	11	15
2	4	6
3	7	5
4	8	14
5	3	6

State the null hypothesis, indicate what test she should conduct, conduct that test, and describe the results.

11.9   Describe what it means for a difference between groups to be *statistically significant?*

11.10 Define **unexplained variance** and describe how related samples t-tests reduce "unexplained variance" relative to independent sample t-tests?

11.11 Describe the distribution assumed under the null hypothesis (1) for the independent samples t-test and (2) for the related samples t-test.

11.12 A researcher wants to compare television v. newspapers as an effective medium for disseminating the news. Sixty-four participants were assigned to the newspaper only condition (n = 28) or to the television news only condition (n = 36). After a month of receiving news from only one source or another, participants were tested on current events. The mean of the newspaper only group was 7.8 (S^2 = 1.8) and the mean of the television only group was 5.9 (S^2 = 2.1). (1) What would be the null hypothesis regarding this study? (2) What would be the appropriate statistical procedure to test this hypothesis? (3) After conducting the appropriate test, what would the researcher conclude about the null hypothesis?

11.13 A researcher studying student drinking asked participants to indicate how many drinks they consumed on a typical weekend night. Data from a sample of 134 participants indicated the mean of 4.5 drinks per weekend night, with a standard deviation of 3.9. However, the researcher realized that her sample estimate might not reflect the true population value. Construct a 95% confidence interval around the sample mean. What does this confidence interval indicate?

11.14 Over several days, a professor records how long it takes him to drive from his house to school in the morning. His data (in number of minutes) are: 13, 09, 22, 17, 18, 14, 10, 25, 07, 15, 18, and 20. The professor teaches an 8 A.M. class, and wants to know how late he can leave his house and still reach the university in time. Using these data, what is the latest the professor could leave his house such that he is 95% confident of reaching the university in time? What if he wanted to be 99% confident?

One-Way Analysis of Variance

T he independent samples t-test, described in Chapter 11, is the statistical procedure used to test the null hypothesis that two samples were drawn from the same population. Upon rejecting the null hypothesis, we can conclude that group membership predicts (or *causes*, in the case of experiments) meaningful differences on some dependent measure. If we fail to reject the null hypothesis, we must conclude that the groups are not meaningfully different, and that any differences observed among sample means are mere random fluctuations.

It should be clear that the independent sample t-test is limited to the comparison of two groups (as indicated by $\bar{X}1 - \bar{X}2$ in the numerator). But researchers may have hypotheses that involve more than two groups. For example, a researcher might wish to compare the effectiveness of two types of painkillers against a no-medicine control. Or, as mentioned in Chapter 3, the researcher may wish to cross together two variables such type of painkiller (Medicine A v. Medicine B) and type of pain (Headache v. Backache) and create four groups.

In such a study, the null hypothesis states that each group in the study was sampled from the same population (or from populations with identical μ). Formally, H0: $\mu1 = \mu2 = \mu3$

. . . μ_K, where k = the number of groups in the study. The alternative hypothesis states that at least two groups were sampled from populations with different means (same as the t-test scenario). Rejecting the null hypothesis indicates that not all of the population means are equal, but it does not imply that all of the population μs are different.

Faced with the task of comparing more than two groups, a researcher may be tempted to conduct a series of independent sample t-tests. For example, in a study involving groups A, B, and C, a researcher could use t-tests to conduct all of the possible comparisons: A v. B, A v. C, B v. C. This approach would address any research question relevant to the study. Given, however, that each hypothesis test that rejects the null hypothesis incurs a 5% chance of making a Type I error, the process of conducting multiple t-tests increases the risk of a Type I error occurring to above the stated alpha-level. Thus, researchers are discouraged from comparing multiple groups using multiple t-tests because the risk of making a Type I error increases as the result.

Analysis of Variance (ANOVA) refers to a single-test procedure with which researchers can reject or retain the null hypothesis when the study involves more than two groups. For a one-way ANOVA, which is described in this chapter, it is assumed that the three or more groups that we are analyzing represent different levels of a single independent variable; that is, our groups vary on one common dimension. If our research is concerned with the relative efficacy of different pain medicines, our independent variable may be "type of pain killer", with our research groups differing on whether they received medicines A, B, or C. In a study where "introversion" is the independent variable of interest, we may select three groups that consist of people who are strongly introverts, people who are strongly extroverts, and people who neither strongly introverts or strongly extroverts.

The logic of ANOVA mirrors what was described in Chapter 11 regarding independent samples t-tests; in fact, t-tests can be thought about as special cases of ANOVA. In Chapter 11, the t-test was described as a ratio of the distance *between* two group means relative to the variability *within* the groups. The standard error used in the independent samples t-test is computed from the within group variability, and can be thought of as a measure of "natural" variability: variability due to all of the factors (e.g., personality, intelligence, luck) that might influence the dependent measure *excluding* the researchers' independent variable that defines the groups (e.g., medicine A v. medicine B; high self-esteem v. low self-esteem) or any other variable explicitly measured as part of the study. The t-test ratio tells us the following: we expect scores to vary naturally to a degree equal to S_{X1-X2}; do our group means vary above and beyond what we would expect to find if they were simply the result of this "natural" variation (error). A large t-score indicates the group means are much further from each other than we would expect if only "natural" variability was involved.

We extend this logic to ANOVA by computing the variability between the groups. When confronted with three or more groups, we cannot conduct simple mean differences (i.e., $\bar{X}1 - \bar{X}2$) as with the independent sample t-test to indicate the difference among our means. Rather, ANOVA involves treating the means of three or more groups as data points, and computing the variance among the points. Recall that variance describes the extent to which data points are spread out, or clustered around, the center of the distribution. A variance concerning group means (between-groups variance) would describe whether these means are relatively close together or relatively spread apart. Thus, a single variance value can indicate the size of differences among any number of sample means. Between-groups variance serves as the numerator (conceptually equivalent to $\bar{X}1 - \bar{X}2$) in ANOVA.

Computationally, ANOVA begins by pooling all data scores from all of the groups and calculating the total sums of squares (SS$_{TOT}$). This uses the same formula for sums of squares as introduced in Chapter 7; it is labeled "Total" because it involves all the data across groups. Total SS is based on the squared deviation of each data point from the mean of the distribution, and reflects the maximum amount of variability within the data set:

$$SS_{TOT} = \Sigma X^2 - (\Sigma X)^2/N$$

Following computation of the total sums of squares, the between-groups sums of squares (SS$_{BET}$) is calculated. The SS$_{BET}$ will indicate the extent to which the group means are spread out from each other. If there is no variability among the means (i.e., all sample group means are identical) then the SS$_{BET}$ will be 0. As group means become further and further apart, the SS$_{BET}$ will increase.

SS$_{BET}$ is calculated as follows:

$$SS_{BET} = \Sigma\, T_j^2/n_j - (\Sigma X)^2/N$$

where T_j is the total (sum) of group j, and n_j is the sample size of group j. The first part of the equation ($\Sigma\, T_j^2/n_j$) involves, for each group, taking the group sum, squaring that sum, dividing by the number of people in each group, and adding together resulting product across all four groups.

Note that the "$(\Sigma X)^2/N$" portion of the formula is identical to that found in the formula for SS$_{TOT}$. The value obtained during computation of the SS$_{TOT}$ can simply be inserted in the formula for SS$_{BET}$.

Recall that the null hypothesis states that there are no meaningful differences among the groups, and that any observed mean differences are due to random error. Thus, if the null hypothesis is true, our estimate of between-groups variability (SS$_{BET}$) consists entirely of unexplained (error) variance. There is nothing intrinsic about the groups themselves that predicts or causes the means to vary from each other. The group means are different from each other for the same reasons that scores within the groups are different from each other: random error.

According to the alternative hypothesis (HA), the existence of between-groups variability is due at least in part to meaningful differences among the groups—that some feature or characteristic of the groups explains variability among scores. The alternative hypothesis does not deny that unexplained variance also contributes to mean differences; only that between-groups variance is not entirely unexplained.

Accordingly:

H0: Between-groups variance is 100% unexplained variance (random error)

H1: Between-groups variance is unexplained variance + variance *explained* by group membership

After computing *total* and *between-groups* sums of squares, the third step is to compute the sums of squares within the groups (SS$_{WITHIN}$). SS$_{WITHIN}$ can be computed directly by computing the sums of squares for each group separately and adding them together.

Thus:

$$SS_{WITHIN} = SS1 + SS2 + SS3 . . . + SSk$$

There is a much simpler method to compute the sums of square within groups. A special feature of the ANOVA procedure is that it involves a full *partitioning of variance*. After estimating the total amount of variability in the sample, that variability can be split orthogonally (i.e., without overlap) into one portion that is computed from the differences between sampled group mean, and another portion that is computed from variability of scores within the groups.

Accordingly:

$$SS_{TOT} = SS_{BET} + SS_{WITHIN}$$

Note that we already have provided the formulas for computing SS_{TOT} and SS_{BET}.

Once these have been calculated, we can compute SS_{WITHIN} simply through subtraction:

$$SS_{WITHIN} = SS_{TOT} - SS_{BET}$$

Readers should remember that sums of squares and variances can never be negative (if you ever compute a negative variance, it implies that you have made a mistake in your calculations). The previous formula implies that SS_{TOT} will always be larger than SS_{BET}. Total sums of squares reflects the total amount of variability among the scores, while sums of squares between groups reflects a portion of that total variability that is determined by differences among sample means. If SS_{BET} ever exceeds SS_{TOT} it should be clear that a computational error has been made.

Ratio of Variances

Recall from Chapter 11 that variability within the groups can be considered 100% unexplained variance (i.e., the effect of being in one group or another cannot explain why scores vary within each group). In ANOVA we also compute SS_{WITHIN}, and from that calculate within-groups variance. According to the null hypothesis, within-groups and between-groups variance *both* are independent estimates of *unexplained* variance. These estimates are independent in that while we expect them to be the same (because they both should reflect the amount of random error on our dependent measure) they might not be exactly the same in this particular sample.

Given this, creating a ratio of between-groups variance and within-groups variance may inform us as to whether the null hypothesis is true.

Accordingly:

H0:
$$\text{Expected value } \frac{\text{Between-groups variance}}{\text{Within-groups variance}} = 1$$

This is because we would expect a ratio of 100% random error/100% random error to approximate 1.

However:

H1:
$$\text{Expected value } \frac{\text{Between-groups variance}}{\text{Within-groups variance}} > 1$$

Because according to the alternative, between-groups variance includes not only unexplained variance, but also explained variance—variability due to real differences among the groups—as well. We would expect that (random error + explained variance)/100% random error should exceed 1.

Of course, because between-groups and within-groups variance are considered independent samples, it is possible that between-groups S^2/within-groups S^2 could exceed 1 simply due to chance—even if the null hypothesis is true. In ANOVA, we compute the likelihood that we could randomly generate two estimates of random error that produce a ratio as large as that obtained in our sample even if the null hypothesis is true. If this likelihood is less than our α, then we can reject the null hypothesis. If this probability is greater than α, we cannot conclude with sufficient confidence that our results are due to anything more than chance.

The Source Table

Part of the analysis of variance (ANOVA) procedures includes a formal approach to organizing and presenting different steps to the computations. As the computational steps are completed, the results are written in a source table. Completing a source table is a necessary part of conducting an ANOVA.

Source tables include five columns: (1) Source; (2) SS; (3) df; (4) MS; and (5) F. In the source column we indicate the sources of variability included in our computations. In the case of a one-way ANOVA, our sources include: *Total, Between,* and *Within.* SS refers to sums of squares, and by the time we begin to construct our source table, it is likely we have computed the sums of squares for each of our three sources.

The third column, df, includes *degrees of freedom,* and there is a different df for each source. As a rule of thumb, the df associated with an SS is equal to the number of observations (scores) used to compute the SS, minus 1 (e.g., $N - 1$). In fact, for SS_{TOT}, which describes the summed variability among all of the scores, df does equal $N - 1$. Recall that in the initial discussion of SS_{BET}, we indicated that SS_{BET} describes whether group means were relatively close together or relatively far apart by treating each group mean as a data point and computing the variability among those data points. Following this logic, we can think of SS_{BET} as sums of squares computed using k cases (where k equals the number of groups in the study). Thus, for SS_{BET}, df = $k - 1$. Finally, SS_{WITHIN} is computed from the variability within each group, and can be computed directly by adding together the SS from each group in our study. The df for SS_{WITHIN} therefore can be computed by summing together the df from each sample, i.e., $\Sigma(n_k - 1)$. Alternatively, however, just as it is possible to compute SS_{WITHIN} by subtracting SS_{BET} from SS_{TOT}, we can compute df_{WITHIN} by subtracting df_{BET} from df_{TOT}.

In the fourth column of the source table, MS stands for mean square, which in turn is short for *mean of the squared mean deviations*, which in Chapter 7 was introduced as another term for *variance* (S^2). Recall that S^2 is calculated by dividing the sums of squares by the degrees of freedom (i.e., $SS/(N-1)$. Thus in the source table, we can compute the total variance (MS_{TOT}), the between-groups variance (MS_{BET}), and the within-groups variance (MS_{WITHIN}) by dividing SS for each source by the corresponding df for each source. Thus:

$$MS_{TOT} = SS_{TOT}/df_{TOT}$$

$$MS_{BET} = SS_{BET}/df_{BET}$$

$$MS_{WITHIN} = SS_{WITHIN}/df_{WITHIN}$$

Finally, the fifth column in the source table is the F-column. F is the test statistics for ANOVA (just as Z is the test statistics for Z-tests and t is the test statistics for t-tests). In the previous section we discussed how computing a ratio of between-groups variance over within-groups variance would help us to determine the confidence with which we can reject the null hypothesis.

Thus, our test statistics in ANOVA, F, is computed as:

$$F = MS_{BET}/MS_{WITHIN}$$

Assuming that the null hypothesis is true, both MS_{BET} and MS_{WITHIN} are estimates of unexplained error variance, and thus we would expect the ratio to be 1. *As F-ratios increase, they begin to suggest sample means vary from each other to a greater extent than we would expect if the between-groups variability was entirely due to random error.* The F-ratio tells us how many times larger our sample MS_{BET} happens to be than what we would expect from chance. If this ratio becomes large enough, we can be confident that the difference among the groups is too great to be attributed to unexplained variance alone, and that some feature or quality of the membership in these groups themselves helps *explain* why the group means are different.

The source table for a one-way ANOVA can be summarized as follows:

Source	SS	df	MS	F
Total	$\Sigma X^2 - (\Sigma X)^2/N$	$N - 1$	SS_{TOT}/df_{TOT}	—
Between	$\Sigma\,T_j^2/n_j - (\Sigma X)^2/N$	$k - 1$	SS_{BET}/df_{BET}	MS_{BET}/MS_{WITHIN}
Within	$SS_{TOT} - SS_{BET}$	$df_{TOT} - df_{BET}$ or $(N - k)$	SS_{WITHIN}/df_{WITHIN}	—

Testing the Null Hypothesis

But how large of an F-ratio is necessary to reject the null hypothesis? Like both the Z-test and t-test, in order to determine whether our t-test statistic is sufficiently large, we must compare it against the critical value associated with our designated α. Note that for t-tests, our critical value varied according to the degrees of freedom of our study. In much the same way, we also must use the dfs when determining the critical F-value for testing the null hypothesis with ANOVA. In the case of ANOVA, however, we appear to have multiple dfs, and thus additional consideration is necessary.

A much reduced version of the critical F-table is presented below.

Reduced F-Table

df numerator df denominator	1	2	3
1	161	200	216
	4052	**4999**	**5403**
2	18.51	19.00	19.16
	98.49	**99.00**	**99.17**
3	10.13	9.55	9.28
	34.12	**30.92**	**29.46**
10	4.96	4.10	3.71
	10.04	**7.56**	**6.55**
16	4.49	3.63	3.24
	8.53	**6.23**	**5.29**

Critical value at α = .05
Critical value at α = .01

Along the top row of the critical value table are dfs associated with the numerator, while along the first column are dfs associated with denominator. By cross-indexing the df numerator and df denominator, the table indicates two critical values. The smaller value (not bold) is the critical F-ratio that must be exceed by the computed F-ratio in order to reject the null hypothesis at α = .05. The larger **(bolded)** value is the critical F-ratio that must be exceeded by the computed F-ratio in order to reject the null hypothesis at α = .01. Note that with ANOVA, there are no negative test statistics (no negative F-ratios). This is because the test statistic is computed from the ratio of variances, and because variances cannot be negative, the resulting F-ratio must be positive.

So which df is the numerator df and which is the denominator df? Consider that F is created from a ratio where MS_{BET} is in the numerator, and MS_{WITHIN} is in the denominator. The degrees of freedom associated with the numerator, therefore, is df_{BET}, and the degrees of freedom associated with the denominator is df_{WITHIN}. Consider a study that included three groups (k = 3) and a total of 13 participants (N = 13). The df_{TOT} would be 13 – 1 = 12, the df_{BET} would be 3 – 1 = 2, and the df_{WITHIN} would be 12 – 2 (or 13 – 3) = 10. Cross-indexing dfs of 2 and 10 (in the numerator and denominator, respectively) we find critical F-values of 4.10 when α = .05 and 7.56 when α = .01. Thus, in a study with three groups and a total of 13 participants, assuming α = .05, our F-ratio would need to be at 4.10 or greater in order to reject the null hypothesis.

In the following example, an instructor wishes to study whether the use of visual aids during classroom lectures influences how well students learn. To this end, he created four versions of the same lecture. One version was written as a Power Point Presentation, another version was put onto transparencies (overhead slides), a third version relied on writing on the chalkboard, and a fourth version included no visual aids: the instructor simply stood behind the podium and read. The instructor sampled 20 students, and then randomly assigned five students to receive each of the four versions of the lecture. Afterwards, he administered a test (on a 10-point scale) covering the material in the lecture.

The data are depicted in the table below. Summary statistics (sum, mean, squared sum, and sum and squared score) are provided for each group.

	Group A Power Point	Group B Transparencies	Group C Chalkboard	Group D Lecture only
	4	6	8	3
	1	6	10	1
	7	2	6	3
	2	3	7	2
	6	5	8	4
ΣX	20	22	39	13
$\bar{X}$	4.0	4.4	7.8	2.6
$(\Sigma X)^2$	400	484	1521	169
ΣX^2	106	110	313	30

The first step in conducting an ANOVA is to compute the SS_{TOT}. We already have summed the scores and the squared scores for each group, and thus by summing these across all groups we get the sum and the sum of squared scores for the entire sample of 20 participants.

For the entire sample:

$$\Sigma X = 20 + 22 + 39 + 13 = 94$$

$$\Sigma X^2 = 106 + 110 + 313 + 30 = 559$$

Thus:

$$SS_{TOT} = 559 - (94^2/20) = 559 - (8836/20) = 559 - 441.8 = \mathbf{117.2}$$

Next we compute:

$$SS_{BET} = \Sigma\, T_j^2/n_j - (\Sigma X)^2/N$$

For the first part of the equation, we take the sum (Total) of each group, square it, divide by the sample size of the group, and then add all of the products together.

$$(20^2/5) + (22^2/5) + (39^2/5) + (13^2/5) = (400/5) + (484/5) + (1521/5) + (169/5)$$

$$= 80.0 + 96.8 + 304.2 + 33.8 = 514.8$$

Such that:

$$SS_{BET} = 514.8 - (\Sigma X)^2/N$$

Note that the latter part of the equation—$(\Sigma X)^2/N$—is identical to the latter part of the equation for SS_{TOT}, and this was already determined (see above) to be 441.8.
Thus:

$$SS_{BET} = 514.8 - 441.8 = \textbf{73.0}$$

We now can compute SS_{WITHIN}. Thus:

$$SS_{WITHIN} = SS_{TOT} - SS_{BET} = 117.2 - 73.0 = \textbf{44.2}$$

With sums of squares computed for each of our three sources, we can begin to fill out the source table. With N = 20, our df_{TOT} = 20 – 1 = 19. With four groups our df_{BET} = 4 – 1 = 3. Finally, we can get our df_{WITHIN} from 19 – 3 = 16.

We can compute the MS (variance) for each source by dividing the SS by the df. Thus, MS_{TOT} = 117.2/19 = 5.12, our MS_{BET} = 73.0/3 = 24.33, and our MS_{WITHIN} = 44.2/16 = 2.76.

Finally, we can compute our F-ratio by dividing: MS_{BET}/MS_{WITHIN} = 24.33/2.76 = 8.82. This F-ratio tells us that our between-groups variance is 16.11 times greater than what we would expect to find if the differences among the group means were entirely due to random error.

Source	SS	df	MS	F
Total	117.2	19	6.17	—
Between	73.0	3	24.33	8.82
Within	44.2	16	2.76	—

In order to determine whether this F-ratio is large enough to reject the null hypothesis at an α = .05 level, we must determine the critical F-value for 3 and 16 dfs (in the numerator and denominator) associated with the upper 5% of the F-distribution. Examining the reduced critical F-table on p. 121 and cross-indexing the "3" column with "16" row, we find a critical value (non-bold) of 3.24. In order to reject the null hypothesis, the F-score then computed must exceed the critical F-value from the table. In this case, 8.82 > 3.24, so we can reject the null hypothesis and conclude that there must be meaningful differences among at least two of the group means, that not all mean differences are due solely to random error. Had our computed F-ratio fallen under 3.24, then we would not reject the null hypothesis. We would have concluded that there is no evidence to suggest that the means differ for any reason than random chance. Note that our computed F-score of 8.82 would have been sufficient to reject H0 had $\alpha = .01$.

Interpreting the Means

If, and only if, the null hypothesis is rejected, the researcher is allowed to examine the means of the groups to make sense of the results. In general it is not sufficient to conclude simply that there are some meaningful differences among group means and end there. If there are real (statistically significant) group differences, then we need to identify where these differences lie: which means are different from which means, and what means are not different.

If we examine the means of our four groups, we find that they are:

	$\bar{X}$
Power Point	4.0
Transparencies	4.4
Chalkboard	7.8
Lecture only	2.6

In this example, the means already were computed, but in many cases the researcher would be required to calculate the means of each group himself.

If we simply eyeball the means (which we would do only if first we rejected H0), there appears to be a pattern among the groups. Accordingly, students assigned to attend the lecture delivered using the chalkboard appeared to perform best, those assigned to attend lectures using Power Point or transparencies performed just about the same, and those assigned to the lecture only group performed the worst.

However, we do not wish to rely on eyeballing alone to interpret the results. Therefore, once we reject the null hypothesis we will need to conduct additional follow-up tests, referred to as *post hoc* tests, to further investigate the mean differences. These tests are called post hoc tests because the specific group comparisons that we plan to conduct (i.e., whether we compared $\bar{X}1$ v. $\bar{X}2$, $\bar{X}2$ v. $\bar{X}4$, etc.) are determined <u>after</u> conducting the overall ANOVA and after examining the group means. Post hoc tests are similar to t-tests in that they are used to compare the means of two groups to determine whether or not they are statistically significant, but differ in that they are (1) adjusted to control for the risk of making Type I errors, and (2) use the error-term (i.e., based on within-group variability) based on all of the groups, not just on the two groups that are being compared.

Typically, our α is adjusted such that the risk of making a Type I error remains at α across all the comparisons we make. This is accomplished by reducing the α-level for each individual test. Essentially, if we wanted to make two simple comparisons (e.g., $\bar{X}1$ v. $\bar{X}2$ and $\bar{X}2$ v. $\bar{X}4$) and our overall $\alpha = .05$, we would set the α-level for each of the two comparisons to $.05/2 = .025$. If we wanted to make three comparisons, we would reduce the α-level to $.05/3 = .017$ for each test. This ensures that our chance of making a Type I error across all of our comparisons does not exceed .05. Post hoc tests present a problem, however, in that α should be chosen before the actual means are examined, but by nature, the specific post hoc tests are determined after we have conducted the initial analysis. Thus, when conducting post hoc tests, we must assume that all possible comparisons will be made, and we must adjust our α-level accordingly. Note that in studies with many different groups, the possible number of comparisons can be quite large.

Scheffe's S test is a conservative but very flexible procedure for conducting post hoc tests that keep the risk of making a Type I error at the established α-level. The Scheffe's procedure can be used not only to test whether the means of two specific groups are significantly different, but also can be used to test more complex contrasts of group combinations. For example, a researcher may wish to compare whether the $\bar{X}1$ is significantly different from $\bar{X}2$ and $\bar{X}3$ combined.

The Scheffe S procedure uses data already computed and entered into the ANOVA source table to determine the *minimum mean difference* needed to reject the null hypothesis for any comparisons. The formula is as follows:

$$\psi = \sqrt{(k-1)(F_{CRIT,\, k-1,\, N-k})} * \sqrt{(MS_{WITHIN})(\Sigma\, c^2/n)}$$

ψ represents the size of the mean difference needed to reject H0 (i.e., if two groups are ψ units apart or greater, then H0 can be rejected).

$k - 1$ is the df_{BET}, and $F_{CRIT,\, k-1,\, N-k}$ is the critical F-value for the study (assuming $\alpha = .05$, with $k - 1$ degrees of freedom in the numerator and $N - k$ degrees of freedom in the denominator). In the previous example, $k - 1 = 3$, the F_{CRIT} is 3.24. For the first part of the equation, the square root of 3×3.24 is:

$$\sqrt{(3)(3.24)} = \sqrt{9.72} = 3.12$$

The first part of the equation determines a factor that controls the risk of making a Type I error across all of our tests, and it will remain constant across all of the comparisons that we make. The second part of the equation may change according to the specific comparison, varying as a function of how many means will be involved and the sample size (n) of each group.

For the second part of the equation, the MS_{WITHIN} already has been calculated (see source table) and it, too, will remain constant across comparisons. In the previous example, our MS_{WITHIN} was calculated to equal 1.51.

The final $(\Sigma\, c^2/n)$ portion of the equation will change depending on the precise comparison that is conducted. "c" represents **contrast coefficient** for a specific group, and n represents the sample size of that group. In the case where we are comparing the means of two groups, the contrast coefficient (c) for one group will be 1 and the contrast coefficient for the other group will be –1. By assigning a positive coefficient to one mean and a negative coefficient to the other mean, we are indicating that we will test the difference between those means. The fact that the coefficients in both cases were ±"1" (as opposed to .05, or 2, etc.) indicates that each mean is given equal weight.

For example, $\bar{X}1 = 4.0$, $\bar{X}2 = 4.4$, and $\bar{X}3 = 7.8$. If we wished to compared groups 1 and 2, and we applied the contrast coefficients of 1 and –1 to those means, our contrast would be $(1)(4.0) + (-1)(4.4)$, or $4.0 - 4.4$. The mean of group 3 does not come into play because a contrast coefficient was not assigned to it. Note that if our comparison was more complex, for example, if we wished to test the hypothesis that groups 1 and 2 were both different than group 3, we would construct a contrast that combines the first two groups and compares it with group 3. Our contrast coefficients might be .5, .5, and –1. Applying these contrasts to our group means would produce: $(.5)(4.0) + (.5)(4.4) + (-1)(7.8) = 2 + 2.2 - 7.8$, or $4.2 - 7.8$. Essentially, we are averaging together the means of groups 1 and 2 and contrasting that with the mean of group 3.

As a rule of thumb, if we compare two groups, our contrast coefficients will be 1 and –1; if we combined two groups and compared those with a third group, our coefficients would be .5, .5 and –1. If we combined three groups and compared those with a fourth group, our coefficients would be .33, .33, .33 and –1. If we combined two groups and wished to compare those to another set of two groups, our coefficients would be .5, .5 and –.5, –.5.

Note that in using the Scheffe's S test, we do not actually apply the means to the contrast coefficients (c); however, understanding how many groups will be involved in a comparison, and knowing the sample sizes of the groups in question, is implicit. Using the previous example, imagine that we wanted to test the hypothesis that $\bar{X}1$ and $\bar{X}2$ are meaningfully different. The sample size of each group is the same ($n = 5$).

Thus, for the second part of the Scheffe S equation, $\sqrt{(MS_{WITHIN})(\Sigma\, c^2/n)}$, using the data above we would find:

$$\sqrt{(1.51)[(1^2/5) + (-1^2/5)]} = \sqrt{(1.51)(1/5 + 1/5)}$$
$$= \sqrt{(1.51)(0.4)} = \sqrt{0.604} = 0.778$$

Previously we determined that the first part of the equation, $\sqrt{(k-1)(F_{CRIT,\, k-1,\, N-k})}$, equaled 3.12.

Therefore,

$$\psi = \sqrt{(k-1)(F_{CRIT,\, k-1,\, N-k})} * \sqrt{(MS_{WITHIN})(\Sigma\, c^2/n)} = 3.12 * .778 = \mathbf{2.42}$$

Because the mean difference between groups 1 and 2 is only 0.4 points (i.e., $|4.4 - 4.0| = 0.4$), and because 0.4 is less than 2.42, we cannot conclude that groups 1 and 2 are significantly different. Thus, there is no evidence that a Power Point-based lecture is any more or less effective than a transparencies-based lecture (in terms of students' performance of a post-lecture exam).

Using Scheffe's S, any two groups of $n = 5$ with means that differ by as much as 2.42 can be considered significantly different. Because each group in our sample has the same sample size ($n = 5$), this value of 2.42 holds for all simple comparisons we could make in this example:

Given:

	$\bar{X}$
Power Point	4.0
Transparencies	4.4
Chalkboard	7.8
Lecture only	2.6

All of our possible group comparisons are:

$\bar{X}1$ v. $\bar{X}2 = |4.0 - 4.4| = 0.4$

$\bar{X}1$ v. $\bar{X}3 = |4.0 - 7.8| = 3.8$

$\bar{X}1$ v. $\bar{X}4 = |4.0 - 2.6| = 1.4$

$\bar{X}2$ v. $\bar{X}3 = |4.4 - 7.8| = 3.4$

$\bar{X}2$ v. $\bar{X}4 = |4.4 - 2.6| = 1.8$

$\bar{X}3$ v. $\bar{X}4 = |7.8 - 2.6| = 5.2$

Only the comparison of $\bar{X}3$ v. $\bar{X}1$, $\bar{X}3$ v. $\bar{X}2$, and $\bar{X}3$ v. $\bar{X}4$ exceeds our ψ value of 2.42. This means that the chalkboard condition was significantly different from the other three conditions. These three differences can be considered statistically significant and due to meaningful differences, not merely random error. The other three comparisons produced mean differences smaller than 2.42, thus those differences cannot be considered statistically significant.

Consider an example where the researcher wanted to contrast the chalkboard condition (group 3) to all three other groups (1, 2, and 4) combined. Our contrast coefficients for groups 1 through 4, in order, would be: .33, .33, -1, and .33. Thus, our computations for Scheffe's S would be:

$$\psi = \sqrt{(3)(3.24)} \times \sqrt{(1.51)[(.33^2/5) + (.33^2/5) - (1^2/5) + (.33^2/5)]}$$

$$= \sqrt{9.72} \times \sqrt{(1.51)(.021 + .021 + .200 + .021)}$$

$$= \sqrt{9.72} \times \sqrt{(1.51)(.263)} = \sqrt{9.72} \times \sqrt{.397}$$

$$= 3.12 \times .630 = \textbf{1.97}$$

We are able to reject the null hypothesis if the difference between the mean of $\bar{X}3$ and mean of $\bar{X}1$, $\bar{X}2$, and $\bar{X}4$ is equal to or greater than 1.97. $\bar{X}3 = 7.8$, and the mean of the other three means equals $((4.0 + 4.4 + 2.6)/3) = 3.67$. Because $7.8 - 3.67 = 4.13$, and $4.13 > 1.97$, we can reject the null hypothesis and conclude that delivering a lecture using the chalkboard is significantly more effective than all the other methods (Power Point, transparencies, and lecture only).

Planned v. Post Hoc Comparisons

The assumption underlying post hoc comparisons is that the researcher determines specifically which means to contrast only after conducting the ANOVA and examining the actual group means. Often, by looking at the group means, the researcher may identify which groups might be significantly different and use post hoc procedures to formally compare those. The penalty of using the results to determine which follow-up tests to conduct is that the α-levels for each test must be adjusted as if all possible comparisons were being conducted; this makes post hoc tests considerably less powerful. Recall that power refers to the ability of a test to detect effects that are there (i.e., they reject H0 when in fact H0 is false).

But what if the researcher knows ahead of time which group means she wishes to compare? Often, there may be strong theoretical reasons for comparing certain group means and not others, and in fact the researcher may be interested only in those specific comparisons and not concerned with the overall between-groups F-test at all. Planned comparisons are very similar to post hoc comparisons in that they are used to test the null hypothesis regarding any two group means from among a set of three or more groups involved in a single study.

Imagine a study of an intervention designed to increase the use of safety belts by students. The study involves four groups with "incremental" interventions. For example, the intervention in group 2 has all the features of group 1 plus one additional feature; the intervention in group 3 has all the features of group 2, except one additional feature, etc. The researcher has a large sample of high schools, and randomly assigns these high schools in one of four groups.

The first group is considered the *control condition*. Here, there is no intervention, and the researcher simply measures the use of safety belts by students at these schools. The second group is the *sign condition*. In all schools assigned to the sign condition, the researcher hangs up a large sign in the cafeteria reminding students to wear their safety belts. The third group is the *sign + announcement condition*. A reminder sign also is hung in schools assigned to this condition, but in addition, at each school, at the end of each school day, the principal announces over the intercom that students should remember to wear their safety belts. Finally, the fourth group is the *sign + announcement + enforcement* condition. In schools assigned to this condition, a reminder sign is hung, and the principal makes a daily announcement, but in addition, on randomly selected days each week, a police officer waits outside the school parking lot and issues tickets for students who do not buckle up.

It may be intuitive to some readers that comparing the control condition to the sign condition effactually tests the impact of hanging the signs on student safety belt use (because the sign is the one thing that makes those conditions different); comparing the sign condition to the sign + announcement condition tests the impact of having the principal make the announcement, as that is the one thing that differentiates those conditions). Finally, comparing the sign + announcement to the sign + announcement + enforcement condition effactually tests the impact of random police presence on student safety belt use.

The researcher may be interested explicitly in studying the impact of (1) hanging a reminder sign; (2) making announcements at the end of the day; and (3) using random police presence. Thus, the researcher may be interested only in contrasting the means of groups 1 and 2, groups 2 and 3, and groups 3 and 4. Contrasting groups 1 and 3, for example, might not be of interest to the researcher, because even if safety belt use is different between those groups, it cannot be determined whether those differences are a result of hanging the reminder sign *or* making announcements over the intercom.

In cases such as this, where the researcher has a clear idea of what groups she wishes to compare, she may conduct *planned comparisons* (alternatively called *a priori comparisons*) rather than post hoc comparisons. The advantage of conducting planned comparisons is that the researcher need only correct α for the number of contrasts that actually will be performed, rather than the total number of possible contrasts. Further, it is not even necessary to reject the null hypothesis for the between-groups effect in an ANOVA in order to make these comparisons. Note that it is necessary to compute MS_{WITHIN} to carry out planned comparisons, and so the researcher must conduct the initial steps of the ANOVA; she need not compute an F-ratio for the between-groups variance in order to proceed.

Dunn's multiple comparison procedure uses the MS_{WITHIN} term from the ANOVA table to compute a t-score for any given two-group comparison. Computing **Dunn's t** involves contrast coefficients, as was described for the Scheffe procedure. Like Scheffe's S test, the procedure can be used to make simple contrasts (e.g., group 1 v. group 2) or complex contrasts (e.g., group 1 + group 2 + group 3 v. group 4 + group 5). Recall that when identifying contrast coefficients, whether a contrast is positive or negative determines which side of the contrast the group falls. In the complex contrast of group 1 + group 2 + group 3 v. group 4 + group 5, the first three might be positive and the last two negative (or the first three negative and the last two positive). Finally, the value of the coefficient (.33, .1. 1, etc.) determines the relative weight of each group. A rule of thumb is that all of the positive contrast coefficients should sum to 1, and all of the negative contrast coefficients should sum to 1. Thus, for the comparison of group 1 + group 2 + group 3 v. group 4 + group 5, the contrast coefficients might be: .33, .33., .33 v. –.5, –.5.

Dunn's t, therefore, can be computed as follows:

$$t(D) = \Sigma(c)(\bar{X}) / \sqrt{(MS_{WITHIN}) \, (\Sigma \, c^2/n)}$$

Readers should note that the denominator in this equation is identical to the second part of the equation for Scheffe's S test. In the numerator, the contrast coefficient is applied to the group means in question, and then summed together.

Imagine the following five group means. Also imagine MS_{WITHIN} from this data set is 2.30. (Note that the researcher first would have needed to compute SS_{TOT} and SS_{BET}, and have worked on the source table, to obtain the MS_{WITHIN}.) Also assume the sample sizes of 10, 12, 9, 12, and 8, for groups 1 through 5, respectively.

$\bar{X}1 = 02.3$

$\bar{X}2 = 04.7$

$\bar{X}3 = 06.0$

$\bar{X}4 = 09.3$

$\bar{X}5 = 11.1$

In a planned comparison between the means of group 3 and group 4, the numerator would be:

$$\Sigma(c)(\bar{X}) = (1)(6.0) + (-1)(9.3) = 6 - 9.3 = -3.3$$

The denominator would be:

$$\sqrt{(MS_{WITHIN})\ (\Sigma\ c^2/n)} = \sqrt{(2.30)[(1^2/9) + (-1^2/12)]}$$
$$= \sqrt{(2.30)(.111 + 0.083)} = \sqrt{(2.30)(.194)}$$
$$= \sqrt{.446} = 0.668$$

Thus, Dunn's t would equal:

$$t(D) = -3.3/.668 = \mathbf{-4.94}$$

In order to determine whether a t-score of -4.94 is sufficient to reject the null hypothesis, we must determine the appropriate critical value. However, we must first adjust α by dividing α by the total number of planned comparisons that we intend to make. If this contrast was one of three that we planned to conduct, then our appropriate α-level for determining the critical value would be $.05/3 = .017$. Furthermore, the degrees of freedom associated with this planned comparison is the same as the df_{WITHIN}. In this example, df_{WITHIN} can be calculated by summing the dfs within each group, i.e., $\Sigma(n - 1)$. So $(10 - 1) + (12 - 1) + (9 - 1) + (12 - 1) + (8 - 1) = 46$.

Thus, we must determine the critical t-score associated with an alpha-level of .017 and with 46 dfs. Note that few t-tables will have a critical value for such a non-typical α-level. However, several computer software packages have probabilities calculators that provide critical value for different distributions. In this case, such a program was used to determine that the t_{CRIT} at 46 dfs and using an alpha-level of .017 is $\pm$ 2.48. In order to reject the null hypothesis, our computed t-score would need to exceed that critical value. Because $|-4.94| >$ 2.48, we can reject the null hypothesis regarding the contrast between groups 2 and 3.

For another example, consider the complex contrast of group 1 + group 2 + group 3 v. group 4 + group 5.

Here, the numerator would be:

$$(.33)(2.3) + (.33)(4.7) + (.33)(6.0) + (-.5)(9.3) + (-.5)(11.1)$$
$$= .76 + 1.55 + 1.98 - 4.65 - 5.55 = 4.29 - 10.2 = -5.91$$

The denominator would be:

$$\sqrt{(2.30)[(.33^2/10) + (.33^2/12) + (.33^2/9) + (-.5^2/12) + (-.5^2/8)]}$$
$$= \sqrt{(2.30)(.011 + .009 + .012 + .021 + .031)}$$
$$= \sqrt{(2.30)(.084)} = \sqrt{.193} = 0.44$$

Thus, Dunn's t would equal:

$$t(D) = -5.91/.44 = \mathbf{-13.43}$$

Assuming that this contrast was the 2nd in a group of three planned comparisons, the critical t-value would still be based on $\alpha = .017$ with 46 dfs, and thus $t_{CRIT} = \pm 2.48$. We would reject the null hypothesis that groups 1, 2, and 3 (combined) are significantly smaller than the combination of groups 4 and 5.

PRACTICE PROBLEMS
(unless stated otherwise, assume α = .05)

12.1 Why is the ANOVA procedure viewed as an advantage over the option of using multiple t-tests to compare the means of three or more groups?

12.2 Describe the similarities and differences between MS_{BET} and $\bar{X}1 - \bar{X}2$, and between MS_{WITHIN} and S_{X1-X2}.

12.3 Define **within-group variability?** Where does it come from? How does random assignment of participants to conditions effect within-group variability?

12.4 Unlike t-scores, which can be positive or negative, F-scores can only be positive. Why?

12.5 A study wants to compare the effects of two therapy conditions and one control condition on the weight gain of anorexic girls. The control group gets no treatment, while the two treatment groups include one that gets cognitive behavioral treatment and another that gets family therapy. The dependent variable is the weight gain in pounds. Make a complete source table. Do the data indicate significant differences between conditions? Use Scheffe's S test to determine which groups are responsible for rejecting the null hypothesis:

Family	Cognitive	Control
8	4	1
7	6	4
10	7	2
6	4	2
9	9	3
8	5	3

12.6 A psychologist studied four computer keyboard designs. Four samples of individuals were given materials to type on a particular keyboard, and the number of errors committed by each subject was recorded. The data are as follows:

Keyboard A	Keyboard B	Keyboard C	Keyboard D
0	6	6	8
4	8	5	5
0	5	9	9
0	4	4	3
1	2	6	5

State the null hypothesis for the study. Conduct the appropriate statistical test. Conduct any follow-up tests, if necessary.

12.7 In everyday language, describe what the F-ratio indicates.

12.8 A researcher conducted a study with 7 different groups. Eight people were assigned to each group and the total sample size was 56. The means of these groups are:

$\bar{X}1 = 1.8$

$\bar{X}2 = 2.7$

$\bar{X}3 = 9.5$

$\bar{X}4 = 4.5$

$\bar{X}5 = 0.4$

$\bar{X}6 = 8.7$

$\bar{X}7 = 6.8$

A one-way ANOVA was conducted and the resulting MS_{WITHIN} was 2.1. The F_{CRIT} for this ANOVA (based on 6, 49 dfs) was 2.29.

Assume that the researcher had prepared a total of three *planned comparisons*:

$\bar{X}1$ v. $\bar{X}4$

$\bar{X}3$ v. $\bar{X}6$

$\bar{X}2$ v. $\bar{X}4$

Conduct the appropriate statistical tests to determine whether the researcher can reject the null hypothesis regarding these three comparisons.

12.9 Next, assume that the researcher wants to conduct a series of post hoc comparisons:

$\bar{X}1 + \bar{X}2 + \bar{X}5$ v. $\bar{X}3 + \bar{X}6$

$\bar{X}4$ v. $\bar{X}6 + \bar{X}7$

$\bar{X}1 + \bar{X}2$ v. $\bar{X}4 + \bar{X}7$

Conduct the appropriate statistical tests to determine whether the researcher can reject the null hypothesis regarding these three comparisons.

Factorial Analysis of Variance

One-way analysis of variance (ANOVA), described in the previous chapter, allows researchers to test the null hypothesis that the means of three or more groups come from the same population (or from populations with identical μs). The groups analyzed typically represent different levels of a single independent variable, and rejection of the null hypothesis indicates that the independent variable in question has a meaningful impact on the dependent (outcome) measure. ANOVA tests the null hypothesis by producing two independent estimates of variability. *Between-groups variability,* which reflects the differences among groups (whether the means are close together or spread apart) and *within-group variability,* which reflects the extent to which scores within each group vary around the group mean. According to the null hypothesis, any differences among group means are due to random error, and thus our variability between or among groups is 100% random error. Under the alternative hypothesis, the between-groups variability is due, *at least in part,* to meaningful differences among group means, i.e., membership in one group or another explains or predicts why some scores on the dependent measure are higher or lower than others. Regardless of the null hypothesis, however, it is certain that the variability within groups is 100% random error, because this variability cannot be explained by membership in one group v. another.

If the null hypothesis is true, between-groups and within-groups variability are both independent estimates of random error, and thus a ratio of MS_{BET} over MS_{WITHIN} would be expected to approximate 1. However, if the alternative hypothesis is true and group membership does contribute to differences in group means, then we would expect our between-groups variance to be greater than our estimates of random error (within group variability) alone. Thus, our ratio of MS_{BET} over MS_{WITHIN} should be greater than 1. If this ratio exceeds 1 to an extent very unlikely to have occurred due to chance, we may reject the null hypothesis and conclude that the between-groups variability must include variability explained by group membership. Thus we conclude there are meaningful differences among the groups—that our independent variable meaningfully predicts change in the dependent measure.

Whereas one-way ANOVA assumes a single independent variable, there are many research questions that involve multiple independent variables at the same time. For example, one independent variable may reflect a particular treatment (e.g., Treatment A v. Treatment B v. Treatment C) and a second independent variable may reflect the types of people or specific conditions under which the treatment might be effective (e.g., Condition A v. Condition B). Note that if these two independent variables were crossed in the same study, it would produce six groups.

	Treatment A	Treatment B	Treatment C
Condition A	1	2	3
Condition B	4	5	6

The researcher conducting this study may be explicitly interested in knowing not only whether the three treatments have differential effects, but whether the relative effects of these treatments vary systematically as a function of condition.

For example, imagine that a researcher wishes to conduct a clinical trial comparing two painkillers, Medicine A and Medicine B. In addition to comparing these two medicines to each other, the researcher wishes to compare both to a Control condition where participants receive non-medicinal placebos. If this was the researcher's only concern, he could conduct a study using these three groups (three levels of the independent variable "Type of Painkiller") and analyze the data using a one-way ANOVA. But in this case, the researcher is also interested in a second independent variable, Type of Pain, and wishes to include participants with headaches and with backaches in the study. In such a study, the researcher might recruit some participants with headaches and some participants with backaches, and then randomly assign these participants to take medicine A, medicine B, or the placebo (the placebo condition is important because people might feel better over time, even without medicine). After waiting one hour for the medicine to take effect, the researcher asks participants to record (on the dependent measure) how they feel using a 10-point scale (from "much pain" to "no pain").

It is unlikely that the researcher is really concerned with studying which type of pain, backaches or headaches, is more painful, but rather is interesting in knowing whether the effectiveness of treatments (medicine A v. medicine B v. control) varies as a function of type of pain. It may be the case, for example, that medicine A is more effective than medicine B when it comes to headaches, but that medicine B is more effective than medicine A when it comes to backaches. It is expected that the placebo would be less effective than both medicines A and B, and that it would have the same effect regardless of type of pain.

The described relationship between the two variables—type of painkillers and type of pain—on the dependent variable is called an **interaction.** An interaction occurs when the impact of two (or more) independent variables in combination is not explained entirely by impacts of those variables taken independently. An interaction can be defined as an event where the impact of one independent variable varies as a function of another independent variable. In the previous example, the impact of type of painkiller (i.e., the different effects of the medicines) varies depending on type of pain (i.e., whether the person has a headache or a backache). A third way of describing interactions is in terms of "differences between differences." For example, the difference between medicine A and medicine B is different for people with headaches than it is for people with backaches; for people with headaches, $\overline{X}$ medicine A – $\overline{X}$ medicine B would be positive, whereas for people with backaches, $\overline{X}$ medicine A – $\overline{X}$ medicine B would be negative.

The type of painkiller × type of pain example describes a **crossover interaction;** (see Figure 13.1); here, the difference between medicine A and medicine B is essentially *opposite* for headaches as it is for backaches. If we were to graph the pattern of results described in this example (ignoring the control condition for the moment), it might appear as the figure below. Note that the line for the headache group and the line for the backache group cross over each other.

However, interactions need not necessarily cross over each other. It would be considered an interaction, for example, if medicine A was equally effective for headaches as for

13.1

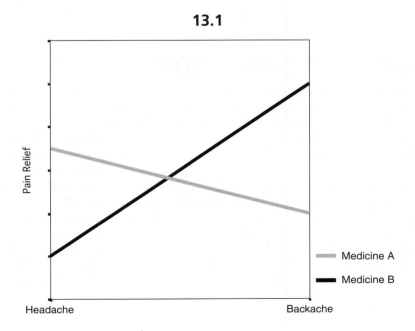

13.2

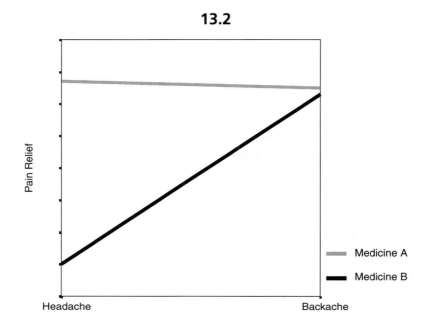

backaches, but medicine B was more effective for one type of pain than another (see Figure 13.2). It also would be considered an interaction if medicine A and medicine B were equally effective for one type of pain, but differentially effective for another type of pain.

Interactions can be extremely useful in research because they can be used to identify the conditions under which particular events occur v. do not occur, when treatments are highly effective v. when they are not effective, etc.

Conducting a Factorial ANOVA

A factorial ANOVA requires that a research design included two or more categories of independent variables and a single measured outcome (dependent variable). The independent variables should be categorical in that the levels within each variable are represented by different groups. In theory, there is no limit to the number of independent variables, nor a limit to the number of levels (groups) within each variable (assuming that there at least are two). However, increasing the number of independent variables included in the analysis will greatly increase the complexity. In this book, we will only consider factorial ANOVAs with two independent variables. Key assumptions underlying a factorial ANOVA are that the participants within each cell are independent (scores within one group help predict scores within another group), and that the population σs underlying the samples are both normally distributed and equal to each other. However, ANOVA generally is not greatly influenced by violations to assumptions of normal and equal distributions. For reasons that are beyond the scope of this book, it is important that sample sizes within each group are equal.

	Medicine A	Medicine B	Placebo
Headache	07	05	01
	09	05	04
	05	06	03
	10	03	02
Backache	03	10	05
	05	08	04
	01	07	01
	03	08	01

Sample data from the "type of painkiller × type of study" study is presented above. Scores reflect how the participants feel (i.e., amount of pain reduction) one hour after taking the medicine.

The research design used in the example is considered a "3 × 2 between-groups design." The design is considered between-groups because each group comprises an independent sample. The "3 × 2" designation indicates that the design includes two independent variables; one variable (type of painkiller) has three levels (medicine A, medicine B, and placebo) and the other independent variable (type of pain) has two levels (headache and backache). In this design there are a total of six groups (2 × 3 = 6), the total sample size (N) equals 24, and there are an even four participants per condition. Note that if we removed the placebo condition from the design and included only medicine A v. medicine B as levels of type of painkiller, the design would be a "2 × 2" (two independent variables, each with two levels). Alternatively, if we included a third independent variable, such as gender (with two levels, men and women), then the design would be a "3 × 2 × 2" design (three independent variables, one with three levels and two with two levels) with a total of 12 groups. However, in this book we do not address computations for factorial ANOVAs including three or more independent variables.

The first steps in conducting a factorial ANOVA in fact are identical to those in conducting a one-way ANOVA. First, we compute the SS_{TOT} by treating all of the scores (N = 24, in this case) as if they are from a single group and computing the SS for those scores. Second, we compute the SS_{BET}, which reflects the extent to which the six sample group means vary from each other. Third, we compute SS_{WITHIN} by subtracting the SS_{BET} from the SS_{TOT}. SS_{WITHIN} reflects the variability of scores within the groups, and is an estimate of the amount of random error in the study.

From the data above, we compute:

N = 24

$\Sigma X = 116$

$(\Sigma X)^2 = 13456$

$\Sigma X^2 = 744$

And thus:

$$SS_{TOT} = 744 - (13456/24) = 744 - 560.67 = \mathbf{183.33}$$

$$SS_{BET} = ((31^2/4) + (19^2/4) + (10^2/4) + (12^2/4) + (33^2/4) + (11^2/4)) - 560.67$$

$$= (240.25 + 90.25 + 25.0 + 36.0 + 272.25 + 30.25) - 560.67 = 694 - 560.67 = 133.33$$

$$SS_{WITHIN} = 183.33 - 133.33 = \mathbf{50}$$

In one-way ANOVA, we are interested in computing an F-ratio for the MS_{BET} in order to test the null hypothesis that all the groups are from the same population (or populations with identical μs). In factorial ANOVA, however, we are not really concerned with the overall between-groups effect. Rather, in the case of a factorial ANOVA with two independent variables, we are interested in three specific tests, and sums of squares must be computed for each of these tests. These three tests of interest include two **main effects** (one for each of the independent variables) and the interaction effect between the two independent variables. A main effect is a test of one independent variable while ignoring the other independent variable. Thus, in the current example, the main effect of "type of painkiller" reflects differences in mean pain-relief scores among medicine A, medicine B, and the placebo, regardless of whether the participant had a headache or backache. Similarly, the main effect of "type of pain" reflects the differences in pain-relief scores between participants with headaches and those with backaches, ignoring which type of painkiller they were given. The interaction effect, as defined previously, reflects whether relative effectiveness of the different painkillers varies between the different types of pain.

It should be noted that these three specific effects in fact are between-groups effects. In the process of conducting a factorial ANOVA, researchers take the SS_{BET} and partition (split) that into the sums of squares for our two main effects and the interaction. Because these effects are subsets of SS_{BET} we can compute them using the same SS_{BET} formula that was introduced in Chapter 12.

$$SS_{BET} = \Sigma\, T_j^2/n_j - (\Sigma X)^2/N$$

In computing SS_{BET}, we took the total of each group, squared it, divided by the number of participants in each group, and then summed across groups. We follow the same approach in computing the main effects for our two independent variables; however, now we configure our groups differently. In the current example, we calculated SS_{BET} by working with the totals of each of six groups. But recall that our main effect of type of painkiller reflects differences among the three groups medicine A, medicine B, and placebo. To compute the sums of squares of type of painkiller (SS_{PK}) we reduce the six groups of our study to three, and work with the totals of medicine A, medicine B, and placebo groups.

If we sum together all eight scores of participants who received medicine A, we get a total (T_A) of 43. If we sum together all eight scores of participants who received medicine B, we get a total (T_B) of 52. Finally, if we sum together all eight scores of participants who received the placebo, we get a total (T_P) of 21. Thus, our SS_{PK} (sums of squares – type of painkiller) is computed as such:

$$SS_{PK} = ((43^2/8) + (52^2/8) + (21^2/8)) - (13456/24) = 231.125 + 338 + 55.125 - 560.67$$

$$= 624.25 - 560.67 = \mathbf{63.58}$$

Note that there are eight participants in each of the three groups. In addition, note that the latter portion of the formula $[(\Sigma X)^2/N]$ is identical to the latter portion of the formulas for computing both SS_{TOT} and SS_{BET}.

Next, we compute the sums of squares associated with our second independent variable, type of pain (SS_{TP}). Here, we take our six groups and combine them to create two groups, one including all of the participants that had headaches, and another group including all of the participants that had backaches. The sum of the headache group (T_H), which we based on scores from 12 participants, equals 60. Similarly, the sum of the backache group (T_B) is 56. Thus, our SS_{TP} equals:

$$SS_{TP} = ((60^2/12) + (56^2/12)) - (13456/24) = 300 + 261.33 - 560.67$$

$$= 561.33 - 560.67 = \mathbf{0.67}$$

Finally, sums of squares for the interaction effect is not computed directly. Recall that earlier in this chapter we hinted that interactions between or among variables occur when the variability between groups cannot be explained by the main effects of those variables alone. In much the same way that we partition our SS_{TOT} perfectly into SS_{BET} and SS_{WITHIN}, in factorial ANOVA we partition our SS_{BET} into the sums of squares of our two main effects as well as the sums of squares of the interaction. Assuming a research design with two independent variables, A and B, our sums of squares for the interaction, SS_{AB}, can be computed from:

$$SS_{AB} = SS_{BET} - (SS_A + SS_B)$$

It is useful to retain the AB-subscript when describing the interaction even when independent variables are not A and B. In our previous example, where the independent variables are type of painkiller and type of pain, symbolizing the sums of squares for the interaction as $SS_{PK.TP}$ can be awkward.

Thus, using data from the previous example:

$$SS_{AB} = SS_{BET} - (SS_{PK} + SS_{TP})$$

$$SS_{AB} = 133.33 - (63.58 + 0.67) = \mathbf{69.08}$$

We now have computed each of the sums of squares necessary to conduct our three tests of interest—the main effects for type of painkiller and type of pain, as well as for the interaction between the two. The next step is to compute the degrees of freedom for each source of variability. Recall that df for SS_{TOT} is equal to $N - 1$, the df for SS_{BET} is $k - 1$, and the df for SS_{WITHIN} is $N - k$ (i.e., $[(N - 1) - (k - 1)]$).

Thus:

$$df_{TOT} = 24 - 1 = 23$$
$$df_{BET} = 6 - 1 = 5$$
$$df_{WITHIN} = 24 - 6 = 18$$

Next, we need to compute the degrees of freedom for our two main effects and the interaction. Recall that these are subsets of our between-groups variability, and thus degrees of freedom can be computed from $k - 1$. Note that our SS_{PK} describes the variability among three groups—medicine A, medicine B, and the placebo. Thus our df_{PK} will be based upon $k - 1 = 3 - 1 = 2$. SS_{TP} describes variability among two groups—headaches and backaches. Thus, our df_{TP} equals $k - 1 = 2 - 1 = 1$. Finally, just as we compute SS_{AB} via subtraction (i.e., $SS_{AB} = SS_{BET} - S_A - SS_B$), we can compute our df_{AB} from $df_{AB} = df_{BET} - (df_A + df_B)$. Thus, $df_{AB} = 5 - (2 + 1) = 2$.

Now that the degrees of freedom for our between-groups effects have been computed, we can compute the mean squares (variances) for each source of variability. Recall that our mean square estimates are computed by dividing our sums of squares by the corresponding degrees of freedom.

Thus, using data already computed:

$$MS_{TOT} = SS_{TOT}/df_{TOT} = 183.33/23 = 7.97$$
$$MS_{BET} = SS_{BET}/df_{BET} = 133.33/5 = 26.67$$
$$MS_{PK} = SS_{PK}/df_{PK} = 63.58/2 = 31.79$$
$$MS_{TP} = SS_{TP}/df_{TP} = 0.67/1 = 0.67$$
$$MS_{AB} = SS_{AB}/df_{AB} = 69.08/2 = 34.54$$
$$MS_{WITHIN} = SS_{WITHIN}/df_{WITHIN} = 50.0/18 = 2.78$$

Finally, now that our mean squares have been calculated, we can compute F-ratios. Recall that for one-way ANOVAS, F is computed from MS_{BET}/MS_{WITHIN}. In factorial ANOVA, however, we are not necessarily interested in our between-groups effect per se; rather than concerning ourselves with the null hypothesis that all groups come from populations with identical μs, we are interested specifically in the main effects of our two independent variables and the interaction between the two. We will compute a separate F-ratio for each of these three effects.

$$F_{PK} = MS_{PK}/MS_{WITHIN} = 31.79/2.78 = 11.44$$
$$F_{TP} = MS_{TP}/MS_{WITHIN} = 0.67/2.78 = 0.24$$
$$F_{AB} = MS_{AB}/MS_{WITHIN} = 34.54/2.78 = 12.42$$

A source table containing all of the values for our computations is provided below.

Source	SS	df	MS	F
Total	183.33	23	07.97	—
Between	133.33	5	26.67	—
Painkiller	63.58	2	31.79	11.44
Type of Pain	00.67	1	00.67	00.24
Interaction	69.08	2	34.54	12.42
Within	50.00	18	02.78	—

These F-ratios can be used to test the null hypotheses for each test: (1) that the samples of our three painkiller groups (medicine A v. medicine B v. placebo) come from the same population, populations with the same μs; (2) that the samples of our two types of pain groups (headache v. backache); and (3) that the differences among painkillers is the same for headaches and backaches.

These three effects are independent of each other. It is possible for all three to be statistically significant, for none of the effects to be statistically significant, or for any one, or any two of the effects to be significant. In order to determine whether we can reject the null hypothesis for any of these effects, we must compare our computed F-ratios to critical values obtained from the F-table.

Note that because our degrees of freedom are different for each different test, our critical values will be different as well. The critical value for the main effect of type of painkiller will be based on 2 dfs in the numerator and 18 dfs in the denominator. The critical value for the main effect of type of pain will be based on 1 dfs in the numerator and 18 dfs in the denominator. Finally, the critical value for the interaction between type of painkiller and type of pain will be based on 2 dfs in the numerator and 18 dfs in the denominator. Examining the F-table, we find the following:

Assuming $\alpha = .05$:

Painkiller main effect: F_{CRIT} (2, 18) = 3.56

Type of Pain main effect: F_{CRIT} (1, 18) = 4.41

Painkiller × Type of Pain interaction: F_{CRIT} (2, 18) = 3.56

For the test of type of painkiller, we find that $F > F_{CRIT}$: 11.44 > 3.56, and thus we reject the null hypothesis regarding differences among the types of painkillers. For the test of type of pain, we find that $F < F_{CRIT}$: 0.67 < 4.41, and thus here we must retain the null hypothesis regarding differences between headaches and backaches. Finally, regarding the interaction effect, we find that $F > F_{CRIT}$: 12.42 > 3.56, and thus we reject the null hypothesis.

Interpreting the Means

The table below presents the means pain-reduction scores of our six groups, along with the marginal means reflecting the comparisons that underlie our two main effects. The means are computed simply by summing the scores in each group and dividing by the sample size of each group.

	Medicine A	Medicine B	Placebo	*Total*
Headache	7.75	4.75	2.50	*5.00*
Backache	3.00	8.25	2.75	*4.67*
Total	*5.38*	*6.50*	*2.62*	

Because the F-score for the main effect of type of painkiller exceeded the appropriate critical value (11.44 > 3.56), we are allowed to reject the null hypothesis. This indicates that among our three sample means (5.375 v. 6.50 v. 2.625) at least two are meaningfully different; i.e., they are different for reasons other than random error. However, this test does not indicate which means are really different. It is unclear, for example, whether medicine A has a significantly different effect (ignoring type of pain) than medicine B, whether medicine A is significantly different from placebo, etc.

Because the F-score for the main effect of type of pain did not exceed the critical value (0.67 < 4.41) we cannot reject the null and must conclude that the mean differences in pain reduction between headaches and backaches (5.00 v. 4.67) is merely an artifact of random error and cannot be attributed to meaningful differences between those two types of pain.

Finally, the F-score for the interaction between type of painkiller and type of pain exceeds the critical value, 12.42 > 3.56, allowing us to reject the null hypothesis. This indicates that the differences between levels of one independent variable vary between or among the levels of the other independent variable. The interaction contrasts explicitly (7.75 – 3.00) v. (4.75 – 8.25) v. (2.50 – 2.75), or (4.75) v. (–3.50) v. (–0.25). In our *sample*, medicine A was 4.75 points more effective for headaches than for backaches, medicine B was 3.50 points more effective for backaches than for headaches, and the placebo was 0.25 points more effective for backaches than for headaches. Rejection of the null hypothesis indicates that at least one of these mean differences is meaningful; however, the overall interaction effect does not specify which comparisons those are.

Thus, factorial ANOVAs that produce statistically significant effects require post hoc testing to fully analyze the results. Note that had the main effect for type of pain been statistically significant, post hoc testing would not be needed to elucidate the pattern of that variable, as only two groups (levels) are involved. However, both the main effect for type of painkiller (3 groups) and the interaction effect require post hoc testing.

Using Sheffe's S, we can compute the critical mean differences required to reject the null hypothesis for any post hoc comparison. Recall that the formula for computed critical mean differences using Scheffe's S is:

$$\psi = \sqrt{(k-1)(F_{CRIT, \, k-1, \, N-k})} \, * \, \sqrt{(MS_{WITHIN})(\Sigma \, c^2/n)}$$

Because our comparisons are post hoc, we compute Scheffe's S using values associated with MS_{BET}. Thus, our $df_{BET} = 5$ and F_{CRIT} (5, 18) = 2.77.

Thus, for the first part of the equation:

$$\sqrt{(5)(2.77)} = \sqrt{13.85} = 3.72$$

For the second part, our MS_{WITHIN} from the source table is 2.78, and the sample size within each group is 8.
Thus:

$$\sqrt{(2.78)((1^2/8) + (-1^2/8))} = \sqrt{(2.78)(.25)} = \sqrt{.70} = .84$$

Our critical mean difference (ψ) for Scheffe's S is thus:

$$\psi = 3.72 \times .84 = \mathbf{3.12}$$

Medicine A – Medicine B = 5.38 – 6.50 = –1.12

Medicine A – Placebo = 5.38 – 2.62 = 2.76

Medicine B – Placebo = 6.50 – 2.62 = 3.88

If we compare the absolute differences among our means to the critical difference value (Ψ) of 2.85, we see we cannot reject the null hypothesis regarding medicine A v. medicine B because $|-1.12| < 3.12$. Nor can we reject the null hypothesis that medicine A was different from placebo because ($|2.76| < 3.12$). However, we can reject the null and say that medicine B works better than placebo ($|3.88| > 3.12$).

	Medicine A	Medicine B	Placebo	Total
Headache	7.75	4.75	2.50	5.00
Backache	3.00	8.25	2.75	4.67
Total	5.38	6.50	2.62	

Next, given that we rejected the null hypothesis regarding the type of painkiller x type of pain interaction, we wish to compare the mean pain-reduction scores among the six groups. First we can compare the relative effect of each medicine on headaches v. backaches (respectively).

Medicine A: 7.75 – 3.00 = 4.75 $|4.75| > 3.12$, thus reject H0

Medicine B: 4.75 – 8.25 = –3.50 $|-3.50| > 3.12$, thus reject H0

Placebo: 2.50 – 2.75 = –0.25 $|-0.25| < 3.12$, thus retain H0

Using Scheffe's S test we can conclude that medicine A is significantly more effective for headaches than for backaches. We also can conclude that medicine B is significantly more effective for backaches than for headaches. However, we must retain the null hypothesis regarding the placebo: we cannot conclude that the placebo affects headaches differently than backaches.

We may wish to make additional comparisons as well. For example, rather than contrasting headaches with backaches for each medicine, we may wish to compare medicines within types of pain. Note that we cannot conclude that medicine A is more effective than medicine B for headaches (7.75 − 4.75 = 3.00, and $|3.00| > 3.12$. However, medicine A is less effective than medicine B for backaches (3.00 − 8.25 = −5.25, and $|-5.25| > 3.12$). Medicine B is not significantly more effective than the placebo for treating headaches (4.75 − 2.50 = 2.25, but $|2.25| < 3.12$), and medicine A is not significantly more effective than the placebo for treating backaches (3.00 − 2.75 = 0.25, but $|0.25| < 3.12$).

PRACTICE PROBLEMS

Presented next are examples of 2 × 2 designs, with the mean score of each group presented. Examine the means of each group and indicate whether or not results suggest an interaction.

13.1

1

	B1	B2
A1	5.4	2.2
A2	9.2	7.4

2

	B1	B2
A1	3.7	5.1
A2	7.8	9.2

3

	B1	B2
A1	8.2	5.5
A2	4.3	5.7

4

	B1	B2
A1	6.5	6.4
A2	6.9	8.8

13.2 The source table below is partially completed from a factorial ANOVA with two independent variables. Using the information provided, complete the source table.

Source	SS	df	MS	F
Total	650		—	—
Between		5		
Effect A				
Effect B	090	2		
AB Interaction			21.67	1.548
Within		35		—

13.3 To study the differential effects of conditioning, an experimenter classically conditions rats using either a tone or a vibratory stimulus as the conditioned stimulus (CS) and one of three levels of foot shock as the unconditioned stimulus (UCS). The dependent variable is the number of trials it takes to press a level in an undetermined situation. Give a complete source table, and conduct any necessary post hoc tests. What do you conclude? Explain in everyday language.

▶

Conditioned Stimulus

		Tone	Vibration
Unconditioned Stimulus	High	20, 22, 19	18, 16, 14
	Medium	03, 05, 04	04, 06, 09
	Low	02, 04, 01	02, 00, 06

13.4 Many people find it difficult to think clearly or work efficiently on hot summer days. You hear comments such as: "It's not the heat; it's the humidity." To evaluate this claim scientifically, you design a study where both heat and humidity are manipulated, and then observe subjects' performance on a problem-solving task (higher scores indicate better performance). Here are the data (just the means) from the study (this is a 2 × 3 factorial design):

▶

	70 degrees	80 degrees	90 degrees
30% humidity	Mean = 80	Mean = 80	Mean = 80
70% humidity	Mean = 80	Mean = 70	Mean = 60

a. Graph the data, with temperature along the x-axis, and the dependent variable on the y-axis—you should have two lines, one for each level of humidity.

b. ANOVA calculations show a significant main effect for both humidity and temperature, and a significant interaction. Interpret (in other words, write a conclusion for) each of these findings separately.

13.5 A scientist has invented a new anti-aging medicine that she guarantees will help keep people looking young and healthy. However, she argues that the medicine will work only for people on a vegetarian diet. To test this, she gives her anti-aging medicine to 12 people, and gives sugar pills to another 12. Half of the people within each group are vegetarians, while the other half are non-vegetarians. After 1 month, she measures the "youthfulness" of each participant. Data are given below. Higher numbers mean the person appears more youthful.

	Anti-Aging	Sugar Pill
	8	5
	12	6
Vegetarian	9	9
	8	7
	7	5
	9	8
	3	1
	7	4
Non-Vegetarian	4	2
	4	4
	7	3
	8	5

Conduct the appropriate statistical test and create a source table. Conduct post hoc tests as necessary.

CHAPTER 14

Repeated Measures and Mixed Model ANOVA

A one-way ANOVA can be conceptualized as an extension of the independent samples t-test (comparing the means of three or more groups instead of only two groups). In much the same way, repeated measures ANOVA (also called within-subjects ANOVA), as described in this chapter, can be conceptualized as an extension of a related samples t-test. In repeated measures ANOVA, we examine the differences among three or more sets of scores that were collected from a single set of participants; thus, our dependent measure is collected from each participant three or more times. In such a study, participants might give ratings of three or more items, or at three points in time (before, during, after).

In addition to requiring that variables be normally distributed in the population, repeated measures ANOVA also assumes *sphericity*, i.e., that errors (deviations between individuals' scores and expected scores) truly are random. Accordingly, some unmeasured factor that causes a measurement in one subject to deviate from the mean should have no affect on the next measurement in the same subject. The assumption of sphericity is violated, for example, when the repeated measurements are made too close together in time such that the factors that cause a particular value to be higher (or lower) than expected do not dissipate before the next measurement.

The advantage of using a repeated measures of ANOVA (relative to conducting a purely between-groups design and using a one-way ANOVA) is that in addition to computing SS_{TOT}, SS_{BET}, and SS_{WITHIN}, we also compute a sum of squares associated with differences among participants, SS_{SUB}. The SS_{SUB} is subtracted from the error term (SS_{WITHIN}); this ultimately reduces the denominator (MS_{WITHIN}) for the F-test can produce larger F-scores. Recall that MS_{WITHIN} is a reflection of error, or unexplained variance. If we can "explain" some of this variance by attributing it to the fact that individual participants vary, that portion is removed from the error term. Note that it is possible to compute this sum of squares only because we have multiple measures of each participant.

Imagine a study of 10 participants enrolled in an exercise program for three months. In addition to measuring baseline, or starting, weight, each participant's weight is recorded at the end of each month. The data are presented below. Note that the sum of each column and each row is presented as well.

	Baseline	Month #1	Month #2	Month #3	Σ
Participant 01	180	177	173	170	700
Participant 02	157	153	147	140	597
Participant 03	209	204	200	196	809
Participant 04	174	182	167	160	683
Participant 05	134	126	120	114	494
Participant 06	107	105	111	114	437
Participant 07	144	144	145	143	576
Participant 08	165	164	162	159	650
Participant 09	235	240	242	236	953
Participant 10	115	113	115	112	455
Σ	1620	1608	1582	1544	

We wish to conduct a repeated measures ANOVA to test the hypothesis that the exercise program is effective in reducing participants' weight, thus we expect mean weights to decrease over time. The null hypothesis is that there is no difference over time in participants' weight. Assume that the assumption of sphericity is tenable.

The first step is to compute SS_{TOT}, computing the total variability among all 40 data points.

If we sum each score, we find that $\Sigma X = 6354$, and thus $(\Sigma X)^2 = 40373316$. If we square the 40 scores, we find that $\Sigma X^2 = 1068886$.

Therefore:

$$SS_{TOT} = 1068886 - (40373316/40) = 1068886 - 1009332.9 = 59553.1$$

Next, we want to compute the sum of squares associated with the *repeated factor*, in this case, the four time points. We will refer to this variable as *Time*, and variability among the different time points indicates that weight scores vary over time. Note that if we were conducting a one-way ANOVA, and the different columns of scores reflected different groups, we would compute the variability among the groups using the formula for SS_{BET}. In the repeated measures ANOVA example, we still use the same SS_{BET} formula, i.e., $SS_{BET} = \Sigma\, T_j^2/n_j - (\Sigma X)^2/N$, but we no longer refer to it as SS_{BET} because the different columns of data do not describe different "groups" per se, but rather sets of scores associated with different points in time. In this example, we will refer to the variability for repeated measures factor as SS_{TIME} to reflect the fact that we are measuring change on time. It also might have been appropriate to label it as SS_{EXC} because presumably any change in weight is due to *exercise;* in other examples, sums of squares for the repeated measure might be labeled SS_{TREAT} as the study involves examining the effect of some *treatment* of time.

We compute our SS_{TIME} (which reflects that variability among the four time points) using the SS_{BET} formula we learned in Chapter 12. We use "10" as the denominator for the column because 10 participants make up the column total.

$$SS_{TIME} = \Sigma\, T_j^2/n_j - (\Sigma X)^2/N$$

$$= (1620^2/10) + (1608^2/10) + (1582^2/10) + (1544^2/10) - 1009332.9$$

$$= 262440 + 258566.4 + 250272.4 + 238393.6 - 1009332.9$$

$$= 1009672.4 - 1009332.9 = \mathbf{339.5}$$

If this was a one-way (between-groups) ANOVA, we could proceed by computing SS_{WITHIN} by subtracting SS_{TIME} from SS_{TOT} (i.e., $SS_{TOT} - SS_{TIME} = 59553.1 - 339.5 = 59213.6$). For there we could compute our appropriating MS (variance) terms, and get an F-ratio for the *time* effect.

Note that there is considerable variability in weight scores because there are considerable differences among participants (initial weights range from 115 to 235); this inevitably will contribute to unexplained variance. However, because we have multiple measures from each participant, we can estimate the amount of variability among scores due to the fact that people are different and remove this from the "unexplained" variance. Because we have multiple measures from each participant, we can compute a total weight for each participant. We can compute a sum of squares associated with differences among participants (subjects) (i.e., SS_{SUB}) by applying the same formula for SS_{TIME} to the totals of each *row* (as opposed to column). We use "4" as the denominator because scores from four time points make up the total for each row.

$$SS_{SUB} = (700^2/4) + (597^2/4) + (809^2/4) + (683^2/4) + (494^2/4) + (437^2/4) + (576^2/4)$$

$$+ (650^2/4) + (953^2/4) + (455^2/4) - 1009332.9$$

$$= (122500 + 89102.25 + 163620.25 + 116622.25 + 61009 + 47742.25 + 82944$$

$$+ 105625 + 227052.25 + 51756.25) - 1009332.9$$

$$= 1067973.5 - 1009332.9 = \mathbf{58640.6}$$

With SS_{TOT}, SS_{TIME}, and SS_{SUB} calculated, we can compute our unexplained sums of squares through subtraction. For both one-way ANOVA and factorial ANOVA, our unexplained variance was based on SS_{WITHIN}, i.e., the variability within each group. In the case of repeated measures ANOVA, however, it is not entirely appropriate to refer to our error term as "within-group" variability. Recall that SS_{WITHIN} is the residual, or remainder, after subtracting SS_{BET} from SS_{TOT}. Part of this "residual" variance is due to the fact that participants differ on any number of variables that might relate to the dependent measure. In repeated measures ANOVA, we compute the sums of squares associated with differences among participants (i.e., SS_{SUB}), and this variability is further subtracted by the SS_{WITHIN} "residual." Once we take SS_{SUB} from SS_{WITHIN}, we are left with a new residual, or remainder, and this is the basis for the appropriate error term: SS_{ERR}.

Thus:

$$SS_{ERR} = SS_{TOT} - (SS_{BET} + SS_{SUB})$$

Thus, in the weight-loss/exercise example:

$$SS_{ERR} = 59553.1 - (339.5 + 58640.6) = \textbf{573.0}$$

Note that if we did not pull out the variability due to participants (SS_{SUB}), our SS_{WITHIN} would have been considerably larger: $SS_{WITHIN} = SS_{TOT} - SS_{TIME} = 59553.1 - 339.5 = 59213.6$.

We now can compute a source table using SS_{TOT}, SS_{TIME}, SS_{SUB}, and SS_{ERR}. Recall that degrees of freedom for SS_{TOT} are based on the *total* number of observations less 1 (NK − 1, where N is the number of participants and k is the number of "groups"—the number of times that each participant is measured). In this example, NK equals 10 participants * 4 "groups" of data, thus 40 − 1 = 39. Degrees of freedom for both SS_{TIME} and SS_{SUB} are based on k −1 and N − 1, respectively. There are 4 "groups" of data (columns) and 10 participants (rows), so the degrees of freedom associated with SS_{TIME} and SS_{SUB} are 4 − 1 = 3, and 10 − 1 = 9, respectively. Finally, given that our SS_{ERR} is a residual (it is what is left over after subtraction), our dfs for the error term also is based on subtraction: $df_{ERR} = df_{TOT} - (df_{TIME} + df_{SUB})$.

Source	SS	df	MS	F
Total	59553.1	39	1527.00	—
Time	339.5	3	113.17	5.33
Subjects	58640.6	9	6515.62	—
Error	573.0	27	21.22	—

Our F_{CRIT} will be based on 3 dfs in the numerator and 27 in the denominator. Assuming $\alpha = .05$, our $F_{CRIT} = 2.96$. Because our computed F-ratio exceeds the critical value, 5.33 > 2.96, we can reject the null hypothesis and conclude the weight scores are significantly different across the four points in time.

We do not often compute an F-test for differences among participants. Testing to determine whether individual participants, on average, differed from each other is not particularly interesting; we only compute the sums of squares for subjects in order to reduce our error term. Note that if we did not pull SS_{SUB} from the error term, and instead used MS_{WITHIN} as our denominator, our F-ratio would have been:

$SS_{WITHIN} = 59213.6$

$MS_{WITHIN} = 59213.6/27 = 2193.10$

$F = 113.17/2193.10 = 0.05$

Clearly, if the analyses had been conducted using a truly one-way, between-groups approach, the difference over time would not have been statistically significant.

After rejecting the null hypothesis (regarding the change in participants' weights over time) we can examine the mean weights of participants over time. We find that mean weights did appear to decrease over time.

	Baseline	Month #1	Month #2	Month #3
$\bar{X}$	162.0	160.8	158.2	154.4

It would appear as if weights decreased significantly over time.

Post Hoc Tests

Note that we can conduct post hoc tests to further clarify the differences among the means. The procedure for Scheffe's S test is described in Chapter 12.

The critical difference between means needed to reject the null hypothesis is computed using the following.

$$\Psi = \sqrt{(df_{BET})(F_{CRIT})} \times \sqrt{(MS_{ERROR})(\Sigma\, c^2/n)}$$

In repeated measures ANOVAs, the "between-groups" effect is substituted by the repeated measures effect (e.g., *Time*). Thus our df_{TIME} for the previous example was 3. The F_{CRIT} for the analysis was 2.96.

Thus, for the first part of the equation:

$$\sqrt{(df_{BET})(F_{CRIT})} = \sqrt{(3 \times 2.96)} = \sqrt{8.88} = \mathbf{2.98}$$

Assuming that we wish to make only pairwise comparisons (one mean v. another mean) rather than complex comparisons, our contrasts will always be based on contrast coefficients of 1 and –1.

Thus, for the second part of the equation:

$$\sqrt{(MS_{ERROR})(\Sigma\, c^2/n)} = \sqrt{(21.22)((1^2/10) + (-1^2/10))}$$
$$= \sqrt{(21.22)(.2)} = \sqrt{4.244} = \mathbf{2.06}$$

The critical mean difference, therefore, is:

$$\Psi = \sqrt{(df_{BET})(F_{CRIT})} \times \sqrt{(MS_{ERROR})(\Sigma\, c^2/n)} = 2.98 \times 2.06 = \mathbf{6.14}$$

If we contrast each mean from each other mean, we find that only the means that are significantly different from each other (i.e., mean difference > 6.14) is the between baseline and at the end of month #3 (162.0 – 154.4 = 7.6) and between the end of month #1 and month #3 (160.8 – 154.4 = 6.4). Every other pairwise comparison produced a difference between means that was smaller than 6.14. Thus, we can conclude that there is a statistically significant reduction in weight after three months of the exercise program, but we cannot discern significantly reductions after only one or two months of the program.

Mixed Model ANOVA

Mixed model ANOVA describes a powerful research design that combines factorial ANOVA and repeated measures ANOVA in a single analysis. It should be noted that mixed model ANOVAs are relatively advanced and typically not taught in introductory statistics courses. The computations involved in conducting the test are no more difficult than factorial ANOVA, but there are more sources of variability (e.g., types of sums of squares) and this adds considerably to the increased complexity of the study.

Recall the previous example where 10 participants went through an exercise-based weight-loss program, and where each participant's weight was measured at four points in time. Now imagine that in addition, before participants began the exercise routine, that half were randomly assigned to a *diet* condition (Condition 1), whereas the other half were not assigned to follow a special diet (Condition 2). The researcher is interested explicitly in the interaction between *time* (repeated measures variable) and *condition* (between-groups variable). The data below are identical to those from the previous example; however, participants clearly are divided into two groups (Condition 1 and Condition 2) as well. In addition to summing the rows and columns (in the previous example), in this example we also sum (in **bold**) the participants' weights within each condition-time combination (e.g., Condition 1-Baseline; Condition 2-Baseline; Condition 1-Month #1, etc.).

	Condition	Baseline	Month #1	Month #2	Month #3	Σ
Participant 01	Diet(1)	180	177	173	170	*700*
Participant 02	Diet(1)	157	153	147	140	*597*
Participant 03	Diet(1)	209	204	200	196	*809*
Participant 04	Diet(1)	174	182	167	160	*683*
Participant 05	Diet(1)	134	126	120	114	*700*
Σ		**854**	**842**	**807**	**780**	*3283*
Participant 06	No Diet(2)	107	105	111	114	*437*
Participant 07	No Diet(2)	144	144	145	143	*576*
Participant 08	No Diet(2)	165	164	162	159	*650*
Participant 09	No Diet(2)	235	240	242	236	*953*
Participant 10	No Diet(2)	115	113	115	112	*455*
Σ		**766**	**766**	**775**	**764**	*3071*

Note that our SS_{TOT}, SS_{TIME}, and SS_{SUB} already have been computed from the previous example. The values are:

$SS_{TOT} = 59553.1$

$SS_{TIME} = 339.5$

$SS_{SUB} = 58640.6$

When computing a mixed model ANOVA, it often is easiest to begin by thinking of the design as a factorial ANOVA and computing the "between-group" effects as such. We can think of the design in this example as a 2×4 design: 4 levels of *time* (containing 10 scores each) crossed with 2 levels of *diet condition* (containing 20 scores each) to create a total of 8 cells (containing 5 scores per cell). Using the standard formula $(\Sigma\ T_j^2/n_j - (\Sigma X)^2/N)$ we can compute the SS_{BET} from the eight groups. This will reflect the total variability among the means of the eight groups.

$$SS_{BET} = (854^2/5) + (842^2/5) + (807^2/5) + (780^2/5) + (766^2/5) + (766^2/5)$$
$$+ (775^2/5) + (764^2/5) - (6354^2/40)$$

$$= (145863.2 + 141792.8 + 130249.8 + 121680 + 117351.2 + 117351.2 + 120125 + 116739.2)$$
$$- 1009332.9$$

$$= 1011152.4 - 1009332.9 = \textbf{1819.5}$$

In factorial ANOVA with two independent variables, after computing SS_{BET} we then compute the main effects of our independent variables represented in the rows and columns of our data. Note that we already have computed the sum of squares for our "column variable," i.e., SS_{TIME}. This reflects the differences between mean weights among the four time points *ignoring* whether or not participants were in the diet or no-diet condition. Following the factorial ANOVA approach, we next can compute the sum of squares for our "row variable," *diet condition.* This reflects the mean differences between the participants assigned to go on a diet v. those who were not assigned to go on a diet, ignoring which point in time the participant was weighed. SS_{DIET} is computed using the total (summed) weights of the 20 scores in the diet condition and the 20 scores in the no-diet condition.

Thus:

$$SS_{DIET} = 3283^2/20 + 3071^2/20 - 6354^2/40 = 1010456.6 - 1009332.9 = \textbf{1123.6}$$

Next, given that we found $SS_{BET} = 1819.5$, $SS_{TIME} = 339.5$, and $SS_{DIET} = 1123.6$, we can compute our interaction term for *Time* $\times$ *Diet* ($SS_{T\times D}$) by subtraction, just as we did for factorial ANOVA.

$$SS_{T\times D} = SS_{BET} - (SS_{TIME} + SS_{DIET}) = 1819.5 - (339.5 + 1123.6) = 1819.5 - 1463.1 = \textbf{356.4}$$

Finally, given we have SS_{TOT} and SS_{BET}, we now can compute SS_{WITHIN} through subtraction, just as we did with factorial ANOVA.

Thus:

$$SS_{WITHIN} = SS_{TOT} - SS_{BET} = 59553.1 - 1819.5 = \mathbf{57733.6}$$

SS_{WITHIN} reflects the variability within each of the eight (Time × Diet) cells, i.e., the extent to which scores vary at a given point in time and in a given condition. It is important to note that some of this within-cell variability is due to the fact that participants vary naturally in how much they weigh. If all participants started the study with approximately the same weight, the variability within each cell (SS_{WITHIN}) would be considerably smaller.

At this stage, we have all sources of SS obtained in a factorial ANOVA: Total; Between; main effect A (Time); main effect B (diet condition); interaction (Time × Diet); and Within.

Unlike factorial ANOVA, however, we have in addition computed (from the example of "one-way" repeated measures) the sum of squares for variability among participants (SS_{SUB} = 58640.6). Recall that this sum of squares reflects the extent to which each participant's mean weight (averaged across time) varies from each other; i.e., it reflects the fact that some participants simply are heavier than others (ignoring time).

In the example of the "one-way" repeated measures ANOVA described previously in this chapter, the variability among participants (SS_{SUB}) was subtracted from the within-group variability to produce an estimate of "natural" unexplained variance. This served as the error term (denominator) in calculating our F-ratio. In the current example, where participants also are nested within condition (diet v. no diet), we can partition this SS_{SUB} even further. Why is it that the mean weight of each participant varies from that of other participants? Of course much of this is due to "natural (unexplained) variability" inherent in all samples, but some of it might be the fact that participants are in different groups (i.e., some participants were on a diet while others were not). We know already that the variability among participants is SS_{SUB} = 58640.6, and that the variability due to differences between conditions (diet v. no diet) is SS_{DIET} = 1123.6. If we subtract variability due to conditions (SS_{DIET}) from variability among participants (SS_{SUB}), the residual is "natural" unexplained variability. We refer to this as variability due to **subjects-within-conditions** (SS_{SWC}). Note that SS_{SWC} ignores the fact that each participant's weight varies over time; it reflects how the mean weight of each participant varies from the overall mean weight of his or her condition (diet v. no diet).

Thus:

$$SS_{SWC} = SS_{SUB} - SS_{DIET} = 58640.6 - 1123.6 = \mathbf{57517}$$

Although we will address this again once we create the source table, we note here that the variability of subjects within conditions (SS_{SWC}) is the appropriate denominator (error term) for testing the condition effect. We will test the main effect of *diet* (diet v. no diet, ignoring *time*) by creating a ratio of variance between the two groups over the variability within each group, i.e., between/within. Conceptually, this is identical to a t-test or one-way ANOVA.

Things get more complicated when we attempt to test the main effect of time and the Time × Diet interaction. Because both of these statistical effects include within-person variability (repeated measures) effects, SS_{SWC} is not the appropriate error term (denominator) for computing an F-ratio for those effects (recall that SS_{SWC} concerns the mean weight of each participant across time and ignores differences in weight over time).

The appropriate error term to test the main effect of Time, and the Time × Diet, interaction is based on within-cell variability. As stated earlier, SS_{WITHIN} indicates the amount of variability among scores within each of the eight cells. However, we also stated this within-cell SS contains variability due to natural differences among participants. We computed SS_{SWC} as a measure of natural variability due to participants (i.e., subjects within conditions). By subtracting the variability due to differences among participants (SS_{SWC}) from the SS_{WITHIN} we get an indicator of the within-group variability controlling for (removing) the natural variability for participants. This residual is the error term (SS_{ERR}) that we use for our denominator in computing F-ratios for time and Time × Diet.

Thus:

$$SS_{ERR} = SS_{WITHIN} - SS_{SWC} = 57733.6 - 57517 = \textbf{216.6}$$

In summary, a mixed model ANOVA with one repeated measure factor (e.g., time) and one between-groups factor (e.g., diet) will involve nine different sources of variability.

Total: total variability among all scores in the data set (where total number of scores equals N * number of repeated levels). For example, 10 participants × 4 time points = 40). Degrees of freedom for SS_{TOT} equals total number of scores − 1; (40 − 1 = 39).

Between Cells: total variability among the means of each cell (where number of cells = # of condition * number of repeated levels). For example, 2 conditions (diet v. no diet) × 4 time points = 8. Degrees of freedom for SS_{BET} equals total number of cells − 1; (8 − 1 = 7).

Diet: variability between our independent conditions (i.e., diet v. no diet) ignoring the four levels of *time*. Degrees of freedom for $SS_{DIET} = k - 1$; (2 − 1 = 1).

Time: variability between our repeated measures (i.e., four time points) ignoring the two *diet* conditions. Degrees of freedom for SS_{TIME} = number of repeated levels − 1; (4 − 1 = 3).

Time × Diet: variability due to the interaction between our independent condition and our repeated measures variable (e.g., does the change in weight over time differ between diet and no-diet conditions); computed as the residual after subtracting the main effect SS from our SS_{BET}. Degrees of freedom for $SS_{T×D} = df_{TOT} - df_{BET}$; (39 − 7 = 32).

Within Cells: total variability of scores *within* each cell (due to all reasons *except* time and diet condition). Degrees of freedom for $SS_{WITHIN} = df_{TOT} - df_{BET}$; (39 − 7 = 32).

Subjects: variability among participants (based on the mean score for each participant, aggregated across repeated measures). This includes "natural" unexplained variability and variability due to diet condition. Degrees of freedom for SS_{SUB} = number of participants (N) − 1; (10 − 1 = 9).

Subjects-Within-Conditions: variability among participants after removing variability due to condition (e.g., diet); reflects the variability in participants' mean scores (aggregated across repeated measures) within each condition. Degrees of freedom for $SS_{SWC} = df_{SUB} - df_{DIET}$; (9 − 1 = 8). Alternatively, SS_{SWC} = number of participants within condition 1 − 1, plus number of participants in condition 2 − 1, or (5 − 1) + (5 − 1) = 8. SS_{SWC} is the error term for testing our between-group condition (e.g., diet) for statistical significance.

Error: variability within each cell after removing the variability due to participants (i.e., the fact that some participants simply are heavier than others). Degrees of freedom for SS_{ERR} = $df_{WITHIN} - df_{SWC}$; (32 − 8 = 24). SS_{ERR} is the error term (denominator) for testing effects that involve the repeated measures variable (e.g., *time* and *Time × Diet*).

Source	SS	df	MS	F
Total	59553.1	39	1527.00	—
Between Cells	1819.5	7	259.93	—
Diet Condition	1123.6	1	1123.6	1123.6/7189.62 = **0.16**
Time	339.5	3	113.17	113.17/9.02 = **12.55**
Time × Diet	356.4	3	118.80	118.8/9.02 = **13.17**
Within Cells	57733.6	32	1804.18	—
Subjects	58640.6	9	6515.62	—
Subjects-within-conditions	57517.0	8	7189.62	*Error term for diet condition*
Error	216.6	24	9.02	*Error term for time and Time × Diet*

Note that SS_{BET} plays no role other than allowing us to compute $SS_{T\times D}$, and SS_{TOT} plays no role other than allowing us to compute SS_{WITHIN}. Our SS_{WITHIN}, in turn, is used to compute SS_{ERR}, and our SS_{SUB} allows us to compute SS_{SWC}.

In order to determine whether we can reject the null hypothesis for the time effect, diet effect, and Time × Diet interaction, we need to determine the appropriate critical value. Note that the degrees of freedom associated with each of the three tests will be different. The test of our between-groups variable, diet condition, is based on 1 df in the numerator, and 8 dfs in the denominator (because MS_{SWC} is the denominator in our test for diet condition. Assuming $\alpha = .05$, our critical value will be 5.32. Because our computed F-ratio of 0.16 < 5.32, we must retain the null hypothesis regarding diet condition. Thus, ignoring the *time* variable, participants randomly assigned to the diet condition did not differ significantly in mean weight ($\overline{X} = 3283/20 = 164.15$) from those assigned to the no-diet condition ($\overline{X} = 3071/20 = 153.55$). Note that the error term for this test ($MS_{SWC} = 57517$) is large relative to the error term for the time effect and Time × Diet interaction (i.e., $MS_{ERR} = 216.6$) because this test ignores the fact that we measured participants at different times and thus the error term contains the "natural" variability in participants' weight.

The main effect for time is based on 3 df in the numerator and 24 in the denominator (because MS_{ERR} is the denominator for the test of time). Assuming $\alpha = .05$, our critical value will be 3.01. Because our computed F-score for time exceeds the critical value, i.e., 12.55 > 3.01, we can reject the null hypothesis and conclude that (ignoring diet condition) mean weight varies as a function of time. Examination of the means suggests that participants' weight decreased over the course of the exercise program.

	Baseline	Month #1	Month #2	Month #3
$\overline{X}$	162.0	160.8	158.2	154.4

Note that this finding replicates the results obtained in the "one-way" repeated measures ANOVA introduced at the beginning of the chapter (that analysis, too, found a statistically significant change in weight as a function of time). If we compare the error terms, however, for the test of time in this from the one-way repeated measures ANOVA and from the current mixed model ANOVA, we find that for the former, the error term is larger than for the latter (one-way repeated measure $MS_{ERR} = 21.22$, mixed model ANOVA $MS_{ERR} = 9.02$). Apparently, including this additional between-groups variable (diet condition) "explained" some of the error variance in the one-way repeated measures ANOVA, thus reducing the denominator.

We could conduct the Scheffe S test to compare the means of our four time periods. examine the means of the specific time intervals.

For the first part of the Scheffe S equation, we use $df_{BET} = 3$ (i.e., 4 times groups – 1) and $F_{CRIT} = 3.01$.

Recall that:

$$\Psi = \sqrt{(df_{BET})(F_{CRIT})} \times \sqrt{(MS_{ERROR})(\Sigma\ c^2/n)}$$

Thus:

$$\sqrt{(df_{BET})(F_{CRIT})} = \sqrt{(3)(3.01)} = \sqrt{9.03} = 3.00$$

For the second part of the Scheffe S equation, assuming only pairwise comparisons:

$$\sqrt{(MS_{ERROR})(\Sigma\ c^2/n)} = \sqrt{(9.02)((1^2.10) + (-1^2/10))} = \sqrt{(9.02)(.2)}$$
$$= \sqrt{1.80} = 1.34$$

Thus:

$$\Psi = \sqrt{(df_{BET})(F_{CRIT})} \times \sqrt{(MS_{ERROR})(\Sigma\ c^2/n)} = (3.00)(1.34) = \textbf{4.02}$$

All group differences (among the four time groups) that exceed 4.02 are statistically significant. Once again, in this example, the differences between baseline weight and month #3 weight, and month #1 and month #3 weight, are statistically significant.

Note that *if* the main effect of diet condition had been statistically significant, *and* had diet condition contained three or more groups (instead of only two), we could have used Scheffe' S test to clarify the mean differences among the levels of diet condition as well. However, in that case, we would have used the MS_{ERR} of 21.22 instead of 9.02 (because 21.22 was the MS_{ERR} used in testing the main effect of diet condition for statistical significance).

We have not yet examined the interaction effect between time and diet. The degrees of freedom associated with the interaction also is based on 3 df in the numerator, and 24 in the denominator, and thus the F_{CRIT} for that test of the interaction is 3.01. Because the F-ratio for the interaction exceeds the critical value, 13.17 > 3.01, we reject the null hypothesis regarding the interaction: the change in weight over time varies as a function of whether participants were assigned to the diet or the no-diet condition.

If we examine the means of our eight cells (computed by dividing the total of each cell by 5), we find the following.

	Baseline	Month #1	Month #2	Month #3
Diet Condition	170.8	168.4	161.4	156
No-Diet Condition	153.2	153.2	155	152.8

At first glance, it appears as if in the diet condition, participants' weight decreases over the course of the exercise program. However, in the no-diet condition, the weights appear not to change.

If we conduct post hoc tests (assuming only pairwise comparisons), we can use the same "critical difference" (from Sheffe's S) score as we did for the test of differences among the *time* groups. This is possible because our MS_{ERR} is the same for the interaction test as it was for the test of time (i.e., $MS_{ERR} = 9.02$). Furthermore, the degrees of freedom and critical value are the same as for the main effect of time (3 df and $F_{CRIT} = 3.01$). Thus, we can conclude that any difference between cell means that exceeds 4.02 can be deemed statistically significant.

From the cell means above, for those in the diet condition, we find that the mean weight of baseline, month #1 and month #2 each differed from month #3. Furthermore, both baseline and month #1 differed significantly from month #2. Overall, the results strongly suggest those participants assigned to the diet condition lost weight over the course of the exercise program. For participants assigned to no-diet condition, however, there was no change in weight as a function of time; for these no-diet participants, none of the four means differed from each other significantly (i.e., no mean differences exceeded 4.02).

In conclusion, we may summarize the results of this mixed model study as follows: *overall*, participants who dieted did not differ significantly from those who did not diet. But this ignores change over time. However, when we examine the Time × Diet interaction, we see that diet does appear to matter. For participants who dieted, they lost weight over the course of the exercise program (going from 170.8 lbs, on average, to 156 lbs on average). For participants who did not diet, however, the exercise program did not appear to produce weight change over time. The bottom line: both exercise and diet are required for weight loss!

PRACTICE PROBLEMS

14.1 Imagine a study where a sample of six participants each viewed five pieces of artwork, and rated each one on its aesthetic quality (using a 5-point scale). Higher ratings indicate that the participant thought the art was more attractive. Thus, each of six participants provided five ratings (one for each piece of art). The data follows on next page.

	Artwork #1	Artwork #2	Artwork #3	Artwork #4	Artwork #5
Participant 1	3	1	2	4	2
Participant 2	2	3	3	5	3
Participant 3	5	1	4	5	4
Participant 4	2	2	4	3	2
Participant 5	5	2	3	5	1
Participant 6	1	1	2	2	1

Conduct the appropriate statistical test to determine whether there are differences in the preference for the five pieces of artwork, and indicate which piece(s) of artwork are considered most attractive.

14.2 A researcher studied the opinions of a small sample of adolescent summer camp attendees regarding their opinion of the summer camp. Opinion ratings were collected at three points in time: before the camp began, during the camp, and then shortly after the camp was over. Some of the participants in the study were assigned to attend a team-building workshop midway through camp (Condition 1), while another set of participants were assigned to extra leisure time instead of the team-building workshop (Condition 2). Ratings (how much they enjoyed the camp) were made on a 7-point scale, where higher scores indicated that they enjoyed the camp more.

	Condition	Before	During	After	Σ
Participant 1	1	5	2	6	10
Participant 2	1	4	4	7	15
Participant 3	1	5	2	5	12
Participant 4	1	5	3	6	14
Σ		16	11	24	
Participant 5	2	3	5	4	12
Participant 6	2	6	6	4	16
Participant 7	2	4	4	4	12
Participant 8	2	2	5	3	10
Σ		15	20	15	
Σ		31	31	39	

A number of the sum of squares computations have been performed for you:

$\Sigma X = 101$

$(\Sigma X)^2 = 10201$

$\Sigma X^2 = 473$

Thus:

$$SS_{TOT} = 473 - (10201/24) = 473 - 425.04 = \textbf{47.93}$$

$$SS_{BET} = (16^2/4) + (11^2/4) + (24^2/4) + (15^2/4) + (20^2/4) + (15^2/4) - 425.04$$
$$= 450.75 - 425.04 = \textbf{25.71}$$

Conduct an analysis that will test the main effect of condition, the main effect of time, and the Condition × Time interaction. What can you conclude about these three effects? Compute a source table that summarizes the results.

14.3 Describe, define, and differentiate SS_{WITHIN}, SS_{SUB}, SS_{SWC}, and SS_{ERR}.

Simple Regression and Correlation

To date, every statistical test that we have discussed shares a common theme: all involve comparison of group means. Whether we are comparing a single sample mean to a population μ, the means of two groups, three or more groups, groups created by crossing independent variables, or groups created measuring the same set of participants more than one time, in each case the statistical test is used to determine whether the differences between or among the groups means are statistically significant (i.e., due to reasons other than random chance).

In some circumstances, the fact that participants are organized into groups is unavoidable. In the case of experimental studies, we must randomly assign participants into groups. In other cases, our variables of interest reflect groups that are naturally occurring (e.g., men v. women; underclassmen v. upperclassmen; Republican v. Democrat; presence or absence of a disease). In these cases, our independent variables clearly are measured on a nominal or ordinal scale, and it makes perfect sense that our statistical tests would be designed to compare these groups on some dependent (outcome) measure. However, there are many circumstances where researchers derive groups from score data. For example, a researcher interested in studying the behavior of introverts and extroverts may measure participants' introversion-extroversion using a standard measure, and from those scores divide the sample into "introverted," "extroverted," and "normal" groups. A researcher interested in student study habits may measure hours spent studying per week and use these data to identify students in the sample as "achievers" or "slackers."

However, there are limitations to using score data to create groups. First, the divisions of the groups may be somewhat arbitrary. In the study habit example, the researcher would need to identify a threshold (cutoff score) in hours spent studying per week that determines which group each participant belongs to. There is no way of knowing, however, whether this threshold really is correct, and whether a different cutoff point would be better. Note that researchers are discouraged from trying different thresholds in order to identify the "best" cutoff point (i.e., the point that produces groups that are most different on the dependent measure); this haphazard approach violates the spirit of scientific inquiry.

Second, the process of creating groups from score data loses information. By creating categories from scores, we essentially are choosing to use a less refined scale of measurement (nominal or ordinal) over a more refined scale (ratio, interval, or ordinal). Imagine that a researcher was studying the relationship between intelligence and interpersonal skills, and had collected IQ scores from a sample of participants. This researcher decided that participants with IQ scores of 115 and above would be placed in the "high intelligence" group, participants with IQ scores between 85 and 114 would be placed in the "average intelligence" group, and those with IQ scores of 84 and below would be placed in the "low intelligence" group. In doing this, the researcher has assumed implicitly that there is no meaningful difference between (for example) a person with an IQ score of 115 and an IQ score of 150 in terms of interpersonal skills, that there is no meaningful difference between a person with an IQ of 85 and an IQ of 114 in interpersonal skills, etc. If, in fact, people with an IQ of 115 tend (on average) to have different interpersonal skills than people with an IQ of 150, and a similar difference occurs between people with IQs of 85 and 114, etc., such differences would be lost by the fact that these participants have been placed into the same group.

Fortunately, there exist a wide variety of statistical tools for relating a continuous (score) predictor (independent) variable with a dependent (outcome) variable. Linear regression is a technique for identifying the nature of the relationship between two score variables (multiple regression, which concerns identifying the nature of the relationship between more than one predictor variable and an outcome variable, is beyond the scope of this book). While regression shares much in common with ANOVA in terms of the underlying concepts, on the surface, and as they often are used, they appear quite different. In t-tests and ANOVA, a researcher may test whether there is a relationship between variables (e.g., whether there is a relationship between taking an SAT prep course and SAT scores) by comparing the means of groups (e.g., mean SAT scores for those who take a prep course v. those who do not). Regression, on the other hand, does not involve comparing group means. Regression involves examining the relationship between variables by examining trends, or patterns, of responses.

Imagine that a researcher is interested in studying whether people who are prone to getting angry also are more likely to drive aggressively. To conduct this study, the researcher first administers a dispositional anger scale to a sample of participants. Next, these participants operate a computerized driving simulator that measures aggressive driving behavior (e.g., excessive speeding, excessive passing, inappropriate lane usage) and computes an aggressive driving score. The researcher may hypothesize that individuals whose scores are relatively high on the dispositional anger scale will tend also to have high aggressive driving scores. It would be possible for the researcher to split the anger scale scores into three groups (e.g., low anger, medium anger, and high anger) and use ANOVA to compare the mean aggressive driving scores among the three groups. However, rather than examine differences among "anger groups," the researcher may prefer to use all of the anger scores and determine whether there is a positive linear relationship between dispositional anger and aggressive driving.

Assume that dispositional anger scores range from 10 to 30 (where 30 reflects very high anger) and aggressive driving scores range from 0 to 15 (where 15 reflects very aggressive driving). Data from a sample of 12 participants may appear as follows:

Dispositional Anger (X)	Aggressive Driving (Y)
12	13
25	05
17	08
10	14
27	03
18	10
13	08
22	01
19	06
25	07
14	04
19	11

Readers should note first that the sample size is 12, and not 24; data were collected on two measures (anger and driving) from the set of 12 participants. In this respect, the data are set up much as we would expect for a related samples t-test (i.e., one sample where each participant provides two scores). However using a related samples t-test on these data would address a very different question than we would address using regression analysis. Recall that t-tests concern differences between groups, and a related samples t-test in this case would be used to determine whether participants' dispositional anger scores are significantly higher or lower than their aggressive driving scores. In this example, the hypothesis underlying μs of a t-test does not make sense: of course anger scores will be higher (on average) than aggressive driving scores because the anger is measured on a larger scale. Imagine if our data consisted of SAT scores ($\mu = 1000$) and IQ scores ($\mu = 100$) from a single sample of participants. It would not be sensible to hypothesize comparing the *differences* between the two.

Regression and correlation are statistical tests that are not concerned with differences or comparisons among group means, but rather are concerned with similarities and trends among responses. We use these tests, for example, to determine whether people who have relatively high anger scores also tend to have relatively high aggressive driving scores (positive relationship), or whether people with relatively high anger scores tend to have low aggressive driving scores (negative relationship), or whether there is no relationship whatsoever.

Regression and correlation are nearly identical tests; the difference between them is that while the former uses variables in its original scale of measurement, the latter uses variables that have been standardized. Readers already may be familiar with the concept of a "correlation," and in some respects it is an easier concept to understand. Nevertheless, we will begin with discussion of regression (rather than correlation), as regression better addresses the conceptual underpinnings of both statistical tests.

Regression

We can get a sense of the nature of the relationship between our two variables by constructing a **scatterplot** (see Figure 15.1). In a scatterplot, each participant's data (on the predictor, variable X, and the outcome, variable Y) is plotted as coordinates on XY axes.

Using the data from the previous page, the first participant has a "12" in terms of dispositional anger (relatively low score), as well as a "13" (relatively high score) on aggressive driving. The first participant's data is expressed as the data point at the 12 and 13 markers along the X and Y axes (respectively). The second participant scored a "25" on anger and a "5" on aggressive driving, and her data is indicated by the point at the 25, 5 intersection, and so forth.

When the data set is large enough, the pattern of responses revealed in the scatterplot can help indicate the nature of the relationship between the variables. Some data sets reveal a clear upward slope in the scatterplot. The scatter plot in Figure 15.2 shows that people who tended to score high on variable X also tended to score high on variable Y, and people who scored low on variable X tended to score low on variable Y. Note that relatively few people who scored high on variable X scored low on variable Y, and relatively few people who

15.1

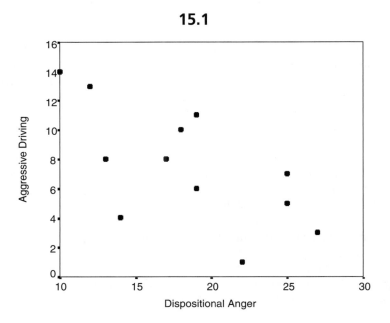

15.2

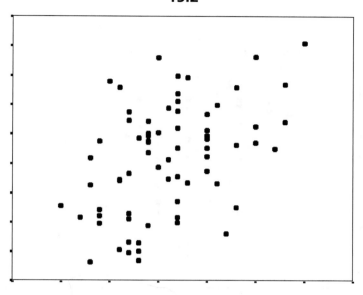

scored low on variable X also scored high on variable Y. The pattern of responses reflected in the scatterplot suggests a positive linear relationship between X and Y. Presumably, if we knew that someone's score on X was relatively high, we would have reason to predict that their Y score also would be relatively high.

Some data sets may produce scatterplots with a clear downward slope. As displayed in Figure 15.3, people who scored relatively high on X tended to score relatively low on Y, and people who scored relatively low on X tended to score relatively high on Y. Few people scored high on X and high on Y, or low on X and low on Y. The pattern of responses in Figure 15.3 suggests a negative linear relationship between X and Y. Presumably, if we knew that someone's score on X was relatively high, we would have reason to predict that their Y score would be relatively low.

Finally, in some data sets there is no apparent relationship between X and Y. Persons who score relatively high on X are equally likely to score high on Y as they are to score low on Y.

In our data set in Figure 15.4 (regarding dispositional anger and aggressive driving), it appears as if the relationship may be negative, as the scores are clustered slightly in the upper-left and lower-right of the scatterplot. In statistics, however, it is rarely sufficient to simply eyeball the data (i.e., scatterplot) and draw conclusions. Rather, we need to quantify this relationship. Regression is a specific procedure for taking data (scores on X and Y for each participant) and from these computing a single statistic that summarizes the relationship between the variables; in essence, regression quantifies the upward or downward slope expressed in the scatterplot, and it is from this quantitative summary that researchers may draw conclusions about the relationship between the variables.

The key to regression is the computation of the **regression line;** it is this line that summarizes the X-Y data, and the slope of the line indicates the strength and direction (positive

15.3

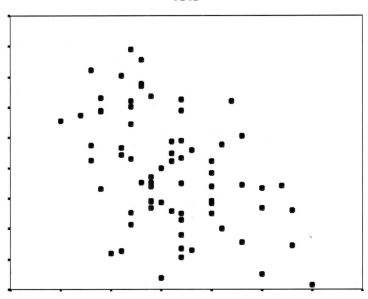

15.4

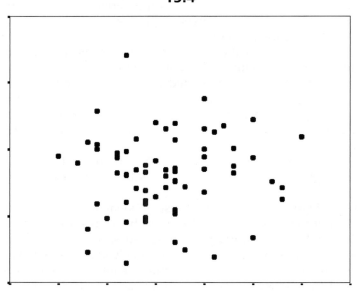

or negative) of this relationship. The formula for plotting a straight line follows the function below:

$$\hat{Y} = A + BX$$

Where $\hat{Y}$ represents a point along the line associated with a given value for X, **A** reflects the **intercept** of the line (i.e., the place on the Y axis where the line begins, and **B** reflects the **slope** of the line. The value for B (i.e., the slope) indicates the extent to which the points on the line increase (or decrease) as X increases. Literally, as our value along the X axis increases by 1, the Y-value of line will change by B; if B is positive, our line will slope by B, and if B is negative our line will slope down by B.

Thus consider the linear equation where A (intercept) is 7.5 and B (slope) is 2.3:

$$\hat{Y} = 7.5 + (2.3)X$$

By selecting arbitrary (random) values for X, we can compute coordinates to form a straight line.

So, when:

$X = 10 \quad \hat{Y} = 7.5 + (2.3)(10) = 30.5$

$X = 06 \quad \hat{Y} = 7.5 + (2.3)(06) = 21.3$

$X = 02 \quad \hat{Y} = 7.5 + (2.3)(02) = 12.1$

We could create a line (see Figure 15.5) by plotting, and then connecting, the X-Y coordinates (10, 30.5), (06, 21.3), and (02, 12.1). Notice that the line begins at the Y axis at 7.5 (the value for the intercept) and increases along the Y axis by 2.3 points (the value of the slope) each time our X increases by 1.

15.5

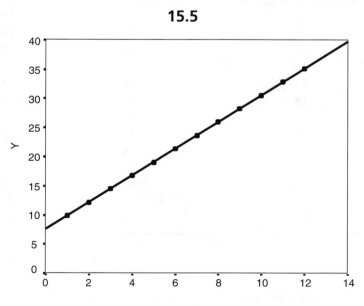

The statistical regression procedure involves computing the value for A (intercept) and the value for B (slope) that produces the equation for a straight line that best fits the data. This line is called a **regression line,** and it is the single straight line (i.e., line of best fit) that comes as close as possible to each point in the data set. In theory, there are an infinite number of straight lines that could be drawn through a scatterplot, but the regression line is the line that fits the data best. Because the regression line best summarizes the data, the slope of this line can be used to interpret the relationship between X and Y in the data set.

Sum of the Cross-Products

In order to compute the slope of a regression line, a researcher first must compute the **sum of cross-products,** or **SP.** The SP is computed as follows:

$$SP = \Sigma XY - ((\Sigma X)(\Sigma Y)/N)$$

Calculating SP involves creating a column of cross-products by multiplying each X by its paired Y, then summing those products. The latter part of the formula involves multiplying the sum of X and the sum of Y, and dividing this product by N. Finally, the latter product is subtracted from the former sum of products.

Using the data from the dispositional anger and aggressive driving study, we find that the sum of anger variable is 221, the sum of the aggressive driving variable is 90, and the sum of the products (anger × driving) is 1498.

Dispositional Anger (X)	Aggressive Driving (Y)	XY
12	13	156
25	05	125
17	08	136
10	14	140
27	03	081
18	10	180
13	08	104
22	01	022
19	06	114
25	07	175
14	04	056
19	11	209
221	**90**	**1498**

Thus:

$$SP = 1498 - ((221)(90)/12) = 1498 - (19890/12) = 1498 - 1657.5 = \textbf{-159.50}$$

Readers may note the formula for SP is very similar to the formula for sums of squares (SS):

$$SS = \Sigma X^2 - ((\Sigma X)^2 / N)$$

In many ways SP and SS are quite similar. In fact, under circumstances where X and Y are identical (X = Y) the sum of cross-products and sum of squares will be the same. One key difference between them is that while sums of squares cannot be negative, sums of cross-products can be negative. A negative SP suggests a negative relationship between X and Y.

Whereas SS describes the variability among a set of scores, the SP reflects the amount of *covariability* among two sets of scores. Recall the raw score formula for SS is $\Sigma(X - \bar{X})^2$, such that to the extent scores deviate further from the mean, the computed SS will be larger.

Similarly, the *raw score formula* for SP—which is mathematically equivalent to $\Sigma XY - ((\Sigma X)(\Sigma Y)/N)$—is:

$$\Sigma(X - \bar{X})(Y - \bar{Y})$$

What happens if in our data set, above average scores on X tend to be paired with above average scores on Y? The mean deviations for X and Y both will tend to be positive (because both scores are greater than the mean), and the products of those mean deviations $[(X - \bar{X})(Y - \bar{Y})]$ will be predominately positive as well (because a positive × positive = positive). Consequently, when we add together these product terms, the sum (SP) will be positive.

On the other hand, if above average scores on X tend to be paired with below average scores on Y, then the mean deviation for one will tend to be positive and the mean deviation for the other will tend to be negative. The product of these mean deviations, therefore, will be predominately negative (because multiplying a positive and a negative number always yields a negative), and the sum of the products (SP) will be negative as well.

Thus, when there is a positive relationship between X and Y in the sample (i.e., high scores are paired with high scores), the resulting SP will be positive. When there appears to be a negative relationship between X and Y in the sample (i.e., high scores are paired with low scores), the resulting SP will be negative.

But what happens when the pairings are inconsistent, i.e., sometimes above average X scores are paired with above average Y scores, and sometimes above average X scores are paired with below average Y scores? In this case, when we multiply the mean deviations, sometimes the product will be positive and other times the product will be negative. If we add together these product terms, the positive and negative products might cancel each other out and produce a sum (SP) close to 0. This is reflected graphically in the fact that the "inconsistent" pairings closely mirror the "no relationship scatterplot" (see Figure 15.3).

The Regression Equation

Thus, the SP reflects the extent to which scores for X and Y vary in a consistent manner (whether Y increases as X increases, or whether Y decreases as X increases). From the SP, we can immediately compute the slope (B) by dividing the SP by the sums of squares for X.

$$B = \frac{\Sigma XY - ((\Sigma X)(\Sigma Y)/N)}{\Sigma X^2 - ((\Sigma X)^2/N)}$$

$$= SP/SS_X$$

The slope (B) indicates the extent to which our regression line changes vertically (along the Y axis) as it increases by 1 along the X axis.

Implicit in regression is that X represents the predictor, or independent, variable (dispositional anger), while Y represents the outcome, or dependent, measure (aggressive driving). Although the SP already has been calculated (SP = –159.50), in order to compute the slope we also need to compute the sums of squares for the dispositional anger variable.

If we square and sum the dispositional anger scores (X) we find that $\Sigma X^2 = 4407$, and that $(\Sigma X)^2 = 221^2 = 48841$.

Thus:

$$SS_X = 4407 - (48841/12) = 4407 - 4070.1 = \textbf{336.92}$$

Finally, we can compute our slope as:

$$B = -159.5/336.9 = \textbf{-0.473}$$

Thus, our regression line decreases by .47 each time X increases by 1.

The intercept (A) indicates the location where the regression line begins at the y axis (where X = 0). The intercept is calculated from the $\bar{X}$, $\bar{Y}$, and B (thus, the slope must be calculated before the intercept (A) is computed).

$$A = \bar{Y} - (\bar{X})(B)$$

Given that N = 12, and $\Sigma X = 221$ and that $\Sigma Y = 90$:

$\bar{X} = 221/12 = 18.417$

$\bar{Y} = 90/12 = 7.500$

$$A = 7.5 - (18.417)(-0.473) = 7.5 + 8.66 = \textbf{16.21}$$

Thus, our regression equation for the line that describes the relationship between X (dispositional anger) and Y (aggressive driving) is:

$$\hat{Y} = \textbf{16.211} + \textbf{(-.473)(X)}$$

By plugging in different values for X, we can produce corresponding $\hat{Y}$ values that generate our regression line. The regression line generated by this equation is the straight line that best fits the data. This line, in fact, indicates the values on Y that we *predict* or *expect* to find for a given value of X.

Using the regression equation $\hat{Y} = 16.211 + (-.473)(X)$, and inserting the X values (dispositional anger) from the data, we produce the following column of predicted Y values (i.e., $\hat{Y}$).

Thus, when the anger score (X) = 12, we predict the aggressive driving score to be: 16.221 + (–.473)(12) = 16.211 – 5.676 = 10.535. When the anger score (X) = 25, we predict the aggressive driving score to be: 16.211 + (–.473)(25) = 16.211 – 11.825 = 4.386, and so forth.

Dispositional Anger (X)	Aggressive Driving (Y)	Ŷ
12	13	10.538
25	05	04.383
17	08	08.171
10	14	11.485
27	03	03.437
18	10	07.697
13	08	10.064
22	01	05.804
19	06	07.224
25	07	04.384
14	04	09.591
19	11	07.224

In the table above, aggressive driving (Y) represents the actual aggressive driving scores, whereas Ŷ reflects the expected aggressive driving scores that we have predicted from participant's dispositional anger (X).

We can connect these predicted Y values to create a regression line, and plot this regression line against the scatterplot of raw scores. This scatterplot reveals participant's *actual* scores compared to the scores that would be predicted from X (see Figure 15.6).

15.6

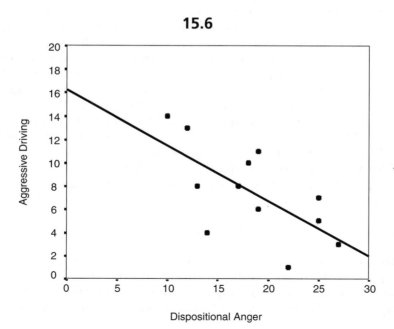

Testing the Null Hypothesis

The utility of regression equation, i.e., the extent to which we can use our regression line to predict Y values from X, depends on whether our slope is statistically significant. According to the null hypothesis, there is no relationship between X and Y in the population: persons who are relatively high on variable X are equally likely also to be relatively high on Y as they are likely to be relatively low on Y. However, in any random sample taken the population, we may just so happen to select individuals where such a relationship appears to exist. It is possible, therefore, that the slope in our sample may not be 0 even if the slope in the population is 0. Before we can use our regression equation to predict Y from X, we must be confident that the slope of our sample is not merely an artifact of sampling.

Before we can test our regression slope to see if it is statistically significant, it is important that a number of assumptions are met. As with t-test and ANOVA, our first assumption is that our variables (X and Y) are normally distributed in the population. Highly skewed data, or samples with outliers, can produce distorted relationships and significance tests. Second, we must assume that the relationship between X and Y is linear (i.e., can be summarized with a straight line) relative to curvilinear. Using linear regression to describe a relationship that actually is curvilinear may produce biased results. Third, there is the assumption of homoscedasticity. This assumption states that the errors (deviations between *actual* Y scores and Y scores *predicted* from the regression line) are equal across all levels of X. This means that the scatterplot should be shaped roughly like an oval or circle. For example, a scatterplot that was shaped like a dumbbell—where scores varied greatly around the regression line for very high and very low values of X, but clustered close to the line around the middle of X— would violate the assumption of homoscedasticity.

Recall that in ANOVA, we measured "natural variability" (i.e., unexplained variability, or error) by examining the extent to which scores varied within each group. This variability is caused or predicted by all possible factors *except* for the variable that defines our groups. We determined whether or not our group means were significantly different by comparing how much those means varied relative to this "natural" variability. In much the same way, we can determine the amount of "natural" variability in regression by measuring the extent to which *actual* Y scores vary around the Y scores predicted from X (i.e., Y – Ŷ). A regression scatterplot where the data points cluster tightly around the regression line is analogous to an ANOVA where the data points cluster tightly around the means of the individual groups. A scatterplot where the data points are spread considerably from the regression line is analogous to an ANOVA where the variability within the groups is relatively large.

It is possible to compute a sum of square for unexplained variability (SS_{ERR}) by computing the difference between actual Y scores and predicted Y scores, squaring those differences, and summing them together:

$$SS_{ERR} = \Sigma(Y - \hat{Y})^2$$

Note that SS_{ERR} is conceptually identical to SS_{WITHIN}. We do not use the term SS_{WITHIN} in this case because we are not really looking "within groups" per se.

From this sum of squares, we can compute a *standard error for the slope* (S_B). This standard error reflects the extent to which we would except slopes (B) to vary if we randomly sampled an infinite number of groups (size N) from the population. This standard error can be used as the denominator (with the slope as the numerator) to compute a t-score to test whether or not the slope is statistically significant.

Computing the standard error of the slope involves two steps. First, we calculate the standard deviation of the errors around the slope (S_E).

The standard deviation of the errors is computed from:

$$S_E = \sqrt{\Sigma(Y - \hat{Y})^2/(N - 2)}$$

Each actual Y value is subtracted from its predicted $\hat{Y}$. These differences scores are squared, and summed. The sum then is divided by N – 2, and the square root is taken to get the standard deviation.

From the error standard deviation, we compute the standard error of the slope (S_B), which serves as the numerator for testing the slope for statistical significance. The standard error of the slope is computed from the error standard deviation divided by the square root of the sum of squares of X. Thus:

$$S_B = S_E/\sqrt{SS_X}$$

The square root of this product is divided by the sum of squares of X (already computed), and the square root of this product is the standard error of the slope:

$$t = B/S_B$$

The t-score is related to the probability that we could have sampled a slope as extreme (from 0) as we did even if the null hypothesis was true. Referring to the t-table, we can find a critical t-score for our selected alpha-level using N – 2 degrees of freedom. If the t-score that we computed exceeds this critical value in absolute value, then we can reject the null hypothesis and conclude that the slope in the population is not 0.

Using the data from the previous example, we can compute $(Y - \hat{Y})$ and $(Y - \hat{Y})^2$.

Dispositional Anger (X)	Aggressive Driving (Y)	$\hat{Y}$	$Y - \hat{Y}$	$(Y - \hat{Y})^2$
12	13	10.538	2.462	06.150
25	05	04.383	0.617	00.348
17	08	08.171	–0.171	00.029
10	14	11.485	2.515	06.452
27	03	03.437	–0.437	00.221
18	10	07.697	2.303	05.290
13	08	10.064	–2.064	04.202
22	01	05.804	–4.804	23.232
19	06	07.224	–1.224	1.5129
25	07	04.384	2.616	06.708
14	04	09.591	–5.591	31.136
19	11	07.224	3.776	14.213

Summing the squared deviations we get:

$$\Sigma(Y - \hat{Y})^2 = \textbf{99.49}$$

Recall that N = 12 (i.e., 12 pairs of X-Y data). Our standard deviation of the errors (around the slope) is:

$$S_E = \sqrt{\Sigma(Y - \hat{Y})^2/(N - 2)}$$

Thus:

$$S_E = \sqrt{99.491/(12 - 2)} = \sqrt{99.491/(10)} = \sqrt{9.949} = \textbf{3.15}$$

From this, we compute the standard error of the slope. Recall that SS_X (computed on page 172) is **336.92.**

$$S_B = S_E/\sqrt{SS_X} = 3.154/\sqrt{336.92} = 3.154/18.355 = \textbf{0.172}$$

Once we have computed the standard error, we can compute a t-score. Recall that our slope (B) was found to be –0.473 (see page 172).

$$t = B/S_E = -0.473/0.172 = \textbf{–2.75}$$

Our T_{CRIT} (assume two-tailed α = .05 and df = 12 – 2 = 10) is 2.23.

Because our computed t-score exceeds the T_{CRIT} (in absolute value), $|-2.76| > 2.23$, we reject H0 and can conclude that the relationship (slope) between dispositional anger and aggressive driving in the population is not 0. In fact, because our slope is negative, we conclude that the relationship in the population is *negative;* as dispositional anger increases, measures of aggressive driving decrease. Recall at the beginning of this chapter we hypothesized a positive relationship between the two variables. Thus, although we rejected the null hypothesis (that the relationship in the population was 0), the results did not support our own hypothesis about the relationship being positive.

Note that if we do not reject the null hypothesis, we must assume that the slope (B) in the population is 0, as there is not enough evidence for us to be confident that the slope obtained in our sample is due to anything other than random error. If B = 0, then we must re-compute our intercept because the formula for the intercept also includes the value for the slope.

If A = $\bar{Y}$ – ($\bar{X}$)(B) and B = 0, then our intercept becomes the mean of Y ($\bar{Y}$).

Thus, our new regression equation under the null hypothesis is:

$$\hat{Y} = \bar{Y} + BX = \bar{Y}$$

If the null hypothesis is true and we wish to predict a person's score on Y, the mean of Y is our best guess. Only if the slope is statistically significant can we use X to help our prediction of Y.

Regression and ANOVA

The purpose of this section is to demonstrate that significance tests for regression can be obtained via the ANOVA approach, as well as the t-test approach.

Another way to conceptualize the slope (B) is to consider the extent to which lines on the slope deviate from the mean Y scores $(\hat{Y} - \bar{Y})$. $\bar{Y}$, of course, is a constant; in the data above, the sum of aggressive driving scores is $\Sigma Y/N = 90/12 = 7.5$. For each participant, we could compute the difference between that person's predicted score $(\hat{Y})$ from the mean $(\bar{Y})$, square that difference score, and sum them together. This is the sum of squares associated with the regression slope (SS_{REG}).

$$SS_{REG} = \Sigma(\hat{Y} - \bar{Y})^2$$

If our regression slope was very shallow, as depicted in the figure below, the deviation between the points on the regression slope and the mean of Y will be quite small. Consequently, the sum of the squared deviations (between $\hat{Y} - \bar{Y}$) will be small. If the slope is quite steep, some points along the regression will deviate from the constant $\bar{Y}$ by a relatively large margin. Consequently, the sum of the squared deviations (between $\hat{Y} - \bar{Y}$) will be relatively large. SS_{REG} is conceptually similar to SS_{BET} in ANOVA; it reflects the variability in Y attributable to participants' scores on X.

If we consider our data on dispositional anger and aggressive driving:

Dispositional Anger (X)	Aggressive Driving (Y)	$\bar{Y}$	$\hat{Y} - \bar{Y}$	$(\hat{Y} - \bar{Y})^2$
12	13	7.5	3.038	09.228
25	05	7.5	−3.117	09.713
17	08	7.5	0.671	00.450
10	14	7.5	3.985	15.877
27	03	7.5	−4.063	16.512
18	10	7.5	0.197	00.039
13	08	7.5	2.564	06.576
22	01	7.5	−1.696	02.878
19	06	7.5	−0.276	00.076
25	07	7.5	−3.117	09.713
14	04	7.5	2.091	04.372
19	11	7.5	−0.276	00.076

The sum of squared deviations between the regression line and the mean of Y is:

$$SS_{REG} = \Sigma(\hat{Y} - \bar{Y})^2 = \mathbf{75.51}$$

Recall that we already computed the sums of squares for the errors (see page 176):

$$SS_{ERR} = \Sigma(Y - \hat{Y})^2 = \textbf{99.49}$$

Given that these sums of squares are known, we could compute a source table for regression much like we did for ANOVA, where SS_{REG} is treated as our SS_{BET} and SS_{ERR} is treated as SS_{WITHIN}. Note that we have not computed SS_{TOT} but instead computed our SS_{ERR} directly.

Because we have both SS_{REG} and SS_{ERR} we do not need to compute SS_{TOT}. However, we will compute it nevertheless in this example. If we square and sum our Y scores (ΣY^2) we get 850. The sum of Y is 90, and $\Sigma(Y^2)$ is 8100. Thus, our SS_{TOT} equals 850 – (8100/12) = **175**. Note that if we add together our SS_{REG} and SS_{ERR} we also get 175.0. In regression as well as ANOVA, the sums of squares that we *attempt to explain* with X (either membership in a particular group or a score on variable X) plus the sums of squares that we *cannot explain* (variability around the group means or around the regression line) equals the sums of squares total. Both ANOVA and regression are based on partitioning variance into an explained portion and an unexplained portion.

The degrees of freedom associated with the variability due to the slope (SS_{REG}) is equal to 1. The degrees of freedom associated with the unexplained, or error, variability (SS_{ERR}) is equal to N – 2 (one df is lost because of the slope, and another df is lost because of the intercept).

Source	SS	df	MS	F
Total	175*	11	15.91	—
Regression	75.51	1	75.51	7.59
Error	99.49	10	9.95	—

The F-score that we computed (7.59) is statistically analogous to our t-test in the previous section of –2.75. In fact, it is no coincidence that the square root of our F-score equals the t-score, i.e., $\sqrt{7.59}$ = 2.75. For a test involving 1 df (either a single regression slope or comparing the means of two groups), the t-score computed using a t-test will equal the square root of the F-score computed using the ANOVA approach.

Correlation

The regression procedure produces a straight line that best fits a set of X-Y data; the points on this line reflect expected or predicted values for the outcome (Y) for each level of the predictor variable (X). By plugging an X value into our regression equation, we can solve for the predicted $\hat{Y}$.

Sometimes, however, the researcher is not interested in making predictions per se, but rather is interested more in better understanding the relationship between the two variables. A researcher may wish to draw conclusions about the strength of the relationship between X and Y. Note that null hypothesis states only that the relationship between X and Y is 0 in the population; even if the null hypothesis is rejected, and we can conclude confidently that some meaningful relationship between X and Y exists, it does not quantify whether the relationship is relatively weak, moderate, or strong. Note that a stronger relationship indicates relatively more precision in our predictions; i.e., if we know someone's score for X, we can be quite accurate in our estimate of their score for Y. In an extreme sense, a perfect relationship between X and Y indicates that the two variables are redundant. If we measure the heights of students in a class in inches (X) and then again in centimeters (Y), we would be able to perfectly predict one from the other. If we measured the length of each student's right arm (X) and then their left arm (Y), we would anticipate finding a very strong relationship between the two, as people tend to have two arms that are equal in length), but chances are this relationship is not perfect (sometimes people's left and right arms are not always of 100% equal length). A *weak* relationship might indicate that knowing a person's X score gives a very general indication of their Y score, but does so with very little precision.

Unfortunately, we cannot simply eyeball a regression slope (B), even if we know it to be statistically significant, and determine whether the relationship between X and Y is weak, moderate, or strong. It is true that all things being equal, the magnitude of the slope (steepness) reflects the strength of the relationship, whereas steeper slopes indicate a relatively stronger relationship; however, the slope also is greatly influenced by the scale of the Y variable. Recall that the slope literally indicates the extent to which our expected Y scores change as X increases by 1. For example, a researcher might use regression to assess the relationship between college GPA (X) and annual income one year after graduation (Y). It is likely that our Y variable will be measured in thousands of dollars (since people earn tens of thousands of dollars per year). Our slope (B), therefore, would reflect how much we expect income to change as GPA increases by 1. Because our outcome (Y) concerns thousands of dollars, we would expect our slope (B) to also be in the range of several thousand dollars.

Conversely, imagine that a researcher used college GPA to predict a person's blood alcohol concentration (BAC) on a given night in order to understand whether scholastic success relates to drinking behavior. BACs are measured on a very small scale (e.g., .000, .080, .124). If we wanted to determine how much we might expect BACs (Y) to change as GPAs increase by 1, our slope (B) invariably will be small simply because the scale of our outcome variable is small.

The slope predicting annual income from GPA, of course, will be larger than the slope predicting BAC from GPA because the scores for annual income are on a larger scale than are scores for BAC. This does not imply, however, that the relationship between GPA and annual income is stronger (a better predictor) than the relationship between GPA and BAC. Accordingly, our slope values are *scale dependent* in that they depend largely on the unit of measurement used for Y. Thus we cannot use the magnitude of the regression slope to assess the strength or magnitude of the relationship between X and Y.

In a previous chapter we were confronted with the issue of making comparisons of scores measured on different scales (e.g., a sprinter's speed to a weight lifter's bench press, or a score on an organic chemistry test to a score on an introduction to psychology test). In such cases, we standardized the scores by transforming them into Z-scores; i.e., we represented each score in terms of the number of standard deviations it varied from the mean of the distribution. In the case of regression, we could standardize our regression slope by first transforming our X and Y data into Z-scores. If we conducted regression using Z-scores instead of raw scores, the slopes that resulted from our analyses would always be comparable; there no longer would be concern over the fact that slopes are scale dependent, because using Z-scores for our data puts everything onto the same scale.

Pearson correlation is simply regression where the X and Y values first are standardized. The end result of a correlation analysis is the correlation coefficient (r), the slope obtained when using standardized data. When computed correctly, correlations will range in magnitude from –1 to 1; a correlation that exceeds +1 or exceeds –1 indicates that a mistake in the calculations has been made. The closer the correlation (r) is to 0, the weaker the relationship (a correlation of 0 indicates no relationship). As the correlation approaches 1, it suggests a stronger and stronger positive relationship, and as it approaches –1 it suggests a stronger and stronger negative relationship. Note that correlations of +1 and –1 indicate perfect relationships; i.e., Y may be predicted from X without error (e.g., height in centimeters can be predicted perfectly from height in inches). Because the correlation is based on standardized data, we can use the magnitude of the correlation (how close it is to +1 or –1) to suggest the strength of the relationship between X and Y. Note that Pearson correlation is the only type of correlation discussed in this book, and is used when both X and Y are continuous or score variables. Other types of correlation, such as Spearman and point biserial correlation, are used when one variable (X) is score/continuous, and the other variable (Y) is ordinal, or binary (dichotomous), respectively.

If our data already are in Z-score form, the correlation coefficient can be computed from:

$$r = \Sigma Z_X Z_Y / N$$

The paired Z-scores are multiplied together, and products are summed together across participants. This sum then is divided by N to produce the correlation coefficient. This formula is quite simple because we know that the variances of the standardized X and Y variables are 1, and thus we need to compute these separately. Note, however, that we rarely will have data already transformed into Z-scores, and that it would be quite tedious to first compute the means and standard deviations of X and Y, and then compute Z-scores for the Xs and the Ys, before using the formula above.

Fortunately, we do not need to go through the process of computing Z-scores for our X and Y scores because the computational formula for the Pearson correlation standardizes those in the process. The computational formula for **r** in fact is quite similar to that for the slope in regression:

$$r = SP / \sqrt{(SS_X \times SS_Y)}$$

where:

$$SP = \Sigma XY - ((\Sigma X)(\Sigma Y)/N)$$

Thus computing the correlation coefficient (r) is similar to computing the regression slope (B) in that it involves the sum of cross-products (SP) in the numerator and the sums of square for X in the denominator. In addition, however, correlation requires the sum of squares for Y. The sum of squares for X and Y are multiplied together, and the square root serves as the denominator in the equation.

Using the data from the dispositional anger and aggressive driving example, we already know:

N = 12

SP = –159.50

SS_X = 336.92

Referring back to aggressive driving scores (Y), we know that ΣY = 90, that $(\Sigma Y)^2$ = 8100, and we square and then sum each Y score, ΣY^2 = 850.

Aggressive Driving (Y)	Y²
13	169
05	025
08	064
14	196
03	009
10	100
08	064
01	001
06	036
07	049
04	016
11	121
90	**850**

Our SS_Y = 850 – (8100/12) = 175.0.
Therefore, our correlation (r) equals:

$$r = SP/\sqrt{(SS_X \times SS_Y)} = -159.50/\sqrt{(336.92 \times 175.0)}$$
$$= -159.50/\sqrt{58,961} = -159.5/242.82 = \textbf{–.657}$$

As expected, our correlation coefficient falls between –1 and +1. Before we use it to assess the strength of the relationship between dispositional anger and aggressive driving, we need to determine whether or not it is statistically significant. According to the null hypothesis, the correlation between X and Y in the population is 0, and thus any correlation we obtain in our sample is simply the result of random fluctuation. Note that because the correlation (r) and the slope (B) are fundamentally the same things (the former is the version of the latter based on standardized data), the significance test for the slope will indicate the same results as will the significance test of the correlation. We know from the previous section that we can reject H0 regarding the regression slope (B), and thus we also will reject the null hypothesis for the correlation (r). Nevertheless, we will demonstrate the steps for testing the statistical significance of the correlation coefficient directly.

Whereas regression relied on t-scores or F-scores to test the null hypothesis, it is possible to determine whether the correlation is statistically significant by comparing the computed r-value to a critical r-value (R_{CRIT}) obtained from a table.

Below is a greatly reduced table of critical correlation values. The far left column lists the degrees of freedom for the test (which are based on N – 2), and the remaining four columns reflect two-tailed α-levels. By cross-indexing the degrees of freedom with the appropriate α-level, we can obtain the R_{CRIT} for the test. If the absolute value of our computed r-score exceeds the critical value from the table, we can reject the null hypothesis and conclude it is unlikely enough that we could have obtained our correlation coefficient simply due to chance under the null hypothesis, that there must be a relationship between X and Y in the population.

Reduced Pearson Correlation Table

df = (N – 2)	.10	.05	.02	.01
1	.988	.997	.999	.999
5	.669	.754	.833	.874
10	.497	.576	.658	.708
20	.360	.423	.492	.537
50	.231	.273	.322	.354
100	.164	.195	.230	.254

Our computed correlation was **–.657,** and we find in the table the R_{CRIT} for our study is .576 (assuming two-tailed α-level = .05 and 12 – 2 = 10 dfs). Because $|-.657| > .576$, we can reject the null hypothesis. Note that if our correlation (in absolute value) had not exceeded the critical value of .576, we would have concluded that there is not enough evidence to be confident (at the α = .05 level) that our results are anything more than random error, and thus we must assume that the correlation between X and Y in the population is 0.

Given that we have rejected the null hypothesis, we can interpret the magnitude of the correlation coefficient. A common rule of thumb suggests the following:

Absolute correlations ($|r|$) between **0.1 – 0.29** are considered small, and suggest a weak (albeit statistically significant) relationship between X and Y.

Absolute correlations ($|r|$) between **0.30 – 0.49** are considered moderate, and suggest a moderate relationship between X and Y.

Absolute correlations ($|r|$) of **0.50 – 1.0** are considered large, and suggest a strong relationship between X and Y.

Correlations below 0.1, even if statistically significant, are considered trivial.

Note from the R_{CRIT} table above that with a large sample size (e.g., when N = 102, df = 100) the critical value to reject the null hypothesis is only .195 (assuming two-tailed α = .05). Thus, a weak correlation can still be statistically significant. We can conclude the observed correlation is not entirely random error (i.e., that there is some relationship between X and Y in the population), although this relationship may be quite weak. X scores are related to Y scores; however, there is considerable imprecision in that relationship.

PRACTICE PROBLEMS

15.1 Consider the X – Y data below. Draw a scatterplot that summarizes the 11 data points.

X	Y
17	12
12	3
09	4
14	7
11	9
07	10
16	8
12	4
12	3
03	1
20	10

15.2 Calculate the regression equation that best fits the data. Assuming this regression line was statistically significant, what would you predict someone's Y score to be if their score on X was 11? Assuming the this regression line was not statistically significant, what would you predict someone's Y score to be if their score on X was 11?

15.3 Using the regression equation, compute the predicted score for each score in the data set.

15.4 Compute the deviation between predicted and actual scores $(\hat{Y} - Y)$ for each score. Next, square and sum each of these deviations to compute an SS_{ERR} term, i.e., $\Sigma((\hat{Y} - Y)2$.

15.5 Define the standard deviation of the errors and the standard error of the slope.

15.6 Using the data above, compute the standard deviation of the errors and the standard error of the slope. Test the slope (B) for statistical significance.

15.7 Describe the similarities between ANOVA and regression.

15.8 Using the data above, compute SS_{REG} from the slope.

15.9 Compute the correlation between X and Y. Test this correlation for statistical significance.

Chi-Square Analysis

To date, each statistical test that we have discussed—Z-tests, t-tests, ANOVA, regression, and correlation—are similar in that each requires that the dependent variable (outcome) be a score or continuous variable. In the case of Z-tests, t-tests, and ANOVA, the mean of the outcome variable is compared between or among groups; if a mean cannot be computed for a variable (i.e., because it is nominal, or possibly ordinal), then it cannot be used as the outcome in a Z-test, t-test, or ANOVA. Similarly, in correlation and regression, the scores of the independent or predictor variable are used to indicate an expected value in the outcome. This assumes that the variable score has some relative meaning (i.e., higher scores indicate more of the variable). In cases where the outcome is categorical, and the value or score indicate membership in a group (e.g., 1 = men, 2 = women), regression and correlation are not appropriate. Note further that for each of these tests, there always is an explicit assumption that the variables are normally distributed and nominal and ordinal data rarely follow a normal distribution.

However, there are many research questions where the outcome measure of interest in fact is categorical; we may wish to study whether people voted "Yes" or "No" on a particular issue, whether there is the presence or absence of some feature in a given environment, whether or not a participant previously engaged in specific behavior, etc. **Chi-square tests** (χ^2) are described as *non-parametric* tests if they do not require that outcomes variables be normally distributed. In fact, they specifically are used to examine relationships between categorical variables. Chi-square tests can also be used to determine whether the proportion of scores falling in different categories is significantly different from some hypothesized value.

Whereas Z-tests, t-tests, ANOVA, regression, and correlation involve participant's scores, the chi-square test concerns *frequencies,* i.e., the number of participants (counts) that fall into different categories.

As a rule of thumb, chi-square is computed from the following formula:

$$\chi^2 = \Sigma \,((f_O - f_E)^2/f_E)$$

where f_O = observed frequencies (i.e., the frequencies of cases that we observe in our data), and f_E = expected frequencies (counts in each group or cell that we would expect if the null hypothesis was true). Chi-square is computed by examining the observed frequencies within a given cell (group), subtracting the expected frequencies, and then squaring this difference. The squared difference then is divided by the expected frequency for that cell. This process is carried out for each cell, and the final product for each cell is summed together to obtain the chi-square. Since observed frequencies are obtained in the data, the key to conducting a chi-square test rests in determining the expected frequencies.

Chi-Square Goodness-of-Fit Test

The purpose of the chi-square goodness of fit test is used to compare counts (proportions) of cases against hypothesized values. Imagine that a political researcher is interested in studying the opinions of registered voters towards "Proposition A." The researcher hypothesizes that Proposition A is quite controversial, and the vote will be split 50/50 (i.e., half will support Proposition A, half will not support Proposition A).

The researcher interviews a random sample of 70 voters and asks them to indicate whether they support "Proposition A." Participants' responses are categorical (i.e., "Yes" or "No").

The study reveals that 44 participants responded "Yes" to the question and the remaining 26 participants responded "No." Thus, although the researcher expected that 35 participants (i.e., 50%) would vote "Yes" and 35 (i.e., 50%) would vote "No," the researcher found that 62.9% (i.e., 44/70) voted "Yes," and 37.1% (i.e., 26/70) voted "No." However, it is not clear whether the proportions in the sample (.629/.371) are significantly different from those expected proportions (.50/.50), or whether they could have been obtained simply due to random chance. In this example, the null hypothesis states that voting preference in the population is 50/50, and the differences found in the sample are due simply to random sampling error. Note that the researcher could have hypothesized proportions other than 50/50 (i.e., 30/70, 40/60).

When the researcher has hypothesized the distribution of cases between or among conditions, expected frequencies can be computed simply by multiplying the proportion hypothesized for each group by the total number of counts. Thus, if the sample size is 70 and we expect 50% to vote "Yes" and 50% to vote "No," our expected frequencies would be 35 and

35. Below we show the observed frequencies (from the data) and the expected frequencies (derived from the researcher's hypothesis).

	Observed	Expected
"Yes" on Proposition A	44	35
"No" on Proposition B	26	35
Total Frequencies	70	70

If we compute chi-square according to:

$$\chi^2 = \Sigma \left((f_O - f_E)^2 / f_E \right)$$

We find:

$$\chi^2 = (44 - 35)^2/35 + (26 - 35)^2/35 = (9^2/35) + (-9^2/35)$$
$$= 81/35 + 81/35 = 2.31 + 2.31 = \mathbf{4.63}$$

Like every other statistical test discussed in this book, the our test statistic (in this case, the chi-square score) must be compared to critical value associated with a particular degrees of freedom and alpha-level in order to determine whether the difference between the observed (data) and expected values is statistically significant. In the case of the chi-square goodness-of-fit test, degrees of freedom are equal to the number of response levels minus one; thus, when there are only two possible levels (e.g., "Yes" and "No") then df = 1.

A greatly reduced table of critical χ^2 values is presented below.

Reduced χ^2 Table

df	.05	.025	.01
1	3.84	5.02	6.64
2	5.99	7.38	9.21
3	7.81	9.35	11.34
4	9.49	11.14	13.28
5	11.07	12.83	15.09
10	18.31	20.48	23.21
20	31.41	34.17	37.57

Assuming α = .05 and 1 df, our critical χ^2 value equals 3.84. In this example, our computed χ^2 (4.63) exceeded the critical value of 3.84; thus the proportion of participants that actually voted "Yes" and "No" was significantly different from the proportion that was hypothesized to vote "Yes" and "No." Essentially, a higher percentage of participants voted "Yes" (62.9%) than was expected (50%).

If the researcher has hypothesized that 70% would vote "Yes" and 30% would vote "No," then our expected values for "Yes" votes would be 70 cases × .70 (hypothesized proportion) = 49 cases. Our expected values for "No" votes would be 70 cases × .30 = 21 cases.

Thus, assuming a hypothesized 70/30 split, our data would look like:

	Observed	Expected
"Yes" on Proposition A	44	49
"No" on Proposition B	26	21
Total Frequencies	70	70

$$\chi^2 = (44 - 49)^2/49 + (26 - 21)^2/21 = (5^2/49) + (-5^2/21)$$
$$= 25/49 + 25/21 = 0.51 + 1.19 = \mathbf{0.70.}$$

This χ^2 clearly does not exceed the critical value of 3.84; the proportion of "Yes" and "No" responses regarding Proposition A did not differ significantly from the hypothesized 70/30 split.

Chi-Square Test of Independence

It is not particularly common, however, for researchers to have a priori hypotheses regarding the proportion of responses. In much the same way that researches typically do not have a priori μs for conducting single sample t-tests, studies are conducted by collecting data from more than one group of which one group may serve as a comparison (similar to using an independent sample t-test instead of a single sample test). The chi-square test of independence is used to test whether there is a relationship between two categorical variables; for example, is there a relationship between voter's political affiliations (Republican v. Democrat v. Independent) and whether they vote "Yes" or "No" on Proposition A; whether or not full length mirrors are present and whether or not an experimental cheats on a task (i.e., mirrors have been found to increase awareness of personal values); whether membership in a fraternity or sorority (v. no Greek affiliation) is associated with engaging in high risk drinking. The chi-square will allow researchers to determine whether knowing which group a person is in will help predict his or her response category.

A relationship between two categorical variables is identified by differences in proportions; for example, whether the proportion of Democrats who vote "Yes" for Proposition A is different from the proportion of Republicans who vote "Yes" for Proposition A; whether a smaller proportion of participants who perform a task in front of a mirror cheat on the task than those who perform the task without a mirror. The null hypothesis for the chi-square test is always that the categorical independent variable and the categorical dependent (response) variable are "independent," i.e., unrelated, to others in the population. If the null hypothesis is retained, then any relationship (i.e., differences in proportions) observed in the sample must be assumed to be the result of random error.

Imagine that the political researcher not only wishes to examine voters' preference of Proposition A, but wishes to determine whether preference for or against the proposition varies as a function of political affiliation. He surveys 100 voters and asks them to determine (1) whether they consider themselves to be Democrats, Republicans, or Independents, and (2) whether they vote "Yes" or "No" for Proposition A. The observed frequencies of surveyed voters that fall in each category are provided below.

	Democrat	Republican	Independent	Total
Yes	35	11	10	*56*
No	18	22	4	*44*
Total	*53*	*33*	*14*	*100*

Recall that in this example we do not have a priori hypotheses regarding the proportions of responses. Rather, for the Test of Independence we can derive the frequencies we would expect to find for each group assuming that the two variables are unrelated from the marginal frequencies (i.e., the number of Democrats, Republicans, and Independents, and the number of Yes and No voters).

The expected frequencies for a given cell (group) is equal to the total frequency of that cell's row multiplied by the total frequency of that cell's column, divided by the total frequency. Thus:

$$f_E = (f_{ROW} \times f_{COL})/f_{TOT}$$

Using the data above, the first cell (Democrats – Yes) has a row total of 56 and a column total of 53, and of course the total frequency is 100. Thus the *expected* frequency for that cell is $(56 \times 53)/100 = 2968/100 = 29.7$. For the second cell (Democrats – No), the row total is 44 and the column total is 53; thus the expected frequency for that cell is $(44 \times 53)/100 = 2332/100 = 23.3$. For the third cell (Republican – Yes), the row total is 56 and the column total is 33; thus, the expected frequency is $(56 \times 33)/100 = 1848/100 = 18.5$. This procedure is computed for each of the six cells.

The observed frequency, row total, column total, and expected frequency for each cell is depicted in the table below. Note that the sum total frequency for each cell is 100. Note that the sum of the expected frequencies equals the total frequency (i.e., 100). Thus our expectation does not change to total sample size, it simply indicates the distribution of counts among the six Political Affiliation × Voting Response category cells.

Political Affiliation	Response Category	Observed Frequency	Row Total	Column Total	Expected Frequency
Democrat	*Yes*	35	56	53	*29.68*
Democrat	*No*	18	44	53	*23.32*
Republican	*Yes*	11	56	33	*18.48*
Republican	*No*	22	44	33	*14.52*
Independent	*Yes*	10	56	14	*07.84*
Independent	*No*	04	44	14	*06.16*

Now that we have the expected frequencies for each cell, we can compute a chi-square using the χ^2 formula.

$$\chi^2 = \Sigma((f_O - f_E)^2/f_E)$$

Recall that the expected frequencies describe the counts we would expect to find in each cell if our independent variable (i.e., political affiliation) and dependent variable (i.e., voting response category) were independent of each other (i.e., unrelated). When in fact there is no relationship between our two variables, then the observed frequencies (based on our data) should be very close to our expected frequencies; the relatively small observed v. expected discrepancies would be reflected in a relatively small χ^2 value. If in fact there is a relationship between our two variables, then our observed frequencies should be quite different from what we expect to find if the null hypothesis was true. These relatively large deviations between observed and expected frequencies will produce a relatively larger χ^2 value.

Political Affiliation	Response Category	Observed Frequency	Expected Frequency	$(f_O - f_E)^2$	$((f_O - f_E)^2/f_E)$
Democrat	Yes	35	29.68	28.30	0.95
Democrat	No	18	23.32	28.30	1.21
Republican	Yes	11	18.48	55.95	3.03
Republican	No	22	14.52	55.95	3.85
Independent	Yes	10	07.84	04.67	0.60
Independent	No	04	06.16	04.67	0.76

We compute χ^2 by summing together the products in the final column.

$$\chi^2 = 0.95 + 1.21 + 3.03 + 3.85 + 0.60 + 0.76 = \mathbf{10.4}$$

In the case of the chi-square Test of Independence, our critical χ^2 value is computed from:

$$df = (\text{\# rows} - 1)(\text{\# columns} - 1)$$

Our original table had two rows (Yes and No) and thee columns (Democrat, Republican, and Independent), thus the df = $(2 - 1)(3 - 1) = (1)(2) = 2$.

Thus, given 2 df and $\alpha = .05$, our $\chi^2_{CRIT} = 5.99$. Because our computed χ^2 exceeds the critical value (10.4 > 5.99) we can reject the null hypothesis and conclude that there is a relationship between political affiliation and voter responses.

Because we rejected the null hypothesis, we now examine the proportion of scores within the cells. If the focus of the researcher is to compare how Democrats, Republicans, and Independent voters voted for Proposition A, we can display the proportion of "Yes" voters and "No" voters for each political party.

	Democrat	Republican	Independent
Yes	.66	.33	.71
No	.34	.66	.29

The statistically significant chi-square test indicates that Democrats voted considerably differently than did Republicans, and in fact the Independents voted quite similar to Democrats. Essentially, the fact that 66% of Democrats voted "Yes" makes them significantly different than Republicans (only 33% of whom voted "Yes"). Knowing whether a participant is a Democrat, Republican, or Independent helps us predict whether the person likely voted "Yes" or "No" on Proposition A. Note that had we failed to reject the null hypothesis, we would have concluded that there is no relationship between political affiliation and voting response category in the population. According to the null hypothesis, the pattern of results in our sample occurred because by chance we sampled Democrats who just happened to favored Proposition A, and sampled Republicans who just happened to oppose Proposition B.

PRACTICE PROBLEMS

16.1 A researcher wants to determine whether or not a coin she has is "fair." If the coin is fair, she would expect that it would land on heads 50% of the time, and on tails 50% of the time. She flips the coin 40 times and gets 26 heads and 14 tails. Conduct the appropriate statistical test to determine whether her results deviate significantly from the expected 50/50 flip.

16.2 How is the chi-square Test of Independence similar, and how is it different, from factorial ANOVA?

16.3 Imagine that a marketing researcher has collected data on footwear preferences for men v. women. She surveyed 50 participants and asked them to indicate which of four types of footwear they prefer most. Conduct the appropriate statistical test to determine whether men and women differ on this area.

	Sandals	Sneakers	Leather Shoes	Boots	Other
Male	12	34	26	18	
Female	26	10	14	32	

16.4 People in serious dating relationships, casual dating relationships and non-dating relationships were asked whether they thought a person described in a picture was highly attractive, moderately attractive, or average. Is there a relationship between dating status and judgment of physical attractiveness? Frequency counts are given in the following table. Conduct the appropriate statistical test and determine whether there is a relationship between dating status and attractiveness ratings of the picture.

	Highly Attractive	Moderately Attractive	Average
Serious	5	12	22
Casual	10	28	23
Non-Dating	34	18	9

Answers

Chapter 1 Answers

1.1   The **population** describes everyone (in some cases, even people past and future) to which the research should generalize. A **sample** is a subset of that population—often drawn at random—that actually participates in the research (i.e., they are our research subjects). A **statistic** is a characteristic, quality, or descriptive value of the sample (for example, the proportion of subjects in our sample that are male is a statistic). A **parameter** is a characteristic, quality, or descriptive value of the population (for example, the proportion of all registered U.S. voters that is male might be a parameter). **Inferential statistics** refers to the process of estimating a population parameter using a sample statistic.

1.2   Some statistics are **descriptive**—the purpose is to describe characteristics or qualities of a target group. Other statistics concern examining the **relationship between or among variables;** for example, is it the case that people who have relatively high SAT scores get relatively high GPAs; does knowing whether someone went through an SAT prep course predict higher SAT scores than if a person did not go through an SAT prep course.

1.3.1 Descriptive

1.3.2 Descriptive

1.3.3 Relationship

1.3.4 Relationship

1.3.5 Descriptive

1.3.6 Relationship

1.4.   **Sampling error** refers to the extent that our sample statistic deviates from the population parameter (because our sample is not entirely representative of the population). For example, we may be interested in knowing what proportion of registered voters support the President, and a sample of 500 voters may indicate 49%. If the true population value (based on all registered voters) was 44% approval, the difference between the 49% statistics and the 44% parameter is due to sampling error.

Chapter 2 Answers

2.1   Measurement is the process of assigning quantitative values that reflect the level of the variable that each individual possesses; we take conceptual numbers and turn them into numbers that we use in analysis.

2.2   A conceptual variable is a variable that reflects an abstract concept, typically not something that is tangible (e.g., a person's level of introversion, self-esteem, intelligence). A measured variable reflects the "scores" (quantitative values) that reflect how much of that variable a person has.

2.3   Reliability refers to the extent that a measurement can be produced. Assuming that the true amount of variable doesn't change, do our measures produce the same score (or approximately the same score) each time we use it? If a measure involves multiple items, do subsets of these items produce similar scores?

2.4   Test-retest procedures determine whether the measure produces similar scores each time it is used to measure the same level of variable in a subject. Inter-item reliability measures whether different subsets of items (from the same scale) produce similar scores.

2.5   Validity concerns the extent to which a measure corresponds (assesses) the conceptual variable in question. For example, does a measure of self-esteem really reflect different levels of self-esteem within people.

2.6   Validity is assessed through convergent and discriminant methods. Convergent validity concerns the extent to which the measured variable correlates to other measured variables that it should (according to theory) correlate with. Discriminant validity concerns the extent to which the measured variable correlates with other measured variables that it should not (according to theory) correlate with.

2.7   A variable that is valid must also be reliable (how can it accurately assess the construct in question if it gives different scores each time); however, just because a measure is reliable does not mean that it is valid. Such a measure could consistently measure a construct other than the one that was intended.

2.8   **Nominal Scale:** The scores reflect what group or category a subject is in; different scores indicate different groups. **Ordinal Scale:** The scores reflect different groups or categories, but these categories have an inherent structure or order; these groups can be ranked, but differences between or among groups cannot be quantified. **Interval Scale:** Scores can reflect the amount of a variable in a subject. Furthermore, differences between or among scores can be quantified. With an interval scale, for example, it is appropriate to say that Person A scored 10 points higher than Person B. **Ratio Scale:** Scores reflect amount of a variable in a subject, and a score of 0 reflects that the subject has none of the variable. For example, something moving 0 MPH has no speed.

2.9.1 ordinal

2.9.2 ratio

2.9.3   ordinal

2.9.4   interval

2.9.5   nominal

2.9.6   interval

2.9.7   ratio

2.9.8   nominal

2.10.1 continuous

2.10.2 categorical

2.10.3 score

2.10.4 score

2.10.5 continuous

2.10.6 categorical

Chapter 3 Answers

3.1   (1) begin with theory; (2) derive hypotheses; (3) design and conduct study to test hypotheses; (4) conduct analyses; (5) interpret and apply results

3.2   **empiricism:** science should be based on observable data; **objectivism:** data collection should minimize bias; **skepticism:** researchers should be willing to question their own theories if inconsistent with the data

3.3   Correlational methods are used to assess the relationship between two variables: if scores on variable X increase do scores on variable Y change systemically? A positive relationship exists if as scores on variable X increase, scores on variable Y tend to increase as well. A negative relationship exits if as scores on variable X increase, scores on variable Y tend to decrease.

3.4   A correlation between X and Y may exist because X causes Y, or because Y causes X, or both X and Y are caused by a 3rd variable.

3.5   In experimental research, independent variables are the variables that are thought to cause change in the outcome variable; in non-experimental research, independent variables are thought to predict the outcome. Dependent variables are those variables that are caused or influenced, or predicted, from the independent variable.

3.6   **Random Assignment** to Condition: this ensures that in the long run, the composition of groups on individual differences variables is equal. **Manipulation of the independent variable:** the researcher does something to one group differently than the other group(s) to increase or decrease the level of some conceptual variable. By combining random assignment and manipulation of the IV, the researchers can be confident that groups are equivalent and differ only on the level of the conceptual variable in question.

3.7.1 IV—level of enforcement; DV—# of alcohol-related crashes; correlational—the researcher does not determine level of enforcement, the counties do

3.7.2 Social skills therapy v. talk therapy; experimental—the researcher controls who receives which therapy

3.7.3 Mandatory v. non-mandatory foreign language/culture class; experimental—the researcher assigns multiple schools to conditions

3.7.4 Attractive speaker v. not-attractive; correlational—although the research assigns "days" to conditions, the students sign up for which day they wish to attend; the researcher cannot be very confident that participants in the two class times are equivalent.

Chapter 4 Answers

4.1 A random sample is one where each individual has an equal probability of being selected.

4.2.1 not mutually exclusive

4.2.2 mutually exclusive

4.2.3 not mutually exclusive

4.2.4 mutually exclusive

4.2.5 not mutually exclusive

4.2.6 mutually exclusive

4.3 Sampling with replacement assumes that all sampled units are returned to the population before sampling again. Thus the total number of events, and the number of specific events, remains unchanged across samples. Sampling without replacement implies that sampled units are not returned to the population. Thus, with each sample, the total number of events, and the number of specific changes, changes. The denominator will always decrease with each sample, and the numerator may also decrease, depending on which specific events were sampled and not returned.

4.4.1 $(45/100) + (17/100) - (14/100) = .48$

4.4.2 $(61/100 + (22/100) = .83$

4.4.3 $(61/100) * (17/100) = .104$

4.4.4 $(22/100) * (21/99) * (20/98) = .0095 = .010$

4.4.5 $(45/100) * (55/100 + 22/100 - 15/100) * (61/100) = .45 * .62 * .61 = .170$

4.4.6 $(55/100) * (45/100 + 61/100 - 24/100) * (17/100 + 22/100) = .55 * .82 * .39 = .176$

4.5 $(1/6 * 1/6) = .028; (2, 6) (3, 5) (4, 4) (5, 3) (6, 2) = 5$ possibilities; $5 \times .028 = .139$

Chapter 5 Answers

5.1

X	f	p	cf	cp
10	1	.05	20	1.00
9	3	.15	19	.95
8	2	.10	16	.80
7	2	.10	14	.70
6	2	.10	12	.60
5	3	.15	10	.50
4	3	.15	7	.35
3	2	.10	4	.20
2	1	.05	2	.10
1	1	.05	1	.05

5.2   The proportion equals the probability of randomly sampling a score of given value.

5.3   **Cumulative frequency** refers to the number of cases that fall in a given category as well as all the categories below that. **Cumulative proportion** refers to the number of cases that fall in a given category as well as all the categories below that.

5.4   Organizing scores in descending order gives definition to cumulative frequency and proportion; i.e., the values reflect cases/proportions in a given category or below. If we organized in ascending order, it would mean that cases should fall in that category or above.

5.5   When there are so many possible values that the rows in the frequency distribution table would become cumbersome; when data are truly continuous and thus have (theoretically) infinite values (frequency distribution tables assume one row per score value).

5.6   (a) between 8–15 rows/intervals; (b) interval widths being values such as 2, 5, 10, 20, 25, 50, etc.; (c) the lowest interval contains the lowest score; (d) the lowest value of the lowest interval is evenly divisible by the interval width

5.7   Interval width of .02, with 11 intervals, will work: $.000 - .019; .020 - .039; .040 - .059;$ $.060 - .079; 080 - .099; .100 - .119; .120 - .139; .140 - .159; .160 - .179; .180 - .199; .200 -$ $.219.$ An interval width of 25 with 9 intervals would work also.

Chapter 6 Answers

6.1 **Mean** = arithmetic center; sum of scores divided by number of scores; mean deviations always sums to zero. **Median** = middle score, score at the 50% of the distribution (equal number of observations above the median as there are below the median); the median is relatively robust and not greatly affected by extreme scores. The median is used with skewed data. **Mode** = most frequent response. The mode is very robust. It also is the only measure usable with nominal data.

6.2 Mean = 256/21 = 12.19; Median = 11; Mode = 11

6.3 Mean = 92/18 = 5.11; Median = 5; Mode = 5

6.4 Mean = 158/21 = 7.52 ; Median = 5; Mode = 5; the median and mode did not change, although the mean did; the median and mode are more robust than the mean.

6.5 Mean = 2107.4/461 = 4.57

6.6

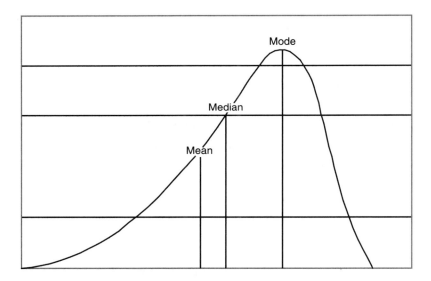

Chapter 7 Answers

7.1 Variability describes the spread of scores in a distribution; are the scores relatively clustered together, or are they dispersed? Are scores pretty much the same, or are they quite different?

7.2 The range is based on the difference between the maximum and minimum scores in a distribution, and to the extent that there is a larger difference between the two, it indicates greater variability. The range is limited in that it is based entirely on two data points (highest and lowest), ignoring the rest of the scores in the distribution. It also ignores whether these high and low scores are outliers. The *inter-quartile range* is the range based on the scores at the 75% and 25%, thus removing outliers or other extreme scores from the calculation.

7.3–7.5

X	$X - \bar{X}$	$|X - \bar{X}|$	$(X - \bar{X})^2$
1	−5.75	5.75	33.0625
13	6.25	6.25	39.0625
7	0.25	0.25	0.0625
8	1.25	1.25	1.5625
12	5.25	5.25	27.5625
3	−3.75	3.75	14.0625
5	−1.75	1.75	3.0625
11	4.25	4.25	18.0625
10	3.25	3.25	10.5625
9	2.25	2.25	5.0625
4	−2.75	2.75	7.5625
4	−2.75	2.75	7.5625
8	1.25	1.25	1.5625
7	0.25	0.25	0.0625
2	−4.75	4.75	22.5625
4	−2.75	2.75	7.5625
$\Sigma X = 108$	$\Sigma = 0$	$\Sigma = 48.5$	$\Sigma = 199$

$\bar{X} = 6.75$

7.6 $S^2 = 199/15 = 13.26; S = 3.64$

7.7 $SS = 2481 - (169^2/12) = 2481 - 2380.083 = 100.92; S^2 = 100.92/11 = 9.17; S = 3.03$

7.8 $5006 - (254^2/15) = 5006 - 4301.07 = 704.93; S^2 = 704.93/14 = 50.34; S = 7.10.$ Adding the outliers more than doubles the standard deviation.

Chapter 8 Answers

8.1 $\bar{X} = 6.33; S = 3.47$

Raw Score	Z-Score
8	0.480
9	0.768
1	−1.54
4	−0.672
2	−1.248
8	0.480
10	1.055
5	−0.384
5	−0.384
4	−0.672
7	0.192
13	1.920

8.2 $SS = 11 - (0^2/12) = 11$; $S^2 = 11/11 = 1$; $S = 1$

8.3 $\bar{X} = 9.69$; $SS = 3114 - (126^2/13) = 3114 - 1221.23 = 1892.77$; $S^2 = 157.73$; $S = 12.56$

Z-Score 1	Z-Score 2
0.480	−0.135
0.768	−0.055
−1.54	−0.692
−0.672	−0.453
−1.248	−0.612
0.480	−0.135
1.055	0.024
−0.384	−0.374
−0.384	−0.374
−0.672	−0.453
0.192	−0.214
1.920	0.263
—	3.209

Except for the outlier, almost all of the Z-scores now are smaller in magnitude. In addition, because the mean was increased as a result of the outlier, there are more negative Z-scores.

8.4 Adding an extreme score can influence the numerator of the Z-score equation $(X - \bar{X})$ because it influences the mean; it may make some scores closer to the mean, and other scores further from the mean. Adding an extreme score also influences the standard deviation of the variable, and thus the denominator. Adding an extreme score will increase the standard deviations, thus increase the denominator, and contribute to smaller Z-scores.

8.5.1 .067

8.5.2 .045

8.5.3 .719

8.5.4 .209

8.5.5 46.15

8.5.6 66.45

Chapter 9 Answers

9.1   The null hypothesis states that there is no phenomenon of interest—no difference between groups, or no relationship between or among variables.

9.2   The fact that this sample has lower-than-average behavioral signs of depression is simply a matter of sampling or random error, and is not due to the therapy; if the study was conducted again, we would not expect the sample to have lower-than-average behavioral signs of depression.

9.3   The null hypothesis states that the sample is drawn from a population with the parameters specified under the null hypothesis; the alternative hypothesis states that the population from which the sample was drawn is different (in terms of μ) than the population with the parameters specified under the null hypothesis.

9.4 μ and σ describe the parameters of the population from which the data were sampled assuming that the null hypothesis is true. The Z-score reflects the location of the data in that population, and consequently indicates the probability that the data *could* have been sampled from the population with mean μ and standard deviation σ. Given that μ and σ describe the population under the null hypothesis, the Z-score indicates the chance that the data could have been sampled even if the null hypothesis was true.

9.5   A Type I error is a "false alarm." It occurs when the researcher rejects the null hypothesis when in fact the null hypothesis is true. This would occur when the researcher just happened (by chance) to sample extreme data even though the treatment had no effect whatsoever. Note that the researcher can only make a Type I error when he or she first decides to reject the null hypothesis. A Type II error is a "miss." This is when the researcher cannot reject the null hypothesis, although in reality the null hypothesis is false. Thus, even if the treatment works, the results may not be extreme enough for the researcher to confidently reject the null hypothesis.

9.6   Alpha (α) level is the maximum probability that the data *could* have been sampled under the null hypothesis, which allows the researcher to reject the null hypothesis with confidence.

9.7   Statistical power refers to the ability of a statistical test to find effects that really exist (i.e., to reject the null hypothesis when the null hypothesis in fact is true).

9.8   By increasing the alpha-level, the researcher is more willing to reject the null hypothesis due to spurious results, and thus make a Type I error. Increasing alpha, however, also increases power, i.e., the ability to find effects that truly exist. By decreasing alpha, the researcher is less willing to reject the null hypothesis due to spurious research (Type I error); the probability that data could have been obtained even if the null hypothesis was true is smaller. The statistical test has less power, however, and is more likely to fail to detect real effects.

Chapter 10 Answers

10.1   P [HHHT or HHTH or HTHH or THHH] = .0625 * 4 = .250

P [6 H and 2 T on 8 coins] = .0039 * 28 = .109

Probability of 75/25 split with 8 coins (p = .109) is less than probability of 75/25 split with 4 coins.

10.2   A **sampling distribution of means** is a theoretical distribution that describes the probability of obtaining a mean ($\overline{X}$) from a sample of size N if drawn from a population of normal scores with mean μ and standard deviation σ. Thus the distribution of scores reflects the characteristics of data set of observations, where a sampling distribution of means reflects the characteristics of group means if we took an infinite number of samples from the distribution of normal scores.

10.3   The **standard error** refers to the variability of a sampling distribution of means (the extent to which we expect sample means to vary). The **standard deviation** refers to the variability of scores (the extent to which the scores in the data set varies).

10.4.1 $Z = (105 - 100)/12/\sqrt{4} = 5/6 = .833$; area above = .203

10.4.2 $Z = (105 - 100)/12/\sqrt{16} = 5/3 = 1.67$; area above = .048

10.4.3 $Z = (110 - 100)/12/\sqrt{9} = 10/4 = 2.5$; area above = .006

10.4.4 $Z = (110 - 100)/12/\sqrt{25} = 10/2.4 = 4.17$; area above = .000

10.5   Z-scores of ±1.96 mark the extreme upper and lower 2.5% of the distribution; combined, the upper and lower proportions of .025 equal alpha of .05

10.6.1 The SAT prep course had no effect; formally, that the population from which the prep course sample was drawn had a population $\mu = 1000$.

10.6.2 $Z = (1080 - 1000)/200/\sqrt{25} = 80/40 = 2$

10.6.3 Because Z of 2.0 > 1.96, we can reject H0 (assuming $\alpha = .05$); people who went through the prep course had higher SAT scores than could be expected by chance.

10.6.4 If N = 12, $Z = (1080 - 1000)/200/\sqrt{12} = 80/57.74 = 1.39$; area above = .084

Chapter 11 Answers

11.1   The t-distribution is similar to the unit normal distribution in that it is symmetric with a mean of 0. Unlike the unit normal distribution, the standard deviation is not necessarily 1, but varies as a function of sample size. The t-distribution is flatter, and has heavier tails than the unit normal distribution. However, when $N = \infty$, the t-distribution is identical to the unit normal distribution.

11.2   There is sampling error in the estimate; the estimate S might not accurately reflect the population σ.

11.3   When $N = \infty$ (i.e., S will equal σ)

11.4   **Single sample t-test:** μ is known and σ is unknown; σ is estimated from S. The null hypothesis states that the sample mean was drawn from a population with a mean of μ. **Independent samples t-test:** neither μ nor σ are known; two group means are compared to each other. The null hypothesis states that two groups were sampled from the same population (or populations with identical means). **Related samples t-test:** neither μ nor σ are known. The study assumes a single sample of participants, each providing a pair of scores (e.g., pre–post).

11.5 $T = (106 - 100)/20/\sqrt{38} = 6/3.24 = 1.85$; T_{CRIT} (37) = 2.026; retain H0

11.6   H0: the sample mean was drawn from a population with $\mu = 6$; use a single sample t-test; $t = 3.25/1.93 = \mathbf{1.68}$; T_{CRIT} (3) = 3.182; retain H0

11.7   H0: there is no difference between the anti-anxiety drug and the placebo in reducing anxiety (i.e., the two samples came from the same population, or population with equal μ); $t = 5.65/2.00 = \mathbf{2.83}$; T_{CRIT} (7) = 2.36; reject H0—the anti-anxiety drug was more effective than the placebo ($\overline{X}$ 9.25 > 3.6) in treating anxiety.

11.8   H0: there is no difference in anxiety ratings between time 1 and time 2; use a related samples t-test; $t = -2.60/1.327 = -1.96$. T_{CRIT} (4) = 2.78; retain H0

11.9   Differences that are *statistically significant* are unlikely enough (i.e., probability $< \alpha$) to have occurred due to random chance alone that the researcher can conclude with confidence that the groups are meaningfully different.

11.10 "Unexplained variance" refers to variability among scores that cannot be explained by the independent variables in our study. Unexplained variance often is due to the fact that individual subjects vary on important characteristics and personality dimensions. In the case of independent samples t-tests, unexplained variance is reflected by variability within the groups. In the case of related samples t-test, the same individuals appear in each group. Thus researchers are able to compare each participant's two scores to each while removing the variability due to individual differences on important characteristics and personality. This approach can greatly reduce the amount of unexplained variability.

11.11 For the **independent samples t-test** the null hypothesis states that the two samples were drawn from the same population (or populations with equal μs); thus we would expect the differences between our two sample means to be 0. The sampling distribution of differences between means describes the probability of sampling two means from the same population and obtained mean differences such as those found in the data. For the **related samples t-test,** the null hypothesis states that the columns of paired scores were sampled from the same population (or populations with equal μs); thus we would expect the mean difference between pairs of scores to be 0. The sampling distribution describes the probability that the same individuals would produce two sets of scores as different as those found in the data.

11.12 The null hypothesis is that television is no more or less effective than newspaper in disseminating the news; this would be examining the independent samples t-test; SS can be obtained by multiplying variances by n − 1, thus $S_P^2 = 1.97$. $S_{X1-X2} = 0.354$; t = 1.9/0.354 = **5.37**. T_{CRIT} (62) = 2.00. Reject H0; people who read the newspaper score significantly higher on a test of current events than those who only watch TV news.

11.13 $S_{\bar{X}} = 3.9/\sqrt{134} = 0.337$; T_{CRIT} (133) = 1.980; Confidence interval = **3.83 − 5.17** (i.e., 4.5 ± 0.667).

11.14 $\bar{X} = 15.67$, N = 12 and S = 5.40; $S_{\bar{X}} = 5.40/\sqrt{12} = 1.56$. T_{CRIT} (11) = 2.201; Confidence interval = **12.24 − 19.10** (i.e., 15.67 ± 3.43). If the professor leaves 19.10 minutes before class, you can be 95% confident of getting to class on time. In order to be 99% confident [T_{CRIT} (11) = 3.106], the professor would need to leave 15.67 + (1.56 * 3.106) = **20.51** minutes early.

Chapter 12 Answers

12.1 It maintains the risk of Type I error as equal to α; conducting multiple t-tests increases the risk of making a Type I error.

12.2 MS_{BET} and $\bar{X}1 - \bar{X}2$ both reflect the variability between or among sample means, and indicate the extent to which group membership informs or predicts scores in our sample. MS_{WITHIN} and S_{X1-X2} is based upon variability within the groups, and estimate random "natural" error that is unexplained by group membership.

12.3 Within-group variability reflects the extent to which scores within each group vary from the mean of that group. This variability in scores within the groups is attributed to the fact that individuals within groups vary in important characteristics (e.g., intelligence, motivation, extroversion). Random assignment does not limit the amount of unexplained variability (error) within the groups, but helps ensure that in the long run, the distribution of participants on these variables is comparable among groups.

12.4 F-scores are computed from ratios of variances, and variances can only be positive. The ratios of positive variances can only be positive.

12.5

Source	SS	df	MS	F
Total	126.44	17	—	
Between (Therapy)	92.11	2	46.06	20.11
Within	34.33	15	02.29	—

F_{CRIT} (2, 15) = 3.68

20.11 > 3.68, thus reject H0

Scheffe: $\psi = \sqrt{(2)(3.68)} * \sqrt{(2.29)((1^2/6) + (-1^2/6))} = (2.71)(0.87) = 2.36$

$\bar{X}1 = 8.00$ (8.00 – 5.83) = 2.17 < 2.36   (8.00 – 2.50) = 5.50 > 2.36

$\bar{X}2 = 5.83$ (5.83 – 2.50) = 3.33 > 2.36

$\bar{X}3 = 2.50$

> There is no significant difference in weight loss between Family and Cognitive therapies. However, Family therapy was significantly better than Control, and Cognitive therapy was also significantly better than Control.

12.6

Source	SS	df	MS	F
Total	126.44	17	—	
Between (Keyboard)	85.00	3	28.33	6.47
Within	70.00	16	04.38	—

F_{CRIT} (3, 16) = 3.24

6.57 > 3.24, thus reject H0

Scheffe: $\psi = \sqrt{(3)(3.24)} * \sqrt{(4.38)((1^2/5) + (-1^2/5))} = (3.12)(1.32) = 4.12$

$\bar{X}1 = 1.00$ (1.00 – 5.00) = –4.00   (1.00 – 6.00) = –5.00   (1.00 – 6.00) = –5.00

$\bar{X}2 = 5.00$ (5.00 – 6.00) = –1.00   (5.00 – 6.00) = –1.00

$\bar{X}3 = 6.00$ (6.00 – 6.00) = 0.00

$\bar{X}4 = 6.00$

> The results indicate that significantly fewer errors were made on keyboard A than on keyboard C, and fewer were made on keyboard A than keyboard D. No other pairwise comparisons were significantly different.

12.7 The F-ratio describes the extent to which our between-groups variance exceeds our within-group variance. Recall that between-group variance may include unexplained error variance, but also may include variance that can be explained by membership in different groups. Within-group variance describes error variance, or unexplained variance. This F-ratio indicates the extent to which the groups means vary from each other above and beyond what we might expect to find simply due to chance.

12.8 For any planned comparison between two groups, the denominator for Dunn's test equals:

$$\sqrt{(MS_{WITHIN})\,(\Sigma\, c^2/n)} = \sqrt{(2.1)((1^2/8)+(-1^2/8))} = \sqrt{(2.1)(.25)} = \sqrt{.525} = .725$$

$\bar{X}1$ v. $\bar{X}4 = 1.8 - 4.5 = -2.7$ $\qquad$ $t = -2.7/.725 = -3.72$

$\bar{X}3$ v. $\bar{X}6 = 9.5 - 8.7 = 0.8$ $\qquad$ $t = 0.8/.725 = 1.10$

$\bar{X}2$ v. $\bar{X}4 = 2.7 - 4.5 = -1.8$ $\qquad$ $t = -1.8/.725 = -2.48$

Given an $\alpha = .05/3 = 0.17$ and 49 df (same as ANOVA), our critical value (obtained via computer) is 2.48.

Our planned comparisons reveal that only the difference between group 1 and group 4 is statistically significant ($|-3.72| > 2.48$) at the .05 α-level (although the comparison of groups 2 and 4 is almost significant!).

12.9 For the post hoc tests (using Scheffe's S), the first part of the equation is: $\sqrt{(6)(2.29)} = 3.71$.

For the contrast coefficients:

$\bar{X}1 + \bar{X}2 + \bar{X}5$ v. $\bar{X}3 + \bar{X}6$: $((.33^2/8)+(.33^2/8)+(.33^2/8)+(-.5^2/8)+(-.5^2/8)) = .104$

$\bar{X}4$ v. $\bar{X}6 + \bar{X}7$: $((1^2/8)+(-.5^2/8)+(-.5^2/8)) = 0.188$

$\bar{X}1 + \bar{X}2$ v. $\bar{X}4 + \bar{X}7$: $((.5^2/8)+(.5^2/8)+(-.5^2/8)+(-.5^2/8)) = 0.125$

Thus, for Scheffe's critical difference:

$\bar{X}1 + \bar{X}2 + \bar{X}5$ v. $\bar{X}3 + \bar{X}6$: $\psi = (3.71) * \sqrt{(2.29)(.104)} = 1.81$

$\bar{X}4$ v. $\bar{X}6 + \bar{X}7$: $\psi = 3.71 * \sqrt{(2.29)(.188)} = 2.43$

$\bar{X}1 + \bar{X}2$ v. $\bar{X}4 + \bar{X}7$: $\psi = 3.71 * \sqrt{(2.29)(.125)} = 1.98$

Using the group means:

$\bar{X}1 + \bar{X}2 + \bar{X}5$ v. $\bar{X}3 + \bar{X}6 = (1.8)(.33) + (2.7)(.33) + (0.4)(.33) + (-.5)(9.5) + (-.5)(8.7)$
$= 1.63 - 9.10 = -7.47$

$\bar{X}4$ v. $\bar{X}6 + \bar{X}7 = (1)(4.5) + (-.5)(8.7) + (-.5)(6.8) = 4.5 - 7.75 = -3.25$

$\bar{X}1 + \bar{X}2$ v. $\bar{X}4 + \bar{X}7 = (.5)(1.8) + (.5)(2.7) + (-.5)(4.5) + (-.5)(6.8) = 2.25 - 5.65 = -3.40$

To test the contrasts:

$\bar{X}1 + \bar{X}2 + \bar{X}5$ v. $\bar{X}3 + \bar{X}6$: $|-7.47| > 1.81$ Reject H0

$\bar{X}4$ v. $\bar{X}6 + \bar{X}7$: $|-3.25| > 2.43$ Reject H0

$\bar{X}1 + \bar{X}2$ v. $\bar{X}4 + \bar{X}7$: $|-3.40| > 1.98$ Reject H0

Chapter 13 Answers

13.1.1 Interaction

13.1.2 No Interaction

13.1.3 Interaction

13.1.4 Interaction

13.2   First solve the degrees of freedom (because the df for Between is 5, the design must be a 2×3).

Once dfs are obtained, compute SS_{AB} by multiplying MS × df.

Because MS_{AB} and F_{AB} are known, MS_{WITHIN} can be obtained by division.

SS_{WITHIN} can be obtained by multiplying MS × df.

With SS_{WITHIN} known, SS_{BET} and SS_A can be obtained.

Now compute the remaining MSs and Fs.

Source	SS	df	MS	F
Total	650	40	—	—
Between	160	5	32	
Effect A	48.33	1	48.33	3.45
Effect B	090	2	45	3.21
AB Interaction	21.67	1	21.67	1.548
Within	490	35	14.0	—

13.3

Source	SS	df	MS	F
Total	930.28	17		—
Between	879.61	5	175.92	—
CS	1.39	1	1.39	0.33
UCS	843.11	2	421.56	99.84
CS × UCS	35.11	2	19.56	4.16
Within	50.67	12	4.22	—

$F_{CRIT} (1, 12) = 4.74$

$F_{CRIT} (2, 12) = 3.89$

The main effect of CS is not statistically significant, $0.33 < 4.74$.

The main effect of UCS is statistically significant, $99.84 > 4.74$.

The interaction between CS and UCS is statistically significant, $4.16 > 3.89$.

Cell means are below:

	Tone	Vibration	
High	20.33	16.00	18.17
Medium	04.00	06.33	05.17
Low	02.33	02.67	02.5
	08.89	08.33	

For the first part of Scheffe's S: $\sqrt{(5)(3.11)} = 3.94$

Note that $F_{CRIT} (5, 12) = 3.11$

For the second part: $\sqrt{(4.22)((1^2/3) + (-1^2/3))} = 1.68$

Thus, $\psi = 3.94 * 1.68 = 6.62$

For the main effect of UCS, we find that High is significantly different from both Medium and Low, but Medium and Low are not different from each other.

For the interaction between CS and UCS, we find that the difference between High and Medium within the Tone condition (16.33) is significantly different from the difference between High and Medium in the Vibration condition (9.67): $16.33 - 9.67 = 6.66$.

13.4

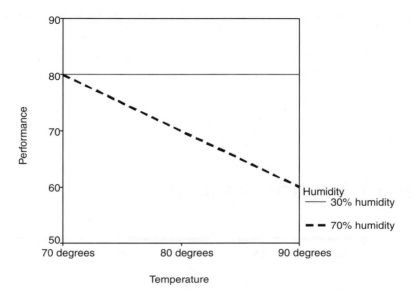

The significant main effect of humidity indicates that performance was better in the low humidity condition than in the high humidity condition, ignoring temperature.

The significant main effect of temperature indicates that performance was better in the lower temperature conditions than in the higher temperature conditions, ignoring level of humidity.

The interaction between humidity and temperature indicates that when the humidity was low, performance did not vary as a function of temperature. But when the humidity was high, performance was worse when temperature levels were higher.

13.5

Source	SS	df	MS	F
Total	160.96	23	—	
Between	100.46	3	33.49	—
Pill	30.38	1	30.38	10.04
Vegetarian	70.04	1	70.04	23.15
Pill × Veg	.042	1	.042	00.01
Within	60.60	20	3.025	—

F_{CRIT} (1, 20) = 4.35

For the main effect of pill, reject H0, 10.14 > 4.35: people who took the pill appear more youthful ($\overline{X}$ = 7.17) than people who took the placebo ($\overline{X}$ = 4.92)

For the main effect of vegetarian, reject H0, 23.15 > 4.35: vegetarians appear more youthful ($\overline{X}$ = 7.75) than non-vegetarians ($\overline{X}$ = 4.33).

For the interaction between pill and vegetarian, retain H0, .042 < 4.35

Only the interaction effect would require post hoc testing, but as it is not statistically significant, Scheffe's S test is not required.

Chapter 14 Practice Problems

14.1

Source	SS	df	MS	F
Total	55.37	29	—	
Artwork	19.20	4	4.80	5.11
Subjects	17.37	5	3.47	
Error	18.80	20	0.94	

F_{CRIT} (4, 20) = 2.87

For the first part of Scheffe' S: $\sqrt{(4)(2.87)} = 3.39$

For the second part: $\sqrt{(0.94)((1^2/6) + (-1^2/6))} = 0.56$

Thus, $\psi = 3.39 * 0.56 = 1.90$

The mean ratings for the five pieces of artwork are below:

Artwork #1   3.00

Artwork #2   1.67

Artwork #3   3.00

Artwork #4   4.00

Artwork #5   2.17

Although artwork #4 has the highest rating, it is not significantly different from artwork pieces #1, #3, or #5. The only two pieces of artwork that are significantly different from each other according to Scheffe's S are pieces #4 and #2.

14.2

Source	SS	df	MS	F
Total	43.33	26	01.67	
Between Cells	26.33	5	05.27	
Condition: Team Building, Leisure	00.67	1	00.67	00.50
Time (Before, During, After)	04.08	2	02.04	02.72
Condition $\times$ Time	21.58	2	10.79	14.39
Within Cells	17.00	18	00.94	
Subjects	08.67	7	01.24	
Subjects-within-conditions	08.00	6	01.33	
Error	9.00	12	0.75	

F_{CRIT} (1, 6) = 5.99

F_{CRIT} (2, 12) = 3.89

Regarding the main effect of condition, retain H0, 0.50 < 5.99

Regarding the main effect of time, retain H0, 2.72 < 3.89

Regarding the interaction between time and condition, reject H0, 14.39 > 3.89

14.3 **Within Cells:** total variability of scores *within* each cell (due to all reasons *except* our conditions).

Subjects: variability between or among participants, ignoring variability within each participant (e.g., over time).

Subjects-within-conditions: variability in participants' mean scores within condition (around the mean of that condition).

Error: variability within each cell after removing the variability due to participants (i.e., the fact that some participants simply are heavier than others).

Chapter 15 Answers

15.1

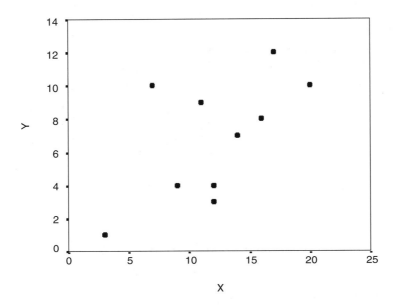

15.2 $SP = 958 - ((133)(71)/11) = 958 - 858.45 = 99.55$

$SS_X = 1833 - (133^2/11) = 1833 - 1608.09 = 224.91$

$B = 99.55/224.91 = 0.44$

$A = 6.45 - (12.09)(0.44) = 1.13$

$\hat{Y} = 1.13 + (0.44)X$

If significant and $X = 11$, $\hat{Y} = 5.97$

If not significant, then $B = 0$, $A = 6.45$, and thus $\hat{Y} = 6.45 + (0)X$; $\hat{Y} = 6.45$

15.3–15.4 *Note that the process of computing SS_{ERR} may produce rounding error.*

X	Y	$\hat{Y}$	$(Y - \hat{Y})$	$(Y - \hat{Y})^2$
17	12	8.61	3.39	11.49
12	3	6.41	−3.41	11.63
09	4	5.09	−1.09	01.19
14	7	7.29	−0.29	00.08
11	9	5.97	3.03	09.18
07	10	4.21	5.79	33.52

16	8	8.17	−0.17	00.03
12	4	6.41	−2.41	05.81
12	3	6.41	−3.41	11.63
03	1	2.45	−1.45	02.10
20	10	9.93	0.07	00.00

$\Sigma(Y - \hat{Y})^2 = SS_{ERR} = \textbf{86.67}$

15.5 The standard deviation of the errors reflects the extent to which actual scores vary "on average" from the predicted scores. The standard error of the slope reflects the variability in slopes (B) that would be expected from an infinite number of random samples (of N cases) from a population where B = 0; in essence, it is the standard deviation of a sampling distribution of slopes.

15.6 Standard Deviation of the Errors $= S_E = \sqrt{\Sigma(Y - \hat{Y})^2/(N-2)} = \sqrt{(86.67/9)} = 3.10$

Recall $SS_X = 224.91$

Standard Error of the Slope $= S_B = S_E/\sqrt{SS_X} = 3.10/\sqrt{224.91} = 0.21$

$t = B/S_B = 0.44/0.21 = 2.10$

$t_{CRIT}(9) = 2.26$

Because 2.10 < 2.26, we retain H0. There is not enough evidence to conclude that there is a relationship between X and Y in the population.

15.7 ANOVA partitions variance into within-group variance (based on the extent to which scores within each group deviate from the mean of that group) and between-group variance—the extent to which the group means vary from each other (actually, the extent to which the group means vary from the overall mean). The ratio of MS_{BET} over MS_{WITHIN} indicates the extent to which our differences among means are above and beyond the differences we might expect to find due to random error (chance).

In regression, we can compute error variance based on the extent to which Y scores associated with a particular X score deviate from the predicted Y score for that X. We also can compute regression variance based on the extent to which points on the regression line (i.e., predicted Y scores) deviate from the overall mean of Y. The ratio of MS_{REG} and MS_{ERR} indicates the extent to which the slope deviates from the mean (i.e., a flat line) above and beyond what we might expect to find due to random error.

Group means in ANOVA are analogous to predicted Y scores in regression.

The difference among group means in ANOVA is analogous to the slope in regression.

The variability within groups in ANOVA is analogous to the variability of scores around the regression line.

15.8 *Note that the process of computing SS$_{REG}$ may produce rounding error.*

X	Y	$\hat{Y}$	$\bar{Y}$	$(\hat{Y} - \bar{Y})$	$(\hat{Y} - \bar{Y})^2$
17	12	8.61	6.45	2.16	04.67
12	3	6.41	6.45	−0.04	00.00
09	4	5.09	6.45	−1.36	01.85
14	7	7.29	6.45	0.84	00.71
11	9	5.97	6.45	−0.48	00.23
07	10	4.21	6.45	−2.24	05.02
16	8	8.17	6.45	1.72	02.96
12	4	6.41	6.45	−0.04	00.00
12	3	6.41	6.45	−0.04	00.00
03	1	2.45	6.45	−4.00	16.00
20	10	9.93	6.45	3.48	12.11

$\Sigma(\hat{Y} - \bar{Y})^2 = SS_{REG} = 43.54$

Recall that $SS_{ERR} = 86.67$

$MS_{REG} = SS_{REG}/df_{REG} = 43.54/1 = 43.54$

$MS_{ERR} = SS_{ERR}/df_{ERR} = 86.67/9 = 9.63$

$F = 43.54/9.63 = 4.52$

$F_{CRIT}(1, 9) = 5.11$

Because $4.52 < 5.11$, retain H0.

15.9 $SS_Y = 130.75$

$R = SP/\sqrt{(SS_X * SS_Y)} = 99.55/\sqrt{(224.91 * 130.75)} = 99.55/171.48 = \mathbf{0.58}$

$R_{CRIT}(9) = .602$

Because $0.58 < 0.602$, retain H0

Chapter 16 Answers

16.1

	Observed	Expected
	26	20
	14	20

$\chi^2 = (26 - 20)^2/20 + (14 - 20)^2/20 = 1.8 + 1.8 = 3.6$

$\chi^2_{CRIT}(1) = 3.84$

Thus, retain H0, $3.6 < 3.84$

The observed distribution of outcomes does not deviate significantly from expected.

16.2 Chi-square and factorial are similar in the way that the data often are presented. Both involve creating "boxes" or cells by crossing categorical variables. In factorial ANOVA, both categorical variables are independent variables, and the participants' scores on the outcome variables are represented inside the boxes. In the case of chi-square, one categorical variable is a dependent (outcome) variable, and the frequencies (number of participants that fall in the combinations of categories) are placed inside the box.

16.3 Expected frequencies are presented below:

	Sneakers	Leather Shoes	Boots	Sandals
Male	19.9	23.0	20.9	26.2
Female	18.1	21.0	19.1	23.8

$\chi^2 = 25.45$

$\chi^2_{CRIT}(3) = 7.81$

Thus, retain H0, $25.45 > 7.81$

Proportions of men and women wearing each type of shoe are presented below.

	Sneakers	Leather Shoes	Boots	Sandals
Male	.316	.773	.650	.360
Female	.684	.227	.350	.640

The results seem to indicate that men tended to prefer leather shoes and boots relative to women, but women tended to prefer sneakers and sandals more than men.

16.4 Expected frequencies are presented below:

	Highly Attractive	Moderately Attractive	Average
Serious	11.9	14.0	13.1
Casual	18.6	22.0	20.5
Non-Dating	18.6	22.0	20.5

$\chi^2 = 36.24$

$\chi^2_{CRIT}(4) = 9.49$

Thus, retain H0, 36.24 > 9.49

Proportions of attractiveness ratings as a function of dating activity are presented below:

	Highly Attractive	Moderately Attractive	Average
Serious	.128	.308	.564
Casual	.164	.459	.377
Non-Dating	.557	.295	.148

The results appear to indicate that as individuals become more seriously involved in relationships, they are more likely to rate the physical attractiveness of a target person as "average" relative to moderately and highly attractive.

Appendix

Unit Normal Table (Z-test critical values)

Z = Z-score
A = proportion in body (larger portion)
B = proportion in tail (smaller portion)
When Z is positive (+), A = area below
When Z is negative (−), A = area above

Z	A	B	Z	A	B	Z	A	B	Z	A	B
0.00	0.5000	0.5000	0.10	0.5398	0.4602	0.20	0.5793	0.4207	0.30	0.6179	0.3821
0.01	0.5040	0.4960	0.11	0.5438	0.4562	0.21	0.5832	0.4168	0.31	0.6217	0.3783
0.02	0.5080	0.4920	0.12	0.5478	0.4522	0.22	0.5871	0.4129	0.32	0.6255	0.3745
0.03	0.5120	0.4880	0.13	0.5517	0.4483	0.23	0.5910	0.4090	0.33	0.6293	0.3707
0.04	0.5160	0.4840	0.14	0.5557	0.4443	0.24	0.5948	0.4052	0.34	0.6331	0.3669
0.05	0.5199	0.4801	0.15	0.5596	0.4404	0.25	0.5987	0.4013	0.35	0.6368	0.3632
0.06	0.5239	0.4761	0.16	0.5636	0.4364	0.26	0.6026	0.3974	0.36	0.6406	0.3594
0.07	0.5279	0.4721	0.17	0.5675	0.4325	0.27	0.6064	0.3936	0.37	0.6443	0.3557
0.08	0.5319	0.4681	0.18	0.5714	0.4286	0.28	0.6103	0.3897	0.38	0.6480	0.3520
0.09	0.5359	0.4641	0.19	0.5753	0.4247	0.29	0.6141	0.3859	0.39	0.6517	0.3483
0.40	0.6554	0.3446	0.50	0.6915	0.3085	0.60	0.7257	0.2743	0.70	0.7580	0.2420
0.41	0.6591	0.3409	0.51	0.6950	0.3050	0.61	0.7291	0.2709	0.71	0.7611	0.2389
0.42	0.6628	0.3372	0.52	0.6985	0.3015	0.62	0.7324	0.2676	0.72	0.7642	0.2358
0.43	0.6664	0.3336	0.53	0.7019	0.2981	0.63	0.7356	0.2644	0.73	0.7673	0.2327
0.44	0.6700	0.3300	0.54	0.7054	0.2946	0.64	0.7389	0.2611	0.74	0.7703	0.2297
0.45	0.6736	0.3264	0.55	0.7088	0.2912	0.65	0.7421	0.2579	0.75	0.7734	0.2266
0.46	0.6772	0.3228	0.56	0.7123	0.2877	0.66	0.7454	0.2546	0.76	0.7764	0.2236
0.47	0.6808	0.3192	0.57	0.7157	0.2843	0.67	0.7486	0.2514	0.77	0.7793	0.2207
0.48	0.6844	0.3156	0.58	0.7190	0.2810	0.68	0.7517	0.2483	0.78	0.7823	0.2177
0.49	0.6879	0.3121	0.59	0.7224	0.2776	0.69	0.7549	0.2451	0.79	0.7852	0.2148

Z	A	B	Z	A	B	Z	A	B	Z	A	B
0.80	0.7881	0.2119	0.90	0.8159	0.1841	1.00	0.8413	0.1587	1.10	0.8643	0.1357
0.81	0.7910	0.2090	0.91	0.8186	0.1814	1.01	0.8437	0.1563	1.11	0.8665	0.1335
0.82	0.7939	0.2061	0.92	0.8212	0.1788	1.02	0.8461	0.1539	1.12	0.8686	0.1314
0.83	0.7967	0.2033	0.93	0.8238	0.1762	1.03	0.8485	0.1515	1.13	0.8707	0.1293
0.84	0.7995	0.2005	0.94	0.8264	0.1736	1.04	0.8508	0.1492	1.14	0.8728	0.1272
0.85	0.8023	0.1977	0.95	0.8289	0.1711	1.05	0.8531	0.1469	1.15	0.8749	0.1251
0.86	0.8051	0.1949	0.96	0.8315	0.1685	1.06	0.8554	0.1446	1.16	0.8770	0.1230
0.87	0.8078	0.1922	0.97	0.8340	0.1660	1.07	0.8577	0.1423	1.17	0.8790	0.1210
0.88	0.8106	0.1894	0.98	0.8364	0.1636	1.08	0.8599	0.1401	1.18	0.8810	0.1190
0.89	0.8133	0.1867	0.99	0.8389	0.1611	1.09	0.8621	0.1379	1.19	0.8830	0.1170
1.20	0.8849	0.1151	1.30	0.9032	0.0968	1.40	0.9192	0.0808	1.50	0.9332	0.0668
1.21	0.8868	0.1132	1.31	0.9049	0.0951	1.41	0.9207	0.0793	1.51	0.9345	0.0655
1.22	0.8887	0.1113	1.32	0.9066	0.0934	1.42	0.9222	0.0778	1.52	0.9357	0.0643
1.23	0.8906	0.1094	1.33	0.9082	0.0918	1.43	0.9236	0.0764	1.53	0.9370	0.0630
1.24	0.8925	0.1075	1.34	0.9099	0.0901	1.44	0.9250	0.0750	1.54	0.9382	0.0618
1.25	0.8943	0.1057	1.35	0.9115	0.0885	1.45	0.9264	0.0736	1.55	0.9394	0.0606
1.26	0.8961	0.1039	1.36	0.9131	0.0869	1.46	0.9278	0.0722	1.56	0.9406	0.0594
1.27	0.8979	0.1021	1.37	0.9146	0.0854	1.47	0.9292	0.0708	1.57	0.9418	0.0582
1.28	0.8997	0.1003	1.38	0.9162	0.0838	1.48	0.9305	0.0695	1.58	0.9429	0.0571
1.29	0.9015	0.0985	1.39	0.9177	0.0823	1.49	0.9319	0.0681	1.59	0.9441	0.0559
1.60	0.9452	0.0548	1.70	0.9554	0.0446	1.80	0.9640	0.0360	1.90	0.9713	0.0287
1.61	0.9463	0.0537	1.71	0.9563	0.0437	1.81	0.9648	0.0352	1.91	0.9719	0.0281
1.62	0.9474	0.0526	1.72	0.9573	0.0427	1.82	0.9656	0.0344	1.92	0.9725	0.0275
1.63	0.9484	0.0516	1.73	0.9582	0.0418	1.83	0.9663	0.0337	1.93	0.9732	0.0268
1.64	0.9495	0.0505	1.74	0.9590	0.0410	1.84	0.9671	0.0329	1.94	0.9738	0.0262
1.65	0.9505	0.0495	1.75	0.9599	0.0401	1.85	0.9678	0.0322	1.95	0.9744	0.0256
1.66	0.9515	0.0485	1.76	0.9608	0.0392	1.86	0.9685	0.0315	1.96	0.9750	0.0250
1.67	0.9525	0.0475	1.77	0.9616	0.0384	1.87	0.9692	0.0308	1.97	0.9755	0.0245
1.68	0.9535	0.0465	1.78	0.9624	0.0376	1.88	0.9699	0.0301	1.98	0.9761	0.0239
1.69	0.9545	0.0455	1.79	0.9632	0.0368	1.89	0.9706	0.0294	1.99	0.9767	0.0233
2.00	0.9772	0.0228	2.10	0.9821	0.0179	2.20	0.9861	0.0139	2.30	0.9892	0.0108
2.01	0.9777	0.0223	2.11	0.9825	0.0175	2.21	0.9864	0.0136	2.31	0.9895	0.0105
2.02	0.9783	0.0217	2.12	0.9830	0.0170	2.22	0.9868	0.0132	2.32	0.9898	0.0102
2.03	0.9788	0.0212	2.13	0.9834	0.0166	2.23	0.9871	0.0129	2.33	0.9901	0.0099
2.04	0.9793	0.0207	2.14	0.9838	0.0162	2.24	0.9874	0.0126	2.34	0.9903	0.0097
2.05	0.9798	0.0202	2.15	0.9842	0.0158	2.25	0.9877	0.0123	2.35	0.9906	0.0094
2.06	0.9803	0.0197	2.16	0.9846	0.0154	2.26	0.9881	0.0119	2.36	0.9908	0.0092
2.07	0.9807	0.0193	2.17	0.9850	0.0150	2.27	0.9884	0.0116	2.37	0.9911	0.0089
2.08	0.9812	0.0188	2.18	0.9853	0.0147	2.28	0.9887	0.0113	2.38	0.9913	0.0087
2.09	0.9817	0.0183	2.19	0.9857	0.0143	2.29	0.9890	0.0110	2.39	0.9915	0.0085

Z	A	B	Z	A	B	Z	A	B	Z	A	B
2.40	0.9918	0.0082	2.50	0.9938	0.0062	2.60	0.9953	0.0047	2.70	0.9965	0.0035
2.41	0.9920	0.0080	2.51	0.9939	0.0061	2.61	0.9954	0.0046	2.71	0.9966	0.0034
2.42	0.9922	0.0078	2.52	0.9941	0.0059	2.62	0.9956	0.0044	2.72	0.9967	0.0033
2.43	0.9924	0.0076	2.53	0.9943	0.0057	2.63	0.9957	0.0043	2.73	0.9968	0.0032
2.44	0.9926	0.0074	2.54	0.9944	0.0056	2.64	0.9958	0.0042	2.74	0.9969	0.0031
2.45	0.9928	0.0072	2.55	0.9946	0.0054	2.65	0.9959	0.0041	2.75	0.9970	0.0030
2.46	0.9930	0.0070	2.56	0.9947	0.0053	2.66	0.9961	0.0039	2.76	0.9971	0.0029
2.47	0.9932	0.0068	2.57	0.9949	0.0051	2.67	0.9962	0.0038	2.77	0.9972	0.0028
2.48	0.9934	0.0066	2.58	0.9950	0.0050	2.68	0.9963	0.0037	2.78	0.9972	0.0028
2.49	0.9936	0.0064	2.59	0.9952	0.0048	2.69	0.9964	0.0036	2.79	0.9973	0.0027
2.80	0.9974	0.0026	2.90	0.9981	0.0019						
2.81	0.9975	0.0025	2.91	0.9982	0.0018						
2.82	0.9976	0.0024	2.92	0.9982	0.0018						
2.83	0.9976	0.0024	2.93	0.9983	0.0017						
2.84	0.9977	0.0023	2.94	0.9983	0.0017						
2.85	0.9978	0.0022	2.95	0.9984	0.0016						
2.86	0.9978	0.0022	2.96	0.9984	0.0016						
2.87	0.9979	0.0021	2.97	0.9985	0.0015						
2.88	0.9980	0.0020	2.98	0.9985	0.0015						
2.89	0.9980	0.0020	2.99	0.9986	0.0014						

The T-Distribution (t-test critical values)

Two-tailed α

df	0.10	0.05	0.02	0.01
1	6.314	12.706	31.821	63.657
2	2.920	4.303	6.965	9.925
3	2.353	3.182	4.541	5.841
4	2.132	2.776	3.747	4.604
5	2.015	2.571	3.365	4.032
6	1.943	2.447	3.143	3.707
7	1.895	2.365	2.998	3.499
8	1.860	2.306	2.896	3.355
9	1.833	2.262	2.821	3.250
10	1.812	2.228	2.764	3.169
11	1.796	2.201	2.718	3.106
12	1.782	2.179	2.681	3.055
13	1.771	2.160	2.650	3.012
14	1.761	2.145	2.624	2.977
15	1.753	2.131	2.602	2.947
16	1.746	2.120	2.583	2.921
17	1.740	2.110	2.567	2.898
18	1.734	2.101	2.552	2.878
19	1.729	2.093	2.539	2.861
20	1.725	2.086	2.528	2.845
21	1.721	2.080	2.518	2.831
22	1.717	2.074	2.508	2.819
23	1.714	2.069	2.500	2.807
24	1.711	2.064	2.492	2.797
25	1.708	2.060	2.485	2.787
26	1.706	2.056	2.479	2.779
27	1.703	2.052	2.473	2.771
28	1.701	2.048	2.467	2.763
29	1.699	2.045	2.462	2.756
30	1.697	2.042	2.457	2.750
40	1.684	2.021	2.423	2.704
60	1.671	2.000	2.390	2.660
120	1.658	1.980	2.358	2.617
∞	1.645	1.960	2.326	2.576

F-Distribution (ANOVA critical values; α = .05)

df Numerator

df Denominator

↓	1	2	3	4	5	6	7	8	9	10
1	161.4	199.5	215.7	224.6	230.2	234.0	236.8	238.9	240.5	241.9
2	18.51	19.00	19.16	9.25	9.30	9.33	9.35	9.37	9.38	9.40
3	10.3	9.55	9.28	9.12	9.01	8.94	8.89	8.85	8.81	8.79
4	7.71	6.94	6.59	6.39	6.26	6.16	6.09	6.04	6.00	5.96
5	6.61	5.79	5.41	5.19	5.05	4.95	4.88	4.82	4.77	4.74
6	5.99	5.14	4.76	4.53	4.39	4.28	4.21	4.15	4.10	4.06
7	5.59	4.74	4.35	4.12	3.97	3.87	3.79	3.73	3.68	3.64
8	5.32	4.46	4.07	3.84	3.69	3.58	3.50	3.44	3.39	3.35
9	5.12	4.26	3.86	3.63	3.48	3.37	3.29	3.23	3.18	3.14
10	4.96	4.10	3.71	3.48	3.33	3.22	3.14	3.07	3.02	2.98
11	4.84	3.98	3.59	3.36	3.20	3.09	3.01	2.95	2.90	2.85
12	4.75	3.89	3.49	3.26	3.11	3.00	2.91	2.85	2.80	2.75
13	4.67	3.81	3.41	3.18	3.03	2.92	2.83	2.77	2.71	2.67
14	4.60	3.74	3.34	3.11	2.96	2.85	2.76	2.70	2.65	2.80
15	4.54	3.68	3.29	3.06	2.90	2.79	2.71	2.64	2.59	2.54
16	4.49	3.63	3.24	3.01	2.85	2.74	2.66	2.59	2.54	2.49
17	4.45	3.59	3.20	2.96	2.81	2.70	2.61	2.55	2.49	2.45
18	4.41	3.55	3.16	2.93	2.77	2.66	2.58	2.51	2.46	2.41
19	4.38	3.52	3.13	2.90	2.74	2.63	2.54	2.48	2.42	2.38
20	4.35	3.49	3.10	2.87	2.71	2.60	2.51	2.45	2.39	2.35
21	4.32	3.47	3.07	2.84	2.68	2.57	2.49	2.42	2.37	2.32
22	4.30	3.44	3.0S	2.82	2.66	2.55	2.46	2.40	2.34	2.30
23	4.28	3.42	3.03	2.80	2.64	2.53	2.44	2.37	2.32	2.27
24	4.26	3.40	3.01	2.78	2.62	2.51	2.42	2.36	2.30	2.25
30	4.17	3.32	2.92	2.69	2.53	2.42	2.33	2.27	2.21	2.16
40	4.08	3.23	2.84	2.61	2.45	2.34	2.25	2.18	2.12	2.08
60	4.00	3.15	2.76	2.53	2.37	2.25	2.17	2.10	2.04	1.99
120	3.92	3.07	2.68	2.45	2.29	2.7	2.09	2.02	1.96	1.91
∞	3.84	3.00	2.60	2.37	2.21	2.0	2.10	1.94	1.88	1.83

Pearson Correlation Critical Values

Two-tailed α

df	0.10	0.05	0.02	0.01
1	.988	.997	.9995	.9999
2	.900	.950	.980	.990
3	.805	.878	.934	.959
4	.729	.811	.882	.917
5	.669	.754	.833	.874
6	.622	.707	.789	.834
7	.582	.666	.750	.798
8	.549	.632	.716	.765
9	.521	.602	.685	.735
10	.497	.576	.658	.708
11	.476	.553	.634	.684
12	.458	.532	.612	.661
13	.441	.514	.592	.641
14	.426	.497	.574	.623
15	.412	.482	.558	.606
16	.400	.468	.542	.590
17	.389	.456	.528	.575
18	.378	.444	.516	.561
19	.369	.433	.503	.549
20	.360	.423	.492	.537
21	.352	.413	.482	.526
22	.344	.404	.472	.515
23	.337	.396	.462	.505
24	.330	.388	.453	.496
25	.323	.381	.445	.487
26	.317	.374	.437	.479
27	.311	.367	.430	.471
28	.306	.361	.423	.463
29	.301	.355	.416	.456
30	.296	.349	.409	.449
35	.275	.325	.381	.418
40	.257	.304	.358	.393
45	.243	.288	.338	.372
50	.231	.273	.322	.354
60	.211	.250	.295	.325
70	.195	.232	.274	.302
80	.183	.217	.256	.283
90	.173	.205	.242	.267
100	.164	.195	.230	.254

Chi-Square (χ^2) Distribution (critical χ^2 values)

Two-tailed α

df	.05	.025	.01
1	3.84	5.02	6.64
2	5.99	7.38	9.21
3	7.81	9.35	11.34
4	9.49	11.14	13.28
5	11.07	12.83	15.09
6	12.59	14.45	16.81
7	14.07	16.01	18.48
8	15.51	17.53	20.09
9	16.92	19.02	21.67
10	18.31	20.48	23.21
11	19.68	21.92	24.72
12	21.03	23.34	26.22
13	22.36	24.74	27.69
14	23.68	26.11	29.14
15	25.00	27.49	30.58
16	26.30	28.85	32.00
17	27.59	30.19	33.41
18	28.87	31.53	34.80
19	30.14	32.85	36.19
20	31.41	34.17	37.57
21	32.67	35.48	38.93
22	33.92	36.78	40.29
23	35.17	38.08	41.64
24	36.42	39.36	42.98
25	37.65	40.65	44.31
26	38.88	41.92	45.64
27	40.11	43.19	46.96
28	41.34	44.46	48.28
29	42.56	45.72	49.59
30	43.77	46.98	50.89
40	55.76	59.34	63.69
50	67.50	71.42	76.15
60	79.08	83.29	88.38
70	90.53	95.02	100.42
80	101.88	106.63	100.43
90	113.15	118.14	124.12
100	124.34	129.56	135.81